**KAPLAN**
PUBLISHING

Kaplan Publishing are constantly finding new ways to make a difference to your studies and our exciting online resources really do offer something different to AAT students looking for exam success.

FOR THE FIRST TIME, KAPLAN'S AAT TEXTS COME WITH FREE EN-gage ONLINE RESOURCES SO THAT YOU CAN STUDY ANYTIME, ANYWHERE

Having purchased this Kaplan Text, you have access to the following online study materials:

- An online version of the Text
- Fixed Online Tests with instant answers

How to access your online resources

- **Kaplan Financial students** will already have a Kaplan EN-gage account and these extra resources will be available to you online. You do not need to register again, as this process was completed when you enrolled. If you are having problems accessing online materials, please ask your course administrator.
- **If you purchased through Kaplan Flexible Learning or via the Kaplan Publishing website** you will automatically receive an e-mail invitation to Kaplan EN-gage online. Please register your details using this e-mail to gain access to your content. If you do not receive the e-mail or book content, please contact Kaplan Flexible Learning.
- **If you are already a registered Kaplan EN-gage user** go to www.EN-gage.co.uk and log in. Select the 'add a book' feature and enter the ISBN number of this book and the unique pass key at the bottom of this card. Then click 'finished' or 'add another book'. You may add as many books as you have purchased from this screen.
- **If you are a new Kaplan EN-gage user** register at www.EN-gage.co.uk and click on the link contained in the e-mail we sent you to activate your account. Then select the 'add a book' feature, enter the ISBN number of this book and the unique pass key at the bottom of this card. Then click 'finished' or 'add another book'.

 **EN-gage**

Your Code and Information

This code can only be used once for the registration of one book online. This registration will expire when the final sittings for the examinations covered by this book have taken place. Please allow one hour from the time you submitted your book details for us to process your request.

i14y-t1O6-j8X7-NRQP

Please be aware that this code is case-sensitive and you will need to include the dashes within the passcode, but not when entering the ISBN. For further technical support, please visit www.EN-gage.co.uk

BASIC ACCOUNTING I

Qualifications and Credit Framework

Level 2 Certificate in Accounting

British Library Cataloguing-in-Publication Data

A catalogue record for this book is available from the British Library.

Published by
Kaplan Publishing UK
Unit 2, The Business Centre
Molly Millars Lane
Wokingham
Berkshire
RG41 2QZ

ISBN 978-0-85732-208-1

Printed in Great Britain by WM Print Ltd, Walsall.

We are grateful to the Association of Accounting Technicians for permission to reproduce past assessment materials and example tasks based on the new syllabus. The solutions to past answers and similar activities in the style of the new syllabus have been prepared by Kaplan Publishing.

CONTENTS

STUDY TEXT AND WORKBOOK

KAPLAN PUBLISHING

INTRODUCTION

HOW TO USE THESE MATERIALS

These Kaplan Publishing learning materials have been carefully designed to make your learning experience as easy as possible and to give you the best chance of success in your AAT assessments.

They contain a number of features to help you in the study process.

The sections on the Unit Guide, the Assessment and Study Skills should be read before you commence your studies.

They are designed to familiarise you with the nature and content of the assessment and to give you tips on how best to approach your studies.

STUDY TEXT

This study text has been specially prepared for the revised AAT qualification introduced in July 2010.

It is written in a practical and interactive style:

- key terms and concepts are clearly defined

- all topics are illustrated with practical examples with clearly worked solutions based on sample tasks provided by the AAT in the new examining style

- frequent practice activities throughout the chapters ensure that what you have learnt is regularly reinforced

- 'pitfalls' and 'examination tips' help you avoid commonly made mistakes and help you focus on what is required to perform well in your examination

- clear advice as to which practice activities can be completed is given at the end of each chapter

WORKBOOK

The workbook comprises:

A question bank of practice activities with solutions, to reinforce the work covered in each chapter.

The questions are divided into their relevant chapters and students may either attempt these questions as they work through the textbook, or leave some or all of these until they have completed the textbook as a final revision of what they have studied.

ICONS

The study chapters include the following icons throughout.

They are designed to assist you in your studies by identifying key definitions and the points at which you can test yourself on the knowledge gained.

 Definition

These sections explain important areas of Knowledge which must be understood and reproduced in an assessment.

 Example

The illustrative examples can be used to help develop an understanding of topics before attempting the activity exercises.

 Activity

These are exercises which give the opportunity to assess your understanding of all the assessment areas.

Test your knowledge

At the end of each chapter these boxes will direct you to the Practice Activities that you can attempt after studying the chapter.

KAPLAN PUBLISHING

UNIT GUIDE

Basic accounting I is the first of two financial accounting assessments at level 2, covering the following units.

Preparing and recording financial documentation (skills)

2 credits

Processing ledger transactions and extracting an initial trial balance (skills)

2 credits

The following unit is assessed in both Basic accounting I and Basic accounting II, and will only be awarded once both assessments have been achieved

Principles of recording and processing financial transactions (knowledge)

2 credits

Purpose of the units

The AAT has stated that the general purpose of this unit is to introduce the learner to the double entry bookkeeping system and associated documents and processes. By studying this unit, the learner is taken to the stage of extracting an initial trial balance, before any adjustments are made.

Learning objectives

On completion of these units the learner will be able to:

- deal with documents that are sent to and from organisations
- code and file those documents appropriately
- make entries in the sales, purchases and returns day books, and to transfer the totals to the sales, purchases and general ledger
- make entries in the cash book and the petty cash book, and to transfer the totals to the sales, purchases and general ledger

Learning Outcomes and Assessment criteria

The unit consists of fourteen learning outcomes, six for Knowledge and eight for Skills, which are further broken down into Assessment criteria. These are set out in the following table with Learning Outcomes in bold type and Assessment criteria listed underneath each Learning Outcome. Reference is also made to the relevant chapter within the text.

Knowledge

To perform this unit effectively you will need to know and understand the following:

Chapter

1   Understand the role of the books of prime entry

1.1	Outline the purpose, content and format of the books of prime entry	6, 8, 13, 15, 16
1.2	Outline the purpose and content of a range of business documents to include:	4, 7, 14, 18

- petty cash voucher
- invoice
- credit note
- remittance advice

1.3	Identify when authorisation is required	14
1.4	Explain how transactions are entered in the following books of prime entry	6, 8, 12, 15, 16

- sales and sales returns day books
- purchases and purchases returns day books
- cash book
- petty cash book

2   Understand the principles of coding

2.1	Describe the need for a coding system for financial transactions within a double entry bookkeeping system	4
2.2	Describe the use of coding within a filing system	4

KAPLAN PUBLISHING

6.2	Describe the specific purpose of the following control accounts	BAII

- sales ledger
- purchases ledger
- sales tax account (e.g. VAT)

6.3	Explain why it is important to reconcile the sales and purchases ledger control accounts regularly	BAII
6.4	Describe the usefulness of an aged debtor analysis for monitoring debtors	9
6.5	Explain the need to deal with discrepancies quickly and professionally	9

Skills

To perform this unit effectively you will need to be able to do the following.

Preparing and recording financial documentation	Chapter
1 Prepare the financial documents to be sent to credit customers	
1.1 Use different source documents to prepare sales invoices and credit notes	4, 5
1.2 Calculate relevant sales tax (e.g. VAT), trade discount and settlement discount	4, 5
1.3 Produce statements of account to be sent to credit customers	9
2 Enter sales invoices and credit notes into the appropriate books of prime entry	
2.1 Code sales invoices and credit notes	4
2.2 Enter invoices and credit notes into the books of prime entry	6
3 Process payments from customers	
3.1 Check the accuracy and validity of receipts against relevant supporting information	7
3.2 Identify and deal with any discrepancies	7

THE ASSESSMENT

The format of the assessment

The assessment will be divided into two sections, with 6 tasks in section 1 and 10 in section 2.

Learners will normally be assessed by computer based assessment (CBA), and will be required to demonstrate competence in both sections of the assessment.

Time allowed

The time allowed for this assessment is **two hours.**

STUDY SKILLS

Preparing to study

Devise a study plan

Determine which times of the week you will study.

Split these times into sessions of at least one hour for study of new material. Any shorter periods could be used for revision or practice.

Put the times you plan to study onto a study plan for the weeks from now until the assessment and set yourself targets for each period of study – in your sessions make sure you cover the whole course, activities and the associated questions in the workbook at the back of the Study Text.

If you are studying more than one unit at a time, try to vary your subjects as this can help to keep you interested and see subjects as part of wider knowledge.

When working through your course, compare your progress with your plan and, if necessary, re-plan your work (perhaps including extra sessions) or, if you are ahead, do some extra revision / practice questions.

Effective studying

Active reading

You are not expected to learn the text by rote, rather, you must understand what you are reading and be able to use it to pass the assessment and develop good practice.

A good technique is to use SQ3Rs – Survey, Question, Read, Recall, Review:

1 **Survey the chapter**

    Look at the headings and read the introduction, knowledge, skills and content, so as to get an overview of what the chapter deals with.

2 **Question**

    Whilst undertaking the survey ask yourself the questions you hope the chapter will answer for you.

3   Read

Read through the chapter thoroughly working through the activities and, at the end, making sure that you can meet the learning objectives shown within the summary.

4   Recall

At the end of each section and at the end of the chapter, try to recall the main ideas of the section / chapter without referring to the text. This is best done after short break of a couple of minutes after the reading stage.

5   Review

Check that your recall notes are correct.

You may also find it helpful to re-read the chapter to try and see the topic(s) it deals with as a whole.

Note taking

Taking notes is a useful way of learning, but do not simply copy out the text.

The notes must:

- be in your own words
- be concise
- cover the key points
- be well organised
- be modified as you study further chapters in this text or in related ones.

Trying to summarise a chapter without referring to the text can be a useful way of determining which areas you know and which you don't.

Three ways of taking notes

1   Summarise the key points of a chapter

2   Make linear notes

A list of headings, subdivided with sub-headings listing the key points.

If you use linear notes, you can use different colours to highlight key points and keep topic areas together.

Use plenty of space to make your notes easy to use.

KAPLAN PUBLISHING

3 Try a diagrammatic form

The most common of which is a mind map.

To make a mind map, put the main heading in the centre of the paper and put a circle around it.

Draw lines radiating from this to the main sub-headings which again have circles around them.

Continue the process from the sub-headings to sub-sub-headings.

Highlighting and underlining

You may find it useful to underline or highlight key points in your study text – but do be selective.

You may also wish to make notes in the margins.

Revision phase

Kaplan has produced material specifically designed for your final assessment preparation for this unit.

These include pocket revision notes and a bank of revision questions specifically in the style of the new syllabus.

Further guidance on how to approach the final stage of your studies is given in these materials.

Further reading

In addition to this text, you should also read the "Student section" of the "Accounting Technician" magazine every month to keep abreast of any guidance from the examiners.

Double entry bookkeeping – introduction

1

Introduction

This chapter introduces the basic concepts and rules of bookkeeping. In particular, we study:

- the dual effect principle;
- the separate entity principle; and
- the accounting equation.

Together these will show how the assets of a business will always equal its liabilities and pave the way for studying double entry bookkeeping in the next chapter.

KNOWLEDGE	CONTENTS
3.1　State the accounting equation	1　Types of accounting
3.2　Explain how the accounting equation relates to a double entry bookkeeping system	2　Management and supervision
	3　The accounting equation: examples

1 Types of accounting

1.1 Management accounting and financial accounting

Depending on why the accounts are being produced, we can describe them as being either **management accounts** or **financial accounts.**

Management accounts

These are usually prepared on a monthly basis to enable the managers to run the business effectively.

Financial accounts

These are prepared annually, mainly for the benefit of people outside the management of the business, such as the owners of the business, HM Revenue and Customs, banks, customers, suppliers and government.

In this text we focus on financial accounting principles, though most of the ideas would also apply to management accounting.

1.2 The two main financial statements

The objective of financial accounting is to provide financial information about a business. This information is given in a set of financial statements (or accounts), which consists of two principal statements:

- The **profit and loss account.** This is a summary of the business's transactions for a given period.

- The **balance sheet.** This is a statement of the financial position of the business at a given date (the end of the period covered by the profit and loss account).

These financial statements are the final product of the accounting system of a business and it is useful to be aware of where all of the double entry bookkeeping that you will study in this chapter is leading. However, you do not need to know anything about the format or rules governing the preparation of the financial statements for Level 2.

KAPLAN PUBLISHING

The following definitions will be used throughout your studies

Definitions

- An **asset** is something owned by a business, available for use in the business.

- **Fixed asset** – an asset which is to be used for the long term in the business and not resold as part of the trading activities, for example the purchase of a delivery van.

- **Current asset** – a short-term asset of the business which is to be used in the business in the near future.

- A **debtor** is an example of a current asset. A debtor is someone who owes the business money.

- A **liability** is an amount **owed** by the business, i.e. an obligation to pay money at some future date.

- A **creditor** is an example of a liability. A creditor is someone the business owes money to.

- **Capital** is the amount which the owner has invested in the business; this is owed back to the owner and is therefore a special liability of the business.

- **Capital expenditure** is the purchase of, or improvement of, fixed assets.

- **Revenue expenditure** is the day to day running costs of the business.

1.3 The difference between 'cash' and 'bank'

A possible confusion in terminology is caused by the apparent interchangeable use of the words 'cash' and 'bank'.

The normal use of the words suggests that a bank account operates by paying money out of the account with a cheque and paying either cash or cheques into the account. In practice you cannot pay 'cash' out of a bank account.

However, accounting terminology does not stick to this distinction, and the terms cash and bank are for the most part interchangeable. Thus the bank account is often referred to as the 'cash book'. Similarly we will often refer to someone 'taking cash out of the bank' or we will say things like 'John bought a car for £5,000 cash', whereas in reality John would have paid for the car using a cheque.

For the early part of your studies all movements of cash/cheques shall be made through the bank account and references to 'cash' or 'cheques' effectively mean the same thing.

2 Management and supervision

2.1 Introduction

Double entry bookkeeping is based upon three basic principles:

- the dual effect principle
- the separate entity principle
- the accounting equation.

2.2 The dual effect principle

This states that every transaction has two financial effects.

(a) If, for example, you spend £2,000 on a car and pay for it by a cheque, you will have £2,000 less money in the bank, but you will also have acquired an asset worth £2,000.

(b) Again, if you owe a creditor £100 and send him a cheque for that amount, you will owe £100 less than before, but you will have £100 less money in the bank.

2.3 The separate entity principle

This states that the owner of a business is, for accounting purposes, a completely separate entity from the business itself. Therefore the money that the owner pays into the business as initial capital has to be accounted for as an amount that the business owes back to the owner. In just the same way, any money that the owner takes out of the business, known as drawings, is treated as a reduction of the initial capital that is owed back to the owner.

The dual effect principle works here as well. If the owner of the business pays £5,000 into his business, one effect is that the business has £5,000 more cash and the second effect is that the business has a £5,000 liability (called 'capital').

Note that we look at this from the point of view of the business, not from the owner's point of view. This is because when studying bookkeeping we are only interested in the business – we are not considering the owner's personal finances.

KAPLAN PUBLISHING

2.4   The accounting equation

At its simplest, the accounting equation simply says that:

Assets = Liabilities

If we treat the owner's capital as a special form of liability then the accounting equation is:

Assets = Liabilities + Capital

Or, rearranging:

Assets – Liabilities = Capital

Profit will increase the proprietor's capital and drawings will reduce it, so that we can write the equation as:

Assets – Liabilities = Capital + Profit – Drawings

3   The accounting equation: examples

 Example 1

John starts his business on 1 July and pays £2,000 into his business bank account.

(a)   What is the dual effect of this transaction?

(b)   What is the accounting equation after this transaction?

Solution

(a)   **The dual effect**

The business bank account has increased by £2,000 (an asset).
The business capital has increased by £2,000 (a liability).

(b)   **The accounting equation**

Assets – Liabilities   = Capital

£2,000 – £0   = £2,000

Example 2

Percy started business on 1 January by paying £20,000 into a business bank account. He then spent £500 on a second-hand van by cheque, £1,000 on purchases of stock for cash, took £500 cash for his own use and bought goods on credit costing £400.

What are the two effects of each of these transactions?

What would the accounting equation look like after each of these transactions?

Solution

(a)   **Percy pays £20,000 into a business bank account**

The bank balance increases from zero to £20,000 (an asset) and the business now has capital of £20,000 (a liability); capital is the amount that is owed back to the owner of the business, Percy.

Accounting equation:

Assets – Liabilities = Capital

£20,000 – £0   = £20,000

(b)   **Percy buys a second-hand van for £500 by cheque**

The bank balance decreases by £500 (a reduction of assets) but the business has acquired a new £500 asset, the van.

The van is a specific type of asset known as a fixed asset as it is for long-term use in the business rather than an asset that is likely to be sold in the trading activities of the business.

The assets of the business are now:

	£
Van	500
Bank (20,000 – 500)	19,500
	─────
	20,000
	─────

The liabilities and capital are unchanged.

Accounting equation:

Assets – Liabilities = Capital

£20,000 – £0   = £20,000

KAPLAN PUBLISHING

(c) **Percy spends £1,000 on purchases of goods for cash**

The bank balance goes down by £1,000 but the business has another asset, stock of £1,000.

Stock is a short-term asset as it is due to be sold to customers in the near future and is known as a current asset.

The assets of the business are now:

	£
Van	500
Stock	1,000
Bank (19,500 – 1,000)	18,500
	20,000

Accounting equation:

Assets – Liabilities = Capital

£20,000 – £0　　= £20,000

(d) **Percy took £500 of cash out of the business**

The bank balance has decreased by £500 and capital has also decreased as the owner has taken money out of the business – this is known as drawings.

Remember that the owner is a completely separate entity from the business itself and if he takes money out of the business in the form of drawings then this means that the business owes him less.

The assets of the business are now:

	£
Van	500
Stock	1,000
Bank (18,500 – 500)	18,000
	19,500

The capital of the business is now £(20,000 – 500) = £19,500.

Accounting equation:

Assets – Liabilities = Capital

£19,500 – £0　　= £19,500

(e) **Purchased goods on credit for £400**

The asset of stock increases by £400 and the business now has a liability of £400, the amount that is owed to the credit supplier. A liability is an amount that is owed by the business.

The assets of the business are now:

	£
Van	500
Stock (1,000 + 400)	1,400
Bank	18,000
	19,900

The liability of the business is £400. The capital is unchanged.

Accounting equation:

Assets – Liabilities = Capital

£19,900 – £400   = £19,500

General notes

1   Each and every transaction that a business undertakes has two effects. The accounting equation reflects the two effects of each transaction and the accounting equation should always balance.

2   The owner is a completely separate entity from the business, any money the owner puts into the business is known as capital and any amounts taken out by the owner are known as drawings.

 Activity 1

State whether each of the following are assets or liabilities:

(i)   Money in the business bank account

(ii)   A creditor

(iii) Stock of goods for resale

(iv)   A computer used in the accounts department

(v)   A debtor

(vi)   A salesman's car

Activity 2

A WORKED EXAMPLE

1   **Introduce capital**

Example 1

You win £10,000 and use it to create a retail business (called TLC) selling hearts and roses. What is the effect?

Answer 1

Dual effect

The business has cash of	£10,000	(asset)
The business owes you	£10,000	(capital)

TLC's position is:

Assets	Capital
£	£

(In this first example, we recorded the dual effect for you just to get you started. In later examples you will need to enter the dual effect yourself, as well as TLC's position after the transaction.)

2   **Buy stock with cash**

Example 2

TLC buys 500 chocolate hearts. The cost of each heart is £5. What is the effect?

Answer 2

Dual effect

TLC's position is:

Assets	Capital
£	£

3   **Buy stock on credit**

In reality a business will not always pay for its purchases with cash but is more likely to buy items on credit.

Example 3

TLC buys stock of 200 red roses on credit. Each red rose costs £10. What is the effect?

Answer 3

Dual effect

TLC's position is:

Net assets	*Capital*
£	£

4   **Buy a delivery van**

The delivery van is bought for ongoing use within the business rather than for resale. Such assets are known as **fixed assets.**

Example 4

TLC buys a delivery van for £1,000 cash. What is the effect?

Answer 4

Dual effect

TLC's position is:

Net assets	*Capital*
£	£

5   **Sell stock for profit**

Example 5

TLC sells 200 red roses for £15 cash each. What is the effect?

Answer 5

Dual effect

TLC's position is:

Net assets	*Capital*
£	£

6   **Sell stock (on credit) for profit**

It is equally likely that a business will sell goods on credit. When goods are sold on credit, an asset of the business called a debtor is generated.

Example 6

TLC sells 400 chocolate hearts to Valentino for £12.50 each on credit. What is the effect?

Answer 6

Dual effect

TLC's position is:

Net assets	*Capital*
£	£

7 **Pay expenses**

Example 7

In reality, TLC will have been incurring expenses from its commencement. TLC received and paid a gas bill for £500. What is the effect?

Answer 7

Dual effect

TLC's position is:

Net assets	*Capital*
£	£

8 **Take out a loan**

In order to fund your future expansion plans for TLC, you persuade your Aunt to lend TLC £2,000.

Example 8

TLC is lent £2,000 cash by your Aunt. She expects to be repaid in two years' time. What is the effect?

Answer 8

Dual effect

TLC's position is:

Net assets	*Capital*
£	£

9   Payment to creditors for purchases

Example 9

TLC pays cash of £1,500 towards the £2,000 owed to the supplier. What is the effect?

Answer 9

Dual effect

TLC's position is:

Net assets £	*Capital* £

10   Receive cash from debtors

Example 10

TLC's debtor sends a cheque for £3,000. What is the effect?

Answer 10

Dual effect

TLC's position is:

Net assets £	*Capital* £

11   Drawings

Example 11

You withdraw £750 from the business. Such a withdrawal is merely a repayment of the capital you introduced. Your withdrawal is called **drawings.** What is the effect?

Answer 11

Dual effect

TLC's position is:

Net assets £	Capital £

4   Test your knowledge

 Test your knowledge

Having completed Chapter 1, you should now be able to attempt Practice activities 1 and 2.

5   Summary

You must understand the basic definitions covered in this chapter. You must also understand the principles of dual effect and separate entity. The accounting equation underlies the whole of bookkeeping and you should re-work the examples in this chapter if you do not fully understand how it works.

Answers to chapter activities

Activity 1

(i)   Asset

(ii)   Liability

(iii)   Asset

(iv)   Asset

(v)   Asset

(vi)   Asset

Activity 2

Answer 1

	Assets £		Capital £
Cash	10,000	Capital introduced	10,000

Answer 2

Dual effect

Increase stock	£2,500	(↑ asset)
Decrease cash	£2,500	(↓ asset)

	Assets £		Capital £
Stock	2,500	Capital introduced	10,000
Cash	7,500		
	10,000		10,000

Answer 3

Dual effect

Increase stock	£2,000	(↑ asset)
Increase creditor	£2,000	(↑ liability)

	Net assets £		Capital £
Stock	4,500	Capital introduced	10,000
Cash	7,500		
	12,000		
Less: Creditors	(2,000)		
	10,000		10,000

Answer 4

Dual effect

Increase fixed asset	£1,000	(↑ asset)
Decrease cash	£1,000	(↓ asset)

	Net assets £		Capital £
Fixed asset	1,000	Capital introduced	10,000
Stock	4,500		
Cash	6,500		
	12,000		
Less: Creditors	(2,000)		
	10,000		10,000

Answer 5

Dual effect

Increase cash	£3,000	(↑ asset)
Decrease stock	£2,000	(↓ asset)
Increase profit	£1,000	(↑ profit)

	Net assets £		Capital £
Fixed asset	1,000	Capital introduced	10,000
Stock	2,500	Profit	1,000
Cash	9,500		
	13,000		
Less: Creditors	(2,000)		
	11,000		11,000

Answer 6

Dual effect

Increase debtors	£5,000	(↑ asset)
Decrease stock	£2,000	(↓. asset)
Increase profit	£3,000	(↑ profit)

	Net assets £		Capital £
Fixed asset	1,000	Capital introduced	10,000
Stock	500	Profit	4,000
Debtors	5,000		
Cash	9,500		
	16,000		
Less: Creditors	(2,000)		
	14,000		14,000

Answer 7

Dual effect

Decrease cash	£500	(↓ asset)
Decrease profit	£500	(↓ profit)

	Net assets £		Capital £
Fixed asset	1,000	Capital introduced	10,000
Stock	500	Profit	3,500
Debtors	5,000		
Cash	9,000		
	15,500		
Less: Creditors	(2,000)		
	13,500		13,500

Answer 8

Dual effect

Increase cash	£2,000	(↑ asset)
Increase creditors	£2,000	(↑ liability)

	Net assets £		Capital £
Fixed asset	1,000	Capital introduced	10,000
Stock	500	Profit	3,500
Debtors	5,000		
Cash	11,000		
	17,500		
Less: Creditors	(2,000)		
Loan	(2,000)		
	13,500		13,500

The loan will be shown separately from creditors for purchases, which are known as trade creditors.

Answer 9

Dual effect

Decrease cash	£1,500	(↓ asset)
Decrease creditors	£1,500	(↓ liability)

	Net assets £			Capital £
Fixed asset	1,000		Capital introduced	10,000
Stock	500		Profit	3,500
Debtors	5,000			
Cash	9,500			
	16,000			
Less: Creditors	(500)			
Loan	(2,000)			
	13,500			13,500

Answer 10

Dual effect

Decrease debtors	£3,000	(↓ asset)
Increase cash	£3,000	(↑ asset)

	Net assets £			Capital £
Fixed asset	1,000		Capital introduced	10,000
Stock	500		Profit	3,500
Debtors	2,000			
Cash	12,500			
	16,000			
Less: Creditors	(500)			
Loan	(2,000)			
	13,500			13,500

Answer 11

Dual effect

Decrease cash	£750	(↓ asset)
Increase drawings	£750	(↓ capital)

	Net assets £		Capital £
Fixed asset	1,000	Capital introduced	10,000
Stock	500	Profit	3,500
Debtors	2,000		
Cash	11,750		
	———		———
	15,250		13,500
Less: Creditors	(500)	Less: Drawings	(750)
Loan	(2,000)		
	———		———
	12,750		12,750
	———		———

We do not simply deduct drawings from profit as we want to show separately the profit or loss for the period before any drawings were made.

Ledger accounting

2

Introduction

Now that we have looked at the basic theory of bookkeeping, it is time to learn and practise how to make the correct double entries for the sorts of transactions that are relevant for the AAT standards.

We shall start with accounting for cash transactions, and will study a series of the different sorts of things that a business can buy or sell (or pay for or receive) in cash.

We shall then study how to deal with purchases and sales made for credit.

SKILLS	CONTENTS
2.1 Balance ledger accounts clearly showing balances carried down and brought down as appropriate	1 Ledger accounting 2 Worked example 3 Examples and activities 4 Credit purchases 5 Credit sales

1 Ledger accounting

1.1 Introduction

The accounting equation does have limitations. In activity 2 in chapter 1, we were able to calculate a profit figure for TLC. We were not able, however, to determine which part of the profit was sales and which part was expenses. We will now account for the movement in sales and purchases, rather than simply the movement of stock.

Another limitation of the accounting equation is that in practice it would be far too time consuming to write up the accounting equation each time that the business undertook a transaction. Instead the two effects of each transaction are recorded in ledger accounts.

1.2 The ledger account

A typical ledger account is shown below:

Title of account							
DEBIT				**CREDIT**			
Date	Details	Folio	Amount £	Date	Details	Folio	Amount £

The important point to note is that it has two sides. The left hand side is known as the **debit** side and the right hand side is known as the **credit** side.

- The date column contains the date of the transaction.

- The details column contains the title of the other account that holds the second part of the dual effect. It may also have a brief description of the nature of the entry (e.g. 'rent 1.1.X3 to 31.3.X3').

- The folio column contains a reference to the source of the information. We shall see some of these sources later on but it could be, for example, 'sales day book p17' or 'payroll month 6'.

- The amount column simply contains the value of the transaction.

- The title of the account is a name that reflects the nature of the transaction ('van account', 'bank account', 'electricity account', etc).

1.3   Simplified account

The ledger account in 1.2 is very detailed and in much of this book we use a simpler form of the account. Part of the reason for this is that it is easier to 'see' the entries being made if there is less detail in the accounts. Thus, we sometimes do without the date or the full description or folio to keep things clear and simple.

For example, we will often use accounts which look like this: Bank account

Bank account			
	£	Van	£
		Van	500

Van account			
	£		£
Bank	500		

It is simple and clearly shows the two sides of the account and the entries that have been made.

1.4   The golden rule for making entries in the ledger accounts

There is a golden rule for making entries in ledger accounts:

Every debit entry must have an equal and opposite credit entry.

This reflects the dual effect of each transaction and causes the accounting equation to always balance.

It is also why we refer to double entry bookkeeping.

1.5 Which accounts to debit and credit

The mnemonic DEAD/CLIC will help you determine if an entry should be made on the debit side or on the credit side of a ledger account

Ledger account	
DEBIT	**CREDIT**
Debtors	**C**reditors
Expenses	**L**iabilities
Assets	**I**ncome
Drawings	**C**apital

We also need to appreciate the effect a debit or a credit entry will have.

Ledger account	
A **debit entry** represents:	A **credit entry** represents:
• An increase in the value of an asset;	• A decrease in the value of an asset;
• A decrease in the value of a liability; or	• An increase in the value of a liability; or
• An item of expenditure	• An item of income (revenue)

1.6 What goes on the debit or credit side?

Step 1

If John pays £2,000 into his business bank account as capital, we need to ask a number of questions

(a) Which accounts are affected?

(b) What type of accounts are they?

(c) Do they increase or decrease?

One of the accounts affected is the bank account, which is an asset account. As we have paid money into the account, the bank account increases. To show an increase in the value of an asset, we would debit that account.

The other account affected is the capital account, which is a special liability of the business. As the John has invested £2,000 into the business, the business owes him this amount back. To show this liability, we would credit this account

Debit Bank Account

Credit Capital Account

Bank account			
	£		£
Capital	2,000		

Capital account			
	£		£
		Bank	2,000

Step 2

If John's business now pays £1,000 out of the bank to buy a van, the double entry will be:

(a) **The bank account**

The bank account needs to show a decrease in the asset, as John has spent some of the money, therefore, Credit Bank Account.

(b) **The van account**

The other half of the transaction must therefore be a debit of £1,000 to the van account, which would show an increase in this fixed asset account.

Bank account			
	£		£
Capital	2,000	Van	1,000

Capital account			
	£		£
		Bank	2,000

Van account			
	£		£
Bank	1,000		

2 Worked example

2.1 Introducing capital into the business – explanation

The owner of a business starts the business by paying money into the business bank account. This is the capital of the business. The business will need this money to 'get going'. It may need to pay rent, buy stock for sale or pay wages to its staff before it has actually sold anything or received any money.

Example

Frankie starts a business and pays £5,000 into the business bank account. What is the double entry for this transaction?

Solution

- £5,000 has been paid into the bank account.

  It represents an asset of the business.

  This is therefore a debit in the bank account.

- The business has a liability because it owes Frankie (the owner) £5,000.

  This liability will be a credit in the capital account.

Bank (or cash book)			Capital		
Capital	£5,000			Bank	£5,000

2.2   Purchasing goods for resale

A business buys goods for resale to customers – that is how most businesses (e.g. shops) make their money. These goods are assets which the business owns.

 Example

Frankie buys £300 of chocolate bars for resale. He pays with a cheque to his supplier.

What is the double entry for this transaction?

Solution

- The business has paid £300 out of its bank account.

  Therefore, the £300 will be credited to the bank account.

- The chocolate bars are an asset.

  This asset will be debited to the purchases account.

Purchases		Bank	
Bank £300			Purchases £300

2.3   Paying office rent

A business will typically rent office space in order to carry out its operations. It will pay rent to the landlord of the offices. Rent is an expense of the business.

 Example

Frankie pays £1,000 per quarter for the rent of his offices. He pays with a cheque to the landlord.

What is the double entry for this transaction?

Solution

- The business has paid £1,000 out of its bank account.

  Therefore, the £1,000 will be credited to the bank account.

- The rent is an expense.

  This expense will be debited to the rent account.

Rent		Bank	
Bank £1,000		Rent £1,000	

2.4 Buying stationery

A business will buy stationery in order to be able to operate. The items of stationery (pens, paper, etc) are not for resale to customers and are used quickly after they are purchased. Stationery is therefore an expense of the business.

 Example

Frankie pays £200 for items of stationery. He pays with a cheque to the supplier.

What is the double entry for this transaction?

Solution

- The business has paid £200 out of its bank account.

  Therefore, the £200 will be credited to the bank account.

- The stationery is an expense.

  This expense will be debited to the stationery account.

Stationery		Bank	
Bank £200		Stationery £200	

2.5 Buying a computer

A business will buy computers in order to streamline its operations. These computers are not bought with a view to re-sale and are to be used in the business for the long term. They are therefore a fixed asset of the business.

Example

Frankie pays £900 to purchase a computer. He pays with a cheque to the supplier.

What is the double entry for this transaction?

Solution

- Once again start with the bank account.

  The business has paid £900 out of its bank account.

  Therefore, the £900 will be credited to the bank account.

- The computer is a fixed asset.

  The £900 will be debited to the fixed asset computer account.

Computer		Bank	
Bank £900			Computer £900

2.6 Receiving income from sales of goods

A business will sell the goods it has purchased for re-sale. This is income for the business and is referred to as 'sales'.

 Example

Frankie sells goods for £1,500. The customer pays cash.

What is the double entry for this transaction?

Solution

- Once again start with the bank account.

  The business has received £1,500 into its bank account.

  Therefore, the £1,500 will be debited to the bank account.

- The cash received is income.

  This income will be credited to the sales account.

Sales		Bank	
	Bank £1,500	Sales £1,500	

2.7 Receiving income for services provided

A business may provide services to its customers, e.g.it may provide consultancy advice. This is income for the business and will usually be referred to as 'sales'.

 Example

Frankie provides consultancy services to a client who pays £2,000 in cash. What is the double entry for this transaction?

Solution

• Once again start with the bank account.

  The business has received £2,000 into its bank account.

  Therefore, the £2,000 will be debited to the bank account.

• The cash received is income.

  This income will be credited to the sales account.

Sales			Bank		
	Bank	£2,000	Sales	£2,000	

3 Examples and activities

 Example

Percy started business on 1 January and made the following transactions.

1 Paid £20,000 into a business bank account.

2 Spent £500 on a second-hand van.

3 Paid £1,000 on purchases of stock.

4 Took £50 cash for his own use.

5 On 5 January bought goods for cash costing £500.

6 Made sales for cash of £2,000.

7 On 15 January paid £200 of rent.

Task 1

Show how the debit and credit entries for each transaction are determined.

Task 2

Enter the transactions into the relevant ledger accounts.

Solution

Task 1

(1) *Capital invested*

Percy has paid £20,000 into the bank account – therefore the bank account is debited.

Debit (Dr)   Bank   £20,000

The business now owes the owner £20,000. Capital is the amount owed by the business to its owner – this is a liability, therefore a credit entry in the capital account.

Credit (Cr)   Capital   £20,000

(2) *Purchase of van*

The business has paid £500 out of the bank account – therefore a credit entry in the bank account.

Cr   Bank   £500

The business now has a van costing £500 – this is an asset therefore a debit entry in the van account. This is a fixed asset of the business.

Dr   Van   £500

(3) *Purchase of stock for cash*

The business has paid out £1,000 out of the bank account – therefore a credit to the bank account.

Cr   Bank   £1,000

The business has made purchases of stock costing £1,000 – this is an item of expenditure therefore a debit entry in the purchases account. Note that the debit entry is to a purchases account not a stock account. The stock account is a different account altogether and will be considered later in this study text.

Dr   Purchases   £1,000

(4) *Drawings*

The business has paid £50 out of the bank account – therefore credit the bank account.

Cr   Bank   £50

The proprietor has made drawings of £50 – this is a reduction of capital and therefore a debit entry to the drawings account.

Dr   Drawings   £50

Drawings should not be directly debited to the capital account. A separate drawings account should be used.

(5) *Purchase of goods for cash*

The business has paid out £500 – therefore credit the bank account.

Cr   Bank   £500

The business has made purchases of stock costing £500 – an expense therefore debit the purchases account.

Dr   Purchases   £500

(6) *Sale for cash*

The business has paid £2,000 into the bank account – therefore a debit to the bank account.

Dr   Bank   £2,000

The business has made sales of £2,000 – this is income therefore a credit to the sales account.

Cr   Sales   £2,000

(7) *Payment of rent*

The business now paid £200 out of the bank account – therefore a credit to the bank account.

Cr   Bank   £200

The business has incurred an expense of rent – as an expense item the rent account must be debited.

Dr   Rent   £200

Task 2

Bank

Date			£	Date			£
1 Jan	Capital	(1)	20,000	1 Jan	Van	(2)	500
5 Jan	Sales	(6)	2,000		Purchases	(3)	1,000
					Drawings	(4)	50
				5 Jan	Purchases	(5)	500
				15 Jan	Rent	(7)	200

Capital

Date			£	Date			£
				1 Jan	Bank	(1)	20,000

Van

Date			£	Date		£
1 Jan	Bank	(2)	500			

Purchases

Date			£	Date		£
1 Jan	Bank	(3)	1,000			
5 Jan	Bank	(5)	500			

Drawings

Date			£	Date		£
1 Jan	Bank	(4)	50			

Sales

Date		£	Date			£
			5 Jan	Bank	(6)	2,000

Rent					
Date			£	*Date*	£
15 Jan	Bank	(7)	200		

Activity 1

Write up the following cash transactions in the ledger accounts.

Transaction	*Details*
1	Set up the business by introducing £150,000 in cash.
2	Purchase property costing £140,000. Pay in cash.
3	Purchase goods costing £5,000. Pay in cash.
4	Sell goods for £7,000. All cash sales.
5	Purchase goods costing £8,000. Pay in cash.
6	Pay a sundry expense of £100, by cheque.
7	Sell goods for £15,000. All cash sales.
8	Pay wages of £2,000 to an employee.
9	Pay postage costs of £100, by cheque.

4 Credit purchases

Definitions

A cash purchase occurs when goods are bought (or a service received) and the customer pays immediately using cash, cheques or credit cards. A receipt is issued for the amount of cash paid.

A credit purchase occurs when goods are bought (or a service received) and the customer does not have to pay immediately but can pay after a specified number of days. An invoice will be issued to act as a reminder of the amount due to be paid.

Example

We have already seen the double entry for a cash purchase and we shall now contrast this with the double entry for a credit purchase by means of an illustration.

John buys goods from Sam for £2,000.

(a) Record the double entry in John's books if John pays for the goods immediately with a cheque.

(b) Record the double entry in John's books if John buys the goods on credit and pays some time later.

Solution

(a) **Cash purchase**

The double entry is simply to:

Credit the bank account with £2,000 because £2,000 has been paid out.

Debit the purchases account with £2,000 because goods have been purchased with £2,000.

Bank

	£			£
		Purchases		2,000

Purchases

	£			£
Bank	2,000			

(b) **Credit purchase**

The double entry will be made at two separate times.

(i) *At the time the purchase is made*

At the time the purchase is made we debit £2,000 to the purchases account because a purchase has been made, but we cannot make any entry in the bank account at the time of the purchase because no cash is paid. However, the dual effect principle means that there must be another effect to this transaction, and in this case it is that the business has a creditor (the supplier to whom the £2,000 is owed).

The double entry is:

Debit the purchases account with £2,000 because expenses have increased by £2,000.

Credit creditors account with £2,000 (this is a liability of the business).

Purchases

	£		£
Creditor	2,000		

Creditors

	£		£
		Purchases	2,000

(ii) *When John pays the £2,000*

The double entry now will be:

Credit the bank account with £2,000 because £2,000 has been paid out.

Debit the creditor account because John has paid and the creditor has been reduced by £2,000.

Creditors

	£		£
Bank	2,000	Purchases	2,000

Purchases

	£		£
Creditor	2,000		

Bank

	£		£
		Creditor	2,000

4.1 Summary

The net effect of the above credit purchase is that the creditor has a nil balance because John has paid, and we are left with a debit in the purchases account and a credit in the cash book. This is exactly as for a cash purchase – we just had to go through the intermediate step of the creditors account to get there.

5 Credit sales

Definitions

A cash sale occurs when goods are sold (or a serviced provided) and the customer pays immediately with cash, cheque or credit card. A receipt is issued for the amount of cash received.

A credit sale occurs when goods are sold (or a service provided) and the customer does not have to pay immediately but can pay after a specified number of days. An invoice is issued to act as a reminder of the amount of money owed.

Example

We have already seen the double entry for a cash sale and we shall now contrast this with the double entry for a credit sale by means of an illustration.

George sells goods to Harry for £1,000.

(a) Record the double entry in George's books if Harry pays for the goods immediately with a cheque.

(b) Record the double entry in George's books if Harry buys the goods on credit and pays some time later.

Solution

(a) **Cash sale**

The double entry is simply to:

Debit the bank account with £1,000 because £1,000 has been paid in.

Credit the sales account with £1,000 because income has increased by £1,000.

Bank

	£		£
Sales	1,000		

Sales

	£		£
		Bank	1,000

(b) **Credit sale**

The double entry will be made at two separate times.

(i) *At the time the sale is made*

At the time the sale is made we credit £1,000 to the sales account because a sale has been made, but we cannot make any entry in the bank account at the time of the sale because no cash is received. However, the dual effect principle means that there must be another effect to this transaction, and in this case it is that the business has acquired a debtor.

The double entry is:

Debit debtors account with £1,000 (this is an asset of the business).

Credit the sales account with £1,000 because income has increased by £1,000.

Debtors

	£		£
Sales	1,000		

Sales

	£		£
		Debtor	1,000

(ii) *When Harry pays the £1,000*

The double entry now will be:

Debit the bank account with £1,000 because £1,000 has been paid in.

Credit the debtors account because Harry has paid and the debtor has been reduced by £1,000.

Debtors

	£		£
Sales	1,000	Bank	1,000

Sales

	£		£
		Debtor	1,000

Bank

	£		£
Debtor	1,000		

5.1   Summary

The net effect of the above credit sale is that the debtor has a nil balance because Harry has paid and we are left with a credit in the sales account and a debit in the cash book. This is exactly as for a cash sale – we just had to go through the intermediate step of the debtor account to get there.

Activity 2

We shall now revisit our worked example from Chapter 1 and record the transactions with debits and credits to ledger accounts.

Date	Detail
1.1.X5	TLC commenced business with £10,000 cash introduced by you, the proprietor
2.1.X5	TLC bought stock of 500 chocolate hearts for £2,500 cash
3.1.X5	TLC bought stock of 200 red roses on credit for £2,000
4.1.X5	TLC bought a delivery van for £1,000 cash
5.1.X5	TLC sold all the red roses for £3,000 cash
6.1.X5	TLC sold 400 chocolate hearts for £5,000 on credit
7.1.X5	TLC paid a gas bill for £500 cash
8.1.X5	TLC took out a loan of £2,000
9.1.X5	TLC paid £1,500 cash to trade creditors
10.1.X5	TLC received £3,000 cash from debtors
11.1.X5	The proprietor withdrew £750 cash

Required:

Record these transactions in the relevant ledger accounts. Make your entries in the ledger accounts below.

Cash

£	£

Capital

£	£

Purchases

	£		£

Creditors

	£		£

Delivery van

	£		£

Sales

	£		£

Debtors

	£		£

Gas		
	£	£

Loan		
	£	£

Drawings		
	£	£

6 Test your knowledge

Having completed Chapter 2, you should now be able to attempt Practice Activities 3 to 8.

7 Summary

In this chapter we have studied cash and credit transactions. It is important to always start with the bank account and remember that cash received is a debit in the bank account and cash paid out is a credit in the bank account. If you get that right then the rest really does fall into place.

You should also be aware of the definitions of assets, expenses and income and the normal entries that you would make in the accounts for these.

Answers to chapter activities

Activity 1

The figures in brackets are used here to indicate the transaction number in the activity. They can be used to match the debit entry for the transaction with the corresponding credit entry.

Capital

	£		£
		Cash at bank (1)	150,000

Property

	£		£
Cash at bank (2)	140,000		

Purchases

	£		£
Cash at bank (3)	5,000		
Cash at bank (5)	8,000		

Sales

	£		£
		Cash at bank (4)	7,000
		Cash at bank (7)	15,000

Sundry expenses

	£		£
Cash at bank (6)	100		

Wages payable

	£		£
Cash at bank (8)	2,000		

Postage

	£		£
Cash at bank (9)	100		

Cash at bank

	£		£
Capital (1)	150,000	Property (2)	140,000
Sales (4)	7,000	Purchases (3)	5,000
Sales (7)	15,000	Purchases (5)	8,000
		Sundry expenses (6)	100
		Wages payable (8)	2,000
		Postage (9)	100

Activity 2

Cash

Date	Narrative	£	Date	Narrative	£
1.1.X5	Capital	10,000	2.1.X5	Purchases	2,500
5.1.X5	Sales	3,000	4.1.X5	Delivery van	1,000
8.1.X5	Loan	2,000	7.1.X5	Gas	500
10.1.X5	Debtors	3,000	9.1.X5	Creditors	1,500
			11.1.X5	Drawings	750

Capital

Date	Narrative	£	Date	Narrative	£
			1.1.X5	Cash	10,000

Purchases

Date	Narrative	£	Date	Narrative	£
2.1.X5	Cash	2,500			
3.1.X5	Creditors	2,000			

Creditors

Date	Narrative	£	Date	Narrative	£
9.1.X5	Cash	1,500	3.1.X5	Purchases	2,000

Delivery van

Date	Narrative	£	Date	Narrative	£
4.1.X5	Cash	1,000			

Sales

Date	Narrative	£	Date	Narrative	£
			5.1.X5	Cash	3,000
			6.1.X5	Debtors	5,000

Debtors

Date	Narrative	£	Date	Narrative	£
6.1.X5	Sales	5,000	10.1.X5	Cash	3,000

Gas

Date	Narrative	£	Date	Narrative	£
7.1.X5	Cash	500			

Loan

Date	Narrative	£	Date	Narrative	£
			8.1.X5	Cash	2,000

Drawings

Date	Narrative	£	Date	Narrative	£
11.1.X5	Cash	750			

Drafting an initial Trial Balance

Introduction

At the end of a period of time, for example a month of trading, the owner of the business might wish to know some details about the performance of the business in the period. For example how much sales revenue was earned, how much does the business owe to its creditors, how much money is left in the bank?

These figures can be found by balancing the ledger accounts. So in this chapter we will look at the procedure for balancing a ledger account as the first step to drafting an initial trial balance.

SKILLS	CONTENTS
2.2 Extract an initial trial balance	1 Procedure for balancing a ledger account
	2 The trial balance

1 Procedure for balancing a ledger account

1.1 Steps to follow

Step 1 Total both the debit and the credit side of the ledger account and make a note of each total.

Step 2 Insert the higher of the two totals as the total on both sides of the ledger account leaving a line beneath the final entry on each side of the account.

Step 3 On the side with the smaller total insert the figure needed to make this column add up to the total. Call this figure the balance carried down (or 'Bal c/d' as an abbreviation).

Step 4 On the opposite side of the ledger account, below the total insert this same figure and call it the balance brought down (or 'Bal b/d' as an abbreviation).

Example

The bank account of a business has the following entries:

Bank

	£		£
Capital	1,000	Purchases	200
Sales	300	Drawings	100
Sales	400	Rent	400
Capital	500	Stationery	300
Sales	800	Purchases	400

Calculate the balance on the account and bring the balance down as a single amount.

Solution

Step 1 Total both sides of the account and make a note of the totals. (Note that these totals that are asterisked below would not normally be written into the ledger account itself. They are only shown here to explain the process more clearly.)

Bank

	£		£
Capital	1,000	Purchases	200
Sales	300	Drawings	100
Sales	400	Rent	400
Capital	500	Stationery	300
Sales	800	Purchases	400
	———		———
*Sub-total debits**	*3,000*	*Sub-total credits**	*1,400*

Step 2 Insert the higher total as the total of both sides.

Bank

	£		£
Capital	1,000	Purchases	200
Sales	300	Drawings	100
Sales	400	Rent	400
Capital	500	Stationery	300
Sales	800	Purchases	400
	———		———
*Sub-total debits**	*3,000*	*Sub-total credits**	*1,400*
	———		———
Total	3,000	Total	3,000
	———		———

Step 3 Insert a balancing figure on the side of the account with the lower sub-total. This is referred to as the 'balance carried down' or 'bal c/d' for short.

Bank

	£		£
Capital	1,000	Purchases	200
Sales	300	Drawings	100
Sales	400	Rent	400
Capital	500	Stationery	300
Sales	800	Purchases	400
	———		———
*Sub-total debits**	*3,000*	*Sub-total credits**	*1,400*
		Bal c/d	1,600
	———		———
Total	3,000	Total	3,000
	———		———

Step 4 Insert the balance carried down figure beneath the total on the other side of the account. This is referred to as 'bal b/d' for short.

Bank

	£		£
Capital	1,000	Purchases	200
Sales	300	Drawings	100
Sales	400	Rent	400
Capital	500	Stationery	300
Sales	800	Purchases	400
	———		———
*Sub-total debits**	*3,000*	*Sub-total credits**	*1,400*
		Bal c/d	1,600
	———		———
Total	3,000	Total	3,000
	———		———
Bal b/d	1,600		

The closing balance carried down at the end of the period is also the opening balance brought down at the start of the next period. This opening balance remains in the account as the starting position and any further transactions are then added into the account. In this case the balance brought down is a debit balance as there is money in the bank account making it an asset.

Example

Consider again the ledger accounts from the example Percy in the previous chapter which are reproduced below and balance them.

Bank

Date			£	Date			£
1 Jan	Capital	(1)	20,000	1 Jan	Van	(2)	500
5 Jan	Sales	(6)	2,000		Purchases	(3)	1,000
					Drawings	(4)	50
				5 Jan	Purchases	(5)	500
				15 Jan	Rent	(7)	200

Capital

Date			£	Date			£
				1 Jan	Bank	(1)	20,000

Van

Date			£	Date			£
1 Jan	Bank	(2)	500				

Purchases

Date			£	Date			£
1 Jan	Bank	(3)	1,000				
5 Jan	Bank	(5)	500				

Drawings

Date			£	Date			£
1 Jan	Bank	(4)	50				

Sales

Date			£	Date			£
				5 Jan	Bank	(6)	2,000

Rent

Date			£	Date		£
15 Jan	Bank	(7)	200			

Solution

(a)   The bank account

Bank

Date		£	Date		£
1 Jan	Capital	20,000	1 Jan	Van	500
5 Jan	Sales	2,000		Purchases	1,000
				Drawings	50
			5 Jan	Purchases	500
			15 Jan	Rent	200

Step 1   Total both the debit and the credit side of the ledger account and make a note of each total – debit side £22,000, credit side £2,250.

Step 2   Insert the higher of the two totals, £22,000, as the total on both sides of the ledger account leaving a line beneath the final entry on each side of the account.

Bank

Date		£	Date		£
1 Jan	Capital	20,000	1 Jan	Van	500
5 Jan	Sales	2,000		Purchases	1,000
				Drawings	50
			5 Jan	Purchases	500
			15 Jan	Rent	200
		22,000			22,000

Step 3   On the side with the smaller total insert the figure needed to make this column add up to the total. Call this figure the balance carried down (or Bal c/d as an abbreviation).

Step 4   On the opposite side of the ledger account, below the total insert this same figure and call it the balance brought down (or Bal b/d as an abbreviation).

Bank

Date		£	Date		£
1 Jan	Capital	20,000	1 Jan	Van	500
5 Jan	Sales	2,000		Purchases	1,000
				Drawings	50
			5 Jan	Purchases	500
			15 Jan	Rent	200
			31 Jan	Balance c/d	19,750
		_____			_____
		22,000			22,000
		_____			_____
1 Feb	Balance b/d	19,750			

This shows that the business has £19,750 left in the bank account at the end of January and therefore also on the first day of February. As the balance that is brought down to start the next period is on the debit side of the account this is known as a debit balance and indicates that this is an asset – money in the bank account.

(b) **Capital**

Capital

Date		£	Date		£
			1 Jan	Bank	20,000

As there is only one entry in this account there is no need to balance the account. The entry is on the credit side and is known as a credit balance. A credit balance is a liability of the business and this account shows that the business owes the owner £20,000 of capital.

(c) **Van**

Van

Date		£	Date		£
1 Jan	Bank	500			

Again, there is no need to balance this account as there is only one entry. This is a debit balance as it is an asset – the fixed asset, the van, which cost £500.

(d)   Purchases

Purchases

Date		£	Date		£
1 Jan	Bank	1,000			
5 Jan	Bank	500	31 Jan	Balance c/d	1,500
		1,500			1,500
1 Feb	Balance b/d	1,500			

This now shows that during the month £1,500 of purchases were made. This is a debit balance as purchases are an expense of the business.

(e)   Drawings

Drawings

Date		£	Date		£
1 Jan	Bank	50			

This is a debit balance as drawings are a reduction of the capital owed to the owner which is a credit balance.

(f)   Sales

Sales

Date		£	Date		£
			5 Jan	Bank	2,000

There is no need to balance the account as there is only one entry – a £2,000 credit balance representing income.

(g)   Rent

Rent

Date		£	Date		£
15 Jan	Bank	200			

As there is only one entry there is no need to balance the account. This is a debit balance indicating that there has been an expense of £200 of rent incurred during the month.

Activity 1

Given below is a bank account ledger account for the month of March. Show the balance b/d at 31st March.

Bank

Date		£	Date		£
1 Mar	Capital	12,000	3 Mar	Purchases	3,000
7 Mar	Sales	5,000	15 Mar	Fixed asset	2,400
19 Mar	Sales	2,000	20 Mar	Purchases	5,300
22 Mar	Sales	3,000	24 Mar	Rent	1,000
			28 Mar	Drawings	2,000

2 The trial balance

2.1 List of balances

The trial balance is a list showing the balances brought down on each ledger account. An example of a simple trial balance is given below:

	Debit £	Credit £
Sales		5,000
Opening stock	100	
Purchases	3,000	
Rent	200	
Car	3,000	
Debtors	100	
Creditors		1,400
	6,400	6,400

The trial balance is produced immediately after the double entry has been completed and balances extracted on the accounts. If the double entry has been done correctly, the total of the debits will equal the total of the credits.

2.2 Reasons for extracting a trial balance

One of the reasons for drafting a trial balance is to ensure that double entry has been correctly completed. It is possible to detect other errors with the trial balance, but this will be discussed in a later chapter.

Example

The following are the balances on the accounts of Ernest at 31 December 20X8.

	£
Sales	47,140
Purchases	26,500
Debtors	7,640
Creditors	4,320
General expenses	9,430
Loan	5,000
Plant and machinery at cost	7,300
Motor van at cost	2,650
Drawings	7,500
Rent and rates	6,450
Insurance	1,560
Bank overdraft	2,570
Capital	10,000

Required:

Prepare Ernest's trial balance as at 31 December 20X8.

Solution

Step 1   Set up a blank trial balance

Step 2   Work down the list of balances one by one using what you have learned so far about debits and credits. Assets and expenses are debit balances and liabilities and income are credit balances.

The mnemonic DEAD CLIC may help.

Debtors	Creditors
Expenses	Liabilities
Assets	Income
Drawings	Capital

TRIAL BALANCE AT 31 DECEMBER 20X8

	£	£
Sales		47,140
Purchases	26,500	
Debtors	7,640	
Creditors		4,320
General expenses	9,430	
Loan		5,000
Plant and machinery at cost	7,300	
Motor van at cost	2,650	
Drawings	7,500	
Rent and rates	6,450	
Insurance	1,560	
Bank overdraft		2,570
Capital		10,000
	69,030	69,030

Take care with drawings. These are a reduction of the capital owed back to the owner therefore as a reduction of a liability they must be a debit balance.

The bank overdraft is an amount owed to the bank therefore it must be a credit balance.

 Activity 2

Continuing with the example above, complete the trial balance for Percy

3 Test your knowledge

Test your knowledge

Now you have completed Chapter 3, you should now be able to attempt Practice Activities 9 to 13.

4 Summary

Balancing an account is a very important technique which you must be able to master for these Units. You must understand how to bring the balance down onto the correct side.

KAPLAN PUBLISHING

Answers to chapter activities

Activity 1

Bank

Date		£	Date		£
1 Mar	Capital	12,000	3 Mar	Purchases	3,000
7 Mar	Sales	5,000	15 Mar	Fixed asset	2,400
19 Mar	Sales	2,000	20 Mar	Purchases	5,300
22 Mar	Sales	3,000	24 Mar	Rent	1,000
			28 Mar	Drawings	2,000
			31 Mar	Balance c/d	8,300
		22,000			22,000
1 Apr	Balance b/d	8,300			

Activity 2

TRIAL BALANCE

	£	£
Bank	19,750	
Capital		20,000
Van	500	
Purchases	1,500	
Drawings	50	
Sales		2,000
Rent	200	
	22,000	22,000

Credit sales: Documents

4

Introduction

Now that we have covered the basics, we can extend on this to include details regarding transactions on credit terms. This chapter will take an outline look at the documents required when making a sale.

KNOWLEDGE

1.2 Outline the purpose and content of a range of business documents to include

Invoice

Credit note

2.1 Describe the need for a coding system for financial transactions within a double entry bookkeeping system

2.2 Describe the use of coding within a filing system

SKILLS

1.1 Use different source documents to prepare sales invoices and credit notes

1.2 Calculate relevant sales tax (e.g. VAT), trade discount and settlement discount

2.1 Code sales invoices and credit notes

CONTENTS

1 The sales documents

2 Summary of credit sales

3 Setting up a credit sale

4 Supplying the goods

5 Issuing credit notes

6 Coding sales invoices

1 The sales documents

1.1 Introduction

Cash sales are relatively straightforward but credit sales are more involved. The details of all of the aspects covered here will be dealt with in greater depth in later chapters.

1.2 Cash sales

A cash sale will normally be made in a retail environment. A customer will enter the shop, choose the goods they wish to buy then come to the till in order to pay for them. The seller will tell the customer the price of the goods and the customer then offers payment for them, in the form or notes and coins. Alternatively, the customer may offer to pay for the goods by cheque or credit or debit card. The detailed procedures for accepting payment by these methods will be considered in later chapters.

Finally, once the customer has paid for the goods, a receipt of some sort will be given to the customer. This may be printed automatically by the till or may be a handwritten receipt in some businesses. The transaction is now complete.

1.3 Credit sales

The procedure for a sale on credit can be rather more involved. The sale process will normally be initiated by the receipt of an order from a customer. This order may be in writing, by fax, over the telephone or by email. When your business receives the order, the first decision that must be made is whether or not to allow the customer credit for this sale; a period of time they can take before paying the invoice.

1.4 Offering credit

Selling goods on credit always involves an element of risk. The goods are being taken away or delivered to the customer now with the promise of payment in the future. Therefore your business must be confident that the payment will be received. The decision process as to whether or not to make the sale on credit will be different depending upon whether this is a sale to an existing credit customer or a new customer.

KAPLAN PUBLISHING

1.5 Existing customers

If an existing credit customer wishes to make a further purchase on credit, it would be normal practice to carry out some basic checks. When the customer was originally taken on as a credit customer, a credit limit will have been set which should not be exceeded. Checks should be made to ensure that the new sale, when added to the amount currently owing, do not take the customer over their credit limit.

It would also be sensible to check that there have been no problems recently with receiving payment from this customer. If the checks are satisfactory then the credit sale can go ahead.

1.6 New customer

If a new customer asks for credit from your business then it would be normal practice to ask the customer to supply some trade references – names of other businesses that they trade with on credit who can vouch for their creditworthiness. Your business may also wish to check the customer's creditworthiness through an agency such as Dun and Bradstreet, or by asking for references from the customer's bank.

If the references and checks are satisfactory then a credit limit will be set for this customer and the sale can go ahead.

2 Summary of credit sales

The main document flows for a credit sale are illustrated below. The various documents are described in the paragraphs that follow.

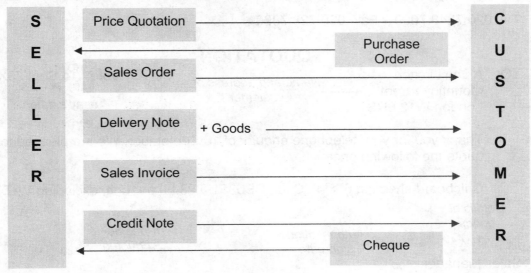

3 Setting up a credit sale

3.1 Price enquiry

The first stage of the process of a credit sale may be the receipt of a price enquiry from a customer.

The price enquiry may be a formal written document or more likely a telephone call. When responding to a price enquiry it is important that you make sure that the price you quote is the correct one as if it is incorrect you may find that you are contracted to sell the goods at that price under contract law (see later chapter in this Study Text).

3.2 Price quotation

In some organisations it is common practice to quote prices to customers over the telephone particularly if there is a catalogue or price list from which there are no deviations in price. However, some businesses will be prepared to offer certain customers goods at different prices. Therefore it is often the case that a price quotation is sent out to a customer showing the price at which the goods that they want can be bought.

A typical price quotation is shown below

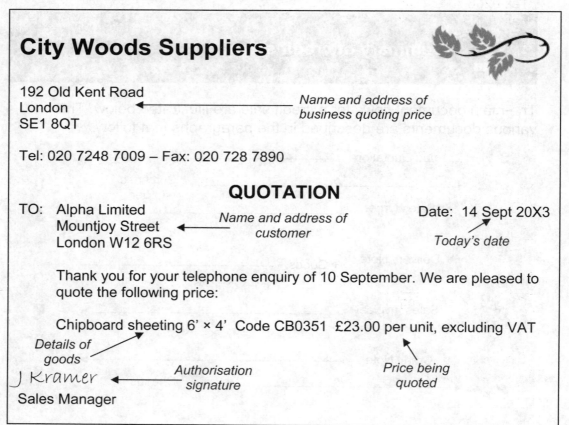

City Woods Suppliers

192 Old Kent Road
London
SE1 8QT
Name and address of business quoting price

Tel: 020 7248 7009 – Fax: 020 728 7890

QUOTATION

TO: Alpha Limited
Mountjoy Street
London W12 6RS
Name and address of customer

Date: 14 Sept 20X3
Today's date

Thank you for your telephone enquiry of 10 September. We are pleased to quote the following price:

Chipboard sheeting 6' × 4' Code CB0351 £23.00 per unit, excluding VAT
Details of goods
Price being quoted

J Kramer
Authorisation signature
Sales Manager

The price quotation is an important document as this is the price that your organisation is now contracted to sell the goods at. Therefore it is important that it is authorised by the appropriate person in the organisation.

3.3   The purchase order

If the customer is happy with the price quotation that they have received from your business then they will place a firm order with you. The order may be by telephone or it may be in writing. Whatever method is used for the purchase order, it is important to check all of the details carefully.

- Is the price that which was quoted to the customer?

- Are the delivery terms acceptable?

- Are any discounts applicable?

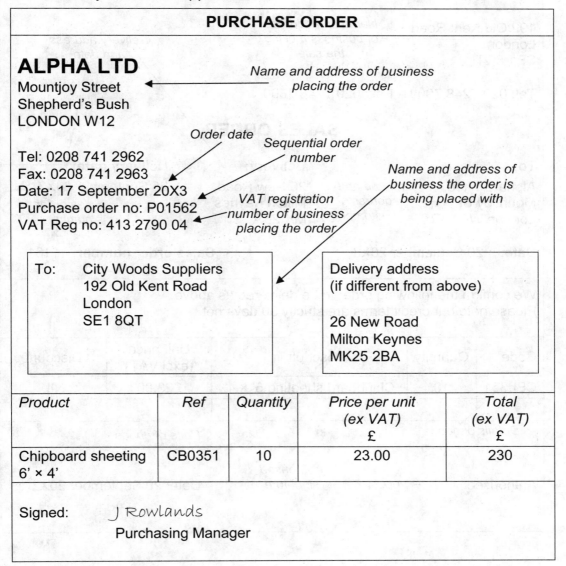

3.4 Confirming sales orders

To avoid misunderstandings, a supplier will normally confirm a customer's order by completing a **sales order**, even if the customer has already sent a written purchase order.

A **sales order** is a document confirming:

- quantity/type of goods or service;
- date of supply;
- location of supply;
- price and terms.

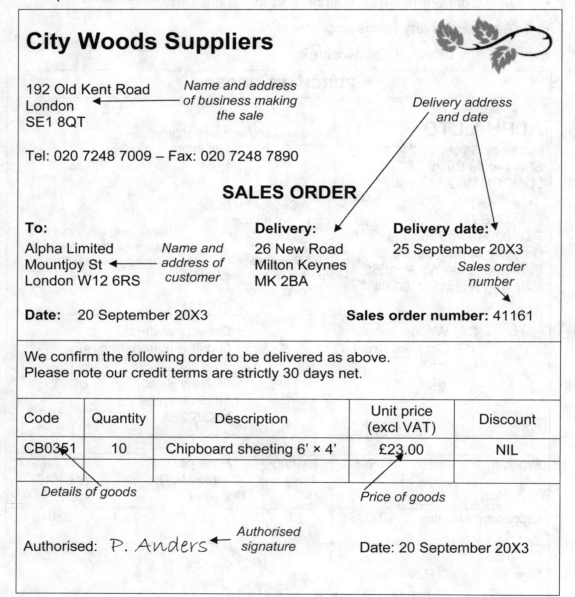

City Woods Suppliers

192 Old Kent Road   *Name and address*
London   *of business making*
SE1 8QT   *the sale*

Delivery address and date

Tel: 020 7248 7009 – Fax: 020 7248 7890

SALES ORDER

To: **Delivery:**   **Delivery date:**

Alpha Limited   *Name and*   26 New Road   25 September 20X3
Mountjoy St   *address of*   Milton Keynes   *Sales order*
London W12 6RS   *customer*   MK 2BA   *number*

Date: 20 September 20X3   **Sales order number:** 41161

We confirm the following order to be delivered as above.
Please note our credit terms are strictly 30 days net.

Code	Quantity	Description	Unit price (excl VAT)	Discount
CB0351	10	Chipboard sheeting 6' × 4'	£23.00	NIL

Details of goods   *Price of goods*

Authorised: *P. Anders*   *Authorised signature*   Date: 20 September 20X3

4 Supplying the goods

4.1 Introduction

Once all of the negotiations over the price and terms of the credit sale have been completed, then the goods themselves must be delivered.

4.2 Delivery notes

Delivery note – a document accompanying goods despatched to a customer.

Delivery notes should have **sequential numbers** that are either pre-printed for a manual system or computer generated in a computer system, and should be used in order. Spoiled delivery notes should be cancelled and kept.

There will normally be three parts to a delivery note:

Part one – This is kept by the customer in order to compare to the purchase order and then to the sales invoice

Part two and three – Signed and returned to the supplier goods as evidence that they have been received by the customer.

City Woods Suppliers

192 Old Kent Road
London
SE1 8QT

Tel: 020 7248 7009 – Fax: 020 7248 7890   DN 005673

DELIVERY NOTE

To:	**Delivery:**	**Delivery date:**
Alpha Limited	26 New Road	25 September 20X3
Mountjoy St	Milton Keynes	
London W12 6RS	MK 2BA	
Date: 25 September 20X3		**Sales order number:** 41161

We confirm the following order to be delivered as above.

Product	Code	Quantity
Chipboard 6' × 4'	CB0351	10

Received in good condition: *A Patel*

4.3 The sales invoice

The next stage is to prepare and send out the sales invoice.

In a manual system, sales invoices must be prepared from the details shown on delivery notes. Delivery notes do not normally show details of prices, discounts or VAT. (This is because the customer might mistake the delivery note for a sales invoice.) Price, discounts and VAT are shown on the sales invoice.

Sales invoices should have pre-printed sequential numbers and should be used in order. Spoiled sales invoices should be cancelled and kept.

In a computer system, the sales invoice will generally be produced at the same time as the delivery note and will be identical except that the delivery note may not have details of price, etc.

City Woods Suppliers

192 Old Kent Road
London
SE1 8QT

Tel: 020 7248 7009 – Fax: 020 7248 7890

Invoice no: 1005673
Tax point: 25 September 20X3
VAT reg no: 618 2201 63
Delivery note: DN005673
Account no: AL6215

INVOICE

To:

Alpha Limited
Mountjoy St
London W12 6RS

Delivery:

26 New Road
Milton Keynes
MK 2BA

Delivery date:

25 September 20X3

Date: 25 September 20X3

Sales order number: 41161

We confirm the following order to be delivered as above.

Product	Code	Quantity	Price per unit £	Total £
Chipboard 6' × 4'	CB0351	10	23.00	230.00
			VAT	40.25
			Total	270.25

4.4 Pricing goods and services

Unit prices for goods or services are kept in master files which must be updated regularly. If a price quotation has been sent to a customer then this must be used to find the price to use on the invoice.

Prices will normally be quoted exclusive of value added tax (VAT), as this is the true selling price to the business.

4.5   Customer details

In order to prepare the sales invoice the customer master file must be found. This will show the details of any discounts, etc offered to this customer (see later in this chapter).

4.6   The effect of value added tax

If the selling business is registered for VAT, VAT must be charged on taxable supplies.

Most goods and services are standard-rated (i.e. 17.5% rate of VAT must be charged). This will be considered in more detail later in the chapter.

 Example

Preparing a sales invoice

Thelma Goody is the sales invoicing clerk for a VAT registered clothing wholesaler. Thelma prepares the sales invoices to be sent to the customer from the price list and a copy of the delivery note sent up to her by the sales department.

Today she has received the following delivery note from the sales department

Delivery note: 2685

To: Kids Clothes Ltd
    9 Port Street
    MANCHESTER
    M1 5EX

A B Fashions Ltd
3 Park Road
Parkway
Bristol
BR6 6SJ
Tel: 01272 695221
Fax: 01272 695222

Delivery date: 20 August 20X6

Quantity	Code	DESCRIPTION	Colour
90	SSB 330	Shawls (babies)	Assorted
30	CJA 991	Cashmere jumpers (adult)	Cream
30	GGC 442	Gloves (children)	Assorted

Received by: ....

Signature: ....   Date: ....

Code	Description	Colour	Unit price £	VAT rate
SSG 001	Skirt (girls)	Black	13.50	Zero
SSW 002	Skirt (women)	Navy	15.90	Standard
TTW 037	Trousers (women)	Black	21.00	Standard
TTW 038	Trousers (women)	Navy	15.60	Standard
TTW 039	Trousers (women)	Red	15.60	Standard
SSB 330	Shawl (babies)	Assorted	11.50	Zero
SSB 331	Shawl (babies)	White	11.50	Zero
CJA 991	Cashmere jumper (adult)	Cream	65.00	Standard
CJA 992	Cashmere jumper (adult)	Pink	65.00	Standard
CJA 993	Cashmere jumper (adult)	Blue	65.00	Standard
CJA 994	Cashmere jumper (adult)	Camel	65.00	Standard
HHB 665	Hat (babies)	White	3.50	Zero
HHB 666	Hat (babies)	Blue	3.50	Zero
GGC 442	Gloves (children)	Assorted	6.20	Zero
GGC 443	Gloves (children)	White	6.50	Zero
GGC 444	Gloves (children)	Black	6.50	Zero

The customer file shows that Kids Clothes Ltd's account number is KC 0055 and that a trade discount of 10% is offered to this customer.

Thelma must now prepare the sales invoice. Today's date is 22 August 20X6.

Solution

INVOICE

Invoice to:
Kids Clothes Ltd
9 Port Street
MANCHESTER
M1 5EX

A B Fashions Ltd
3 Park Road
Parkway
Bristol
BR6 6SJ
Tel: 01272 695221
Fax: 01272 695222

Deliver to:

As above

Invoice no:	95124
Tax point:	22 August 20X6
VAT reg no:	488 7922 26
Delivery note no:	2685
Account no:	KC 0055

Code	Description	Quantity	VAT rate %	Unit price £	Amount excl of VAT £
SSB 330	Shawls (babies) assorted	90	0	11.50	1,035.00
CJA 991	Cashmere jumper (adult) cream	30	17.5	65.00	1,950.00
GGC 442	Gloves (children) assorted	30	0	6.20	186.00
					3,171.00
Trade discount 10%					(317.10)
					2,853.90
VAT at 17.5%					307.12
Total amount payable					3,161.02

Step 1   Enter today's date on the invoice and the invoice number which should be the next number after the last sales invoice number.

Step 2   Enter the customer details – name, address and account number.

Step 3   Refer now to the delivery note copy and enter the delivery note number and the quantities, codes and descriptions of the goods.

Step 4   Refer to the price list and enter the unit prices of the goods and the rate of VAT (note that the VAT rate for children's clothes is zero).

Step 5   Now for the calculations – firstly multiply the number of each item by the unit price to find the VAT exclusive price – then total these total prices – finally calculate the trade discount as 10% of this total, £3,171 × 10% = £317.10 and deduct it.

Step 6   Calculate the VAT – in this case there is only standard rate VAT on the cashmere jumpers but you must remember to deduct the trade discount (£1,950 – £195) before calculating the VAT amount £1,755 × 17.5% = £307.12 – add the VAT to the invoice total after deducting the trade discount.

4.7   Other terms found on invoices

You may also find other terms and conditions shown on invoices or other documents. Here are some of the more common:

E & OE – Errors and omissions excepted. The seller is claiming the right to correct any genuine errors on the invoice (e.g. prices) at a later date.

Carriage paid – The invoice value includes delivery of the goods to the customer's premises.

Ex works – Prices quoted do not include delivery to the customer's premises. The customer must organise and pay for the delivery of the goods.

Cash on delivery – The customer is expected to pay for the goods when they are delivered.

 Activity 1

A purchase order, number 28596, has been received from J Hardy Construction for the following:

    3 Cotswold panels

    5 insulation bricks

    1 red brick roof tile

The file for this customer shows that trade discounts are offered to this customer of 2% and settlement discounts of 3% if payment is within 14 days. The file also includes the customer's address: Poplar Works, Poplar Street, Oldham, OL4 6QB and account number SL07.

An extract from the price list is given.

Description	Code	Unit price £
Insulation bricks	159 SO4	195.50
Red brick roof tiles	874 KL5	56.65
Cotswold panels	950 BB3	300.00

The goods are to be despatched along with despatch note number 68553. The next sales invoice number is 69472. Today's date is 23 August 20X3.

Prepare the sales invoice for this sale on the blank invoice given below.

INVOICE

Invoice to: **A.J. Broom & Company Limited**
59 Parkway
Manchester
M2 6EG
Tel: 0161 560 3392
Fax: 0161 560 5322

Deliver to:

Invoice no:
Tax point:
VAT reg no: 625 9911 58
Order no:
Delivery note no:
Account no:

Code	Description	Quantity	VAT rate	Unit price	Amount excl of VAT
			%	£	£
Trade discount %					
VAT at 17.5%					
Deduct discount of % if paid within					

5 Issuing credit notes

5.1 Introduction

Credit notes are issued as documentary evidence that goods have been returned and that all or part of a previous sales invoice is cancelled. Therefore a business must keep strict control over the credit notes it issues.

Credit note – Document issued by a supplier to a customer cancelling part or all of a sales invoice. Business normally issues a credit note:

- when a customer has returned faulty or damaged goods;
- when a customer has returned perfect goods by agreement with the supplier;
- to make a refund for short deliveries;
- to settle a dispute with a customer.

A credit note is the reversal of a previous invoice or part of the invoice value.

5.2 Return of goods

Returned goods must be inspected, counted and recorded on receipt. They would normally be recorded on a returns inwards note.

5.3 Authorising credit notes

All credit notes must be authorised by a supervisor prior to being issued.

Some credit notes may be issued without a returns inwards note. For example, an error may have been made in pricing on an invoice but the customer is satisfied with the goods and does not need to return them.

These credit notes must be issued only after written authorisation has been received and must be reviewed and approved before being sent to the customer or recorded.

5.4 Preparing credit notes

A credit note is effectively the reverse of an invoice and therefore will tend to include all the details that would normally appear on a sales invoice.

If Alpha Ltd returned two of the chipboard panels, the credit note would be as follows.

City Woods Suppliers

192 Old Kent Road   *Name and address*   *Sequential credit*
London   *of issuer of credit*   *note number*
SE1 8QT   *note*

Tel: 020 7248 7009 – Fax: 020 7248 7890   Credit note no: CN 02542
                                           Tax point: 30 September 20X3
          VAT registration   VAT reg no: 618 2201 63
          number of supplier   Return inwards note no: 01531
                                           Invoice no: 1005673
          Returns inwards   Account no: AL 6215
          note reference
                                                      Date of credit note
CREDIT NOTE

Credit to: *Name and address*
Alpha Limited   *of customer*   *Customer's account*
Mountjoy St   *code*
London W12 6RS

Date: 30 September 20X3

Description	Code	Quantity	VAT rate %	Unit price £	Amount exclusive of VAT £
Chipboard 6' × 4'	CB0351	2	17.5	23.00	46.00

Rate of VAT on goods returned

Goods returned total → 46.00

					46.00
VAT at 17.5%				VAT charged →	8.05
			Total amount of credit →		54.05

Activity 2

You work for A J Broom & Company Limited and have returns inwards note number 01532 in front of you and you have to prepare a credit note to send to K Phipps Builders for one insulation brick, code 159 SO4,that was damaged. The unit price of the insulation brick is £195.50.

The customer file shows that a trade discount of 5% is given to this customer but no settlement discount. The file also shows the customer's address: Hayward House, Manor Estate, Oldham, OL7 4HD, and the customer's account number SL35.

The next credit note number to use is CN 02543 and today's date is 25 August 20X3.

Prepare the credit note on the blank form provided.

CREDIT NOTE

Credit note to: **A.J. Broom & Company Limited**

59 Parkway
Manchester
M2 6EG
Tel: 0161 560 3392
Fax: 0161 560 5322

Credit note no:
Tax point:
VAT reg no: 625 9911 58
Return inwards note no:
Account no:

Code	Description	Quantity	VAT rate	Unit price	Amount excl of VAT
			%	£	£
Trade discount %					
VAT at 17.5%					
Deduct discount of % if paid within					

KAPLAN PUBLISHING

6 Coding sales invoices

6.1 Introduction

Sales invoices should be coded to show:

- product group/type for analysis of sales;
- customer account number.

There are several different systems of coding which can be used by a business and the main ones are outlined below.

6.2 Sequence codes

Allocate a number, or a letter, to items in a simple list.

For example:

Code	Name
01	ADAMS, Joan
02	AITKEN, James
03	ALCOCK, Freda
04	BROWN, Joe

6.3 Block codes

These allocate bands of numbers to particular categories.

For example, consider a tobacco manufacturer who produces several types of cigarettes, cigars and pipe tobaccos. He could assign a code to each particular brand as follows:

Product type	Block code
Cigarette	01 – 19
Cigar	20 – 29
Pipe tobacco	30 – 39

6.4 Significant digit codes

These are a particular type of group classification code where individual digits and letters are used to represent features of the coded item. The example given is one used to describe different kinds of vehicle tyres.

Code	Item
TT67015B	Tube Tyre 670 × 15 Blackwall
LT67015W	Tubeless Tyre 670 × 15 Whitewall

6.5 Faceted codes

Faceted codes are another type of group classification code by which the digits of the code are divided into facets of several digits and each facet represents some attribute of the item being coded. These codes are similar to significant digit codes but are purely numerical.

Example: faceted code for types of carpet

Facet 1	=	type of weave (1 digit)	1	=	Cord
			2	=	Twist
			3	=	Short tufted, etc
Facet 2	=	material (1 digit)	1	=	All wool
			2	=	80% wool, 20% nylon
			3	=	50% wool, 50% nylon, etc
Facet 3	=	pattern (2 digits)	01	=	Self colour (plain)
			02	=	Self colour (embossed)
			03	=	Fig leaf, etc
Facet 4	=	colour (2 digits)	01	=	Off white
			02	=	Bright yellow
			03	=	Scarlet, etc

A typical code would be 220302 representing a twist carpet in 80% wool, 20% nylon, pattern fig leaf and colour bright yellow.

Note that a two-digit facet allows up to 100 different codings (00 to 99).

6.6 Decimal codes (or hierarchical codes)

These are yet another form of a group classification code. The most obvious example of a decimal code is the Universal Decimal Code (UDC) devised by Dewey and widely used for the classification of books in libraries. UDC divides all human knowledge into more and more detailed categories as shown.

Code	Item
3	Social science
37	Education
372	Elementary
372.2	Kindergarten
372.21	Methods
372.215	Songs and games

Whatever the coding system that is used it is important for further accounting purposes that the invoices and credit notes are coded according to type of sales and the particular customer.

You may be expected to code items included on sales invoices or credit notes according to a coding system that is given to you in an assessment.

 Activity 3

Is the cheque number used in a cheque book an example of a sequential code or a hierarchical code?

7 Test your knowledge

 Test your knowledge

Having completed Chapter 4, you should now be able to attempt Practice Activities 14 to 16.

8 Summary

In this chapter we have concentrated on the process of actually preparing sales invoices and credit notes. Before preparing an invoice it is necessary to ensure that this is for a valid sale by checking the order and delivery details. When preparing the invoice you need to understand the difference between trade discounts and settlement discounts and their treatment on the invoice and for VAT purposes. You also need to be able to correctly find the price of items from a price list and to correctly transfer this to the invoice together with correct multiplication to arrive at the total. No invoice or credit note should be sent out unless it has been properly authorised and it will also need to be coded to ensure that it is eventually correctly recorded in the accounting records.

Answers to chapter activities

 Activity 1

INVOICE

Invoice to:
J Hardy Construction
Poplar Works
Poplar Street
Oldham OL4 6QB

A.J. Broom & Company Limited

59 Parkway
Manchester
M2 6EG
Tel: 0161 560 3392
Fax: 0161 560 5322

Deliver to:
As above

Invoice no:	69472
Tax point:	23 August 20X3
VAT reg no:	625 9911 58
Order no:	28596
Delivery note no:	68553
Account no:	SL07

Code	Description	Quantity	VAT rate %	Unit price £	Amount excl of VAT £
950 BB3	Cotswold Panels	3	17.5	300.00	900.00
159 S04	Insulation Bricks	5	17.5	195.50	977.50
874 KL5	Red Brick Roof Tiles	1	17.5	56.65	56.65
					1,934.15
Trade discount 2%					38.68
					1,895.47
VAT at 17.5%					321.75
Total amount payable					2,217.22
Deduct discount of 3% if paid within 14 days					

* VAT is calculated as 17.5% × (£1,895.47 × 0.97), i.e. assuming that the settlement discount is taken.

Note that the trade discount is deducted on the face of the invoice whereas the only effect of the settlement discount is in the calculation of the VAT.

Activity 2

CREDIT NOTE

Credit note to:
K Phipps Builders
Hayward House
Manor Estate
Oldham
OL7 4HD

A.J. Broom & Company Limited
59 Parkway
Manchester
M2 6EG
Tel: 0161 560 3392
Fax: 0161 560 5322

Credit note no: CN02543
Tax point: 25 August 20X3
VAT reg no: 625 9911 58
Return inwards note no: 01532
Account no: SL35

Code	Description	Quantity	VAT rate %	Unit price £	Amount excl of VAT £
159 S04	Insulation brick	1	17.5	195.50	195.50
					195.50
Trade discount 5%					9.77
					185.73
VAT at 17.5%					32.50
Total amount of credit					218.23

 Activity 3

A sequential code (the numbers run in sequential order).

Credit sales – Discounts and VAT

Introduction

In this chapter we will consider, in more detail, the further effects of discounts and VAT when accounting for credit sales.

KNOWLEDGE	CONTENTS
3.5 Define and distinguish between capital income and revenue income	**1** Discounts
	2 Value added tax
3.6 Define and distinguish between capital expenditure and revenue expenditure	**3** Calculating the amount of VAT
	4 Cash (or settlement) discount and VAT
4.1 Explain the difference between settlement, trade and bulk discount	**5** Accounting for credit sales and VAT
4.2 Describe the effect that settlement discount has on the sales tax (e.g. VAT) charged	

SKILLS

1.1 Use different source documents to prepare sales invoices and credit notes

1.2 Calculate relevant sales tax (e.g. VAT), trade discount and settlement discount

1 Discounts

1.1 Introduction

There are three main types of discount that a business might offer to its credit customers, a bulk discount, a trade discount and a cash (or settlement) discount.

1.2 Bulk discounts

A bulk discount is a percentage of the list price of the goods being sold that is deducted from the list price when purchasing large quantities.

1.3 Trade discounts

A trade discount is a percentage of the list price of the goods being sold that is deducted from the list price for certain customers. This discount may be offered due to the fact that the customer is a frequent and valued customer or because the customer is another business rather than an individual.

A trade discount is a definite amount deducted from the list price total of the invoice.

1.4 Cash or Settlement discounts

A cash or settlement discount is offered to customers if they settle the invoice within a certain time period. It is up to the customer to decide whether or not to pay early and therefore take the settlement discount. The discount is expressed as a percentage of the invoice total but is not deducted from the invoice total as it is not certain when the invoice is sent out whether or not it will be accepted. Instead the details of the settlement discount will be noted at the bottom of the invoice.

A settlement discount can be offered but it is up to the customer whether or not to take advantage of it.

2 Value added tax

2.1 The operation of VAT

VAT is a tax levied on **consumer** expenditure. However the procedure is that it is collected at each stage in the production and distribution chain. Most businesses (being **taxable persons** as defined later) avoid having to treat VAT as an expense as they may deduct the VAT they have paid on their purchases **(input tax)** from the VAT they charge to customers on their sales **(output tax)** and pay only the difference to HM Revenue and Customs.

2.2 How VAT works

Let us examine a simple illustration. We will assume a standard rate of 17.5%, and follow one article, a wooden table, through the production and distribution chain.

- A private individual cuts down a tree and sells it to a timber mill for £10. **Tax effect** – none. The individual is not a 'taxable person in this case.

- The timber mill saws the log and sells the timber to a furniture manufacturer for £100 + VAT.

  Tax effect – Being a taxable person, the mill is obliged to charge its customers VAT at 17.5% on the selling price (output tax).There is no input tax available for offset.

  Cash effect – The mill collected £117.50 from the customer (or has a debtor for this sum). Of this, £17.50 has to be paid to HM Revenue and Customs, and therefore only £100 would be recognised as sales.

- The manufacturer makes a table from the wood, and sells this to a retailer for £400 + VAT.

  Tax effect – The manufacturer is obliged to charge VAT at 17.5% on the selling price (i.e. £70), but in this instance would be allowed to reduce this amount by setting off the input tax of £17.50 charged on the purchase of wood from the mill.

  Cash effect – Tax of £52.50 is paid to HM Revenue and Customs (output less input tax = £70 less £17.50). £400 is recognised as sales and £100 as purchases in the accounts.

- The retailer sells the table to a private customer for £851 plus VAT of £149. **Tax effect** – The retailer charges £149 of VAT to the customer but against this output tax may be set off the input tax of £70 charged on the purchase from the manufacturer.

  Cash effect – £79 (£149 – £70) is paid to HM Revenue and Customs. Purchases would be shown in the books at £400 and sales at £851.

- **The private customer** – VAT is a tax levied on consumer expenditure and the chain ends here. The customer is not a taxable person, and cannot recover the tax paid.

You will note that everybody else has passed the VAT on and, though the customer has paid his £149 to the retailer, to HM Revenue and Customs has received its tax by contributions from each link in the chain, as shown below:

	£
Timber mill	17.50
Manufacturer	52.50
Retailer	79.00
	149.00

🔍 Definitions

VAT is charged on the **taxable supply of goods and services** in the United Kingdom by a **taxable person** in the course of a business carried on by him.

Output tax is the tax charged on the sale of goods and services

Input tax is the tax paid on the purchase of goods and services

2.3 Taxable supply of goods and services

Taxable supply is the supply of all items except those which are **exempt.** Examples of exempt items are as follows:

- certain land and buildings, where sold, leased or hired;
- insurance;

- Post Office postal services;
- betting, gaming and lotteries.

Input tax cannot be reclaimed where the trader's supplies are all exempt.

2.4 Rates of VAT

There are three rates of VAT on taxable supplies. Some items are 'zero-rated' (similar to exempt except that input tax can be reclaimed), there is a special rate of 5% for domestic fuel and power, and all other items are rated at the standard rate of 17.5%. Examples of 'zero-rated' supplies include:

- water and most types of food;
- books and newspapers;
- drugs and medicines;
- children's clothing and footwear.

2.5 Non-deductible VAT

VAT on some items is non-deductible. This means that VAT on any purchases of these items cannot be deducted from the amount of tax payable to HM Revenue and Customs. The business has to bear the VAT as an expense.

Non-deductible items include:

- motor cars;
- business entertaining.

For our purposes you will be dealing with taxable supplies at the standard rate of 17.5%.

2.6 Taxable person

A taxable person is any individual, partnership, company, etc who intends to make taxable supplies and is liable to register.

A person is liable to register if the value of his taxable supplies exceeds a specified amount in a 12-month period. Most companies and partnerships and many sole traders are liable to register.

3 Calculating the amount of VAT

3.1 VAT exclusive amounts

If you are given the net price of goods, the price excluding VAT, then the amount of VAT is 17.5/100 of this price.

VAT is always rounded down to the nearest penny.

 Example

A sale is made for £360.48 plus VAT. What is the amount of VAT to be charged on this sale?

Solution

VAT = £360.48 × 17.5/100 = £63.08

Remember to round down to the nearest penny.

3.2 VAT inclusive amounts

If a price is given that already includes the VAT then calculating the VAT requires an understanding of the price structure where VAT is concerned.

	%
Selling price including VAT (gross)	117.5
VAT	17.5
Selling price excluding VAT (net)	100.0

 Example

Goods have a selling price of £2,350 inclusive of VAT. What is the VAT on the goods and the net price of these goods?

Solution

	£
Net price (£2,350 × 100/117.5)	2,000
VAT (£2,350 × 17.5/117.5)	350
Gross price	2,350

Activity 1

What is the amount of VAT on each of the following transactions?

(i)   £145.37 net of VAT

(ii)   £285.47 net of VAT

(iii) £159.80 including VAT

(iv) £575.75 including VAT

4   Cash (or settlement) discount and VAT

4.1   Introduction

When a cash/settlement discount is offered, this makes the VAT calculation slightly more complex.

Invoices should show the VAT payable as 17.5% of the **discounted price**. The amount paid by the customer is either:

(a)   taking discount – discounted amount (excluding VAT) plus discounted VAT; or

(b)   not taking discount – full amount (excluding VAT) plus discounted VAT.

The amount of VAT paid is always based on the discounted amount even though when the invoice is being prepared it is not known whether the customer will or will not take advantage of the cash or settlement discount.

 Example

A purchase is for 20 items @ £15 each. This totals £300. A 2% discount is offered for settlement within 30 days.

(a)   Calculate the VAT.

(b)   Calculate the amounts to be invoiced.

Solution

(a)   The VAT is therefore calculated as:

300 × 98% = 294

294 × 17.5% = 51.45

(b) *Invoice amount*

	£
Net	300.00
VAT (working a)	51.45
Total	351.45

We do not show the discounted amount on the invoice as it is uncertain if the customer will pay within the period required

Example

A sales invoice is to be prepared for two adult Fairisle sweaters at a cost of £50.00 each. A settlement discount of 5% for payment within 30 days is offered. What would the sales invoice look like?

Solution

INVOICE

Creative Clothing

3 The Mall, Wanstead, London, E11 3AY,
Tel: 0208 491 3200, Fax: 0208 491 3220

Invoice to:		VAT Registration:	487 3921 12
Smith & Isaacs		Date/tax point:	14 February 20X0
23 Sloane Street		Invoice number:	149
London		Delivery note no:	41682
SW3		Account no:	SL43

Code	Description	Quantity	VAT rate %	Unit price (£)	Amount (£)
FW168	Fairisle Sweater (adult)	2	17.5	50.00	100.00

Total net amount	100.00
VAT at 17.5%	16.62
Total amount payable	116.62

Terms: **Deduct discount of 5% if paid within 30 days**

The VAT is calculated at 17.5% × (£100 × 95%) = £16.62.

Activity 2

A customer orders 10 Sansui radios priced at £25 each. The customer is given a 20% trade discount and a 10% cash discount for prompt payment. Calculate the VAT charged on the sale and show the figures to be included on the invoice

5 Accounting for credit sales and VAT

5.1 Accounting entries

We have already seen in this chapter that a business makes no profit out of any VAT charged on its sales. Instead this amount of output tax (less any related input tax) is paid over to HM Revenue and Customs. Therefore when a credit sale is recorded in the sales account it must be at the net of VAT amount.

However, when our customer eventually pays us he will pay the full amount due, i.e. the gross amount including the VAT. Therefore when we record a debtor in the ledger accounts it must be at the full gross amount of the invoice.

The difference between these two amounts, the VAT, is recorded in the VAT account.

5.2 Summary of entries

In summary the accounting entries for a credit sale with VAT are:

Debit   Debtors account with the gross amount

Credit   Sales account with the net amount

Credit   VAT account with the VAT

Work through the following examples to practise the double entry for credit sales.

Example 1

C sells £2,000 of goods net of VAT to Z on credit. He offers Z a 5% settlement discount if Z pays within 30 days. Z does not pay his account within 30 days and so does not take the settlement discount. Z pays after 40 days. Enter these transactions in the accounts.

Solution

Step 1   Calculate the VAT on the sale.

	£
Sales value net of VAT	2,000.00
VAT = (2,000 – 5%)x17.5%	332.50
	————
Invoice value	2,332.50
	————

Note   Remember that when a settlement discount is offered, the VAT is calculated on the sales value minus the settlement discount. In this case it turns out that Z does not take the settlement discount but at no stage do we go back to recalculate the VAT.

Step 2   Enter the invoice in the accounts.

Debtors

	£		£
Sales and VAT	2,332.50		

Sales

	£		£
		Debtors	2,000.00

VAT

	£		£
		Debtors	332.50

Step 3   Enter the payment by Z in the accounts.

Debtors

	£		£
Sales and VAT	2,332.50	Bank	2,332.50

Sales

	£		£
		Debtors	2,000.00

VAT

	£		£
		Debtors	332.50

Bank

	£		£
Debtors	2,332.50		

Note   As Z does not take the settlement discount, there is no entry for the settlement discount at all in the accounts.

🔆 Example 2

Two months later C sells another £2,000 of goods net of VAT to Z on credit. He offers Z a 5% settlement discount if Z pays within 30 days. This time Z does pay his account within 30 days and takes the settlement discount. Enter these transactions in the accounts.

Solution

Step 1   Calculate the VAT on the sale.

Note   This is exactly the same as the previous example because the calculation of VAT with a settlement discount is the same whether the customer takes the settlement discount or not.

	£
Sales value net of VAT	2,000.00
VAT = (2,000 – 5%) 17.5%	332.50
	————
Invoice value	2,332.50
	————

Step 2   Enter the invoice in the accounts.

Note   This is exactly the same as the previous example because the value of the invoice is exactly the same as the previous example.

Debtors

	£			£
Sales and VAT	2,332.50			

Sales

	£			£
			Debtors	2,000.00

VAT

	£			£
			Debtors	332.50

Step 3   Calculate the amount paid by Z.

Note   The amount paid by Z will be different from the previous example because Z does take the 5% discount.

	£
Sales value net of VAT	2,000.00
Less: settlement discount = 5% × 2,000	(100.00)
VAT (as per the invoice)	332.50
	————
Amount paid by Z	2,232.50
	————

Step 4 Enter this amount in the accounts.

Debtors

	£			£
Sales and VAT	2,332.50	Bank		2,232.50

Because Z takes the settlement discount, he pays C £100 less than the invoice value. In order to clear the debtors account we have to credit that account with the £100 and debit a discount allowed account with £100. This £100 is an expense of the business as we have allowed our customer to pay less than the invoice value in order to have the benefit of receiving the money earlier.

Sales

	£		£
		Debtors	2,000.00

VAT

	£		£
		Debtors	332.50

Debtors

	£		£
Sales and VAT	2,332.50	Bank	2,232.50
		Discount allowed	100.00

Discount allowed

	£		£
Debtors	100.00		

6 Test your knowledge

Test your knowledge

Having completed Chapter 5, you should now be able to attempt
Practice Activities 17 to 20.

7 Summary

We have covered some fairly tricky ideas in this chapter and it is very
important that you really do understand them.

The calculations of VAT are fairly straightforward but do make sure that
you can calculate the VAT element of a sale when you are given the sales
value gross of VAT.

Also quite tricky is the treatment of settlement discounts. You have to be
able to do two things.

(a)   Calculate the VAT on a sale when a settlement discount is offered.
Remember that it is irrelevant whether the customer takes the
settlement discount or not.

(b)   Calculate the amount paid by the customer if he takes a settlement
discount. This will be less than the invoice value and you therefore
have to account for the discount allowed.

Answers to chapter activities

Activity 1

(i)	£145.37 × 17.5/100	=	£25.43
(ii)	£285.47 × 17.5/100	=	£49.95
(iii)	£159.80 × 17.5/117.5	=	£23.80
(iv)	£575.75 × 17.5/117.5	=	£85.75

Activity 2

Note: The answer is arrived at as follows:

	£
Sales price (10 × £25)	250.00
Less: Trade discount (250 × 20%)	(50.00)
	200.00
Less: Cash discount (200 × 10%)	(20.00)
	180.00
VAT @ 17.5%	31.50

	£
Sales value	200.00
VAT	31.50
	231.50

The sales day book – main and subsidiary ledgers

Introduction

We have already seen how to calculate the amount of a credit sale, including VAT and any relevant discounts. In this chapter we will deal with the initial recording of credit sales before they are entered into the ledger accounts.

KNOWLEDGE

1.1 Outline the purpose, content and format of the books of prime entry

1.4 Explain how transactions are entered in the following books of prime entry: sales and sales returns day books

3.3 Outline how the books of prime entry integrate with a double entry bookkeeping system

3.4 Explain how to process financial transactions from the books of prime entry into the double entry bookkeeping system

SKILLS

2.2 Enter invoices and credit notes into the books of prime entry

1.1 Transfer data correctly from the day books to the ledgers

CONTENTS

1 Accounting for credit sales

2 The main and subsidiary ledgers

3 Sales returns

4 The sales returns day book

1 Accounting for credit sales

1.1 Introduction

In a typical business there will be a great number of sales transactions to be recorded. If we were to record each transaction individually, the accounts would be very cluttered.

In order to simplify the process (and exercise greater control) we divide the recording of the transactions into three parts.

(a) The first part is the books of prime entry. We shall study here the sales day book.

(b) The second part is the main ledger itself where the double entry takes place.

(c) The third part is the sales ledger which contains the individual debtor accounts. (Note that the sales ledger is also sometimes referred to as the subsidiary (sales) ledger.)

Sales invoices and cheques are the source documents which will form the basis of accounting entries in all these three parts.

1.2 Books of prime entry – the sales day book (SDB)

The sales day book is simply a list of the sales invoices that are to be processed for a given period (e.g. a week).

In its simplest form, the sales day book will comprise just the names of the customers and the amount of the invoices issued in the week.

The SDB is not part of the double entry; it is not part of the ledger accounts. It is just a list but we shall use it to perform the double entry. It will look something like this:

Week 1			
Customer	**Total** **£**	**VAT** **£**	**Net** **£**
X	1,175	175	1,000
Y	2,350	350	2,000
Z	3,525	525	3,000
Total	7,050	1,050	6,000

1.3   The analysed sales day book

The sales day book is usually analysed with 'analysis columns' showing how the total value of each customer's invoice is made up.

SALES DAY BOOK								
Date	Customer	Reference	Invoice number	Total £	VAT £	Product 1 £	Product 2 £	Product 3 £
			TOTALS					

(a)   The date and customer columns are self explanatory.

(b)   The reference number is the code number of the customer's account in the sales ledger.

(c)   The invoice number is the number of the invoice issued for this sale.

(d)   The total column is the total value of the goods sold as shown on the invoice:

- after deducting any trade discount that may have been offered;

- including VAT.

Example

An invoice to customer A is made up as follows:

	£
Sale of 50 units at £2 per unit	100.00
Less: 20% trade discount	(20.00)
	80.00
VAT @ 17.5% (£80 × 17.5%)	14.00
Total invoice value	94.00

The £94 would be entered in the 'total' column.

(e)   The VAT column – this column is the value of the VAT on the invoice – in this case £14.00.

(f)   Product 1, 2, etc columns – these are columns that analyse the net sales value (i.e. the total value after deducting VAT) into groupings that are of interest to the business.

In this introductory section we shall not complicate things by considering more than one type of product so that there will only be one column for sales.

In this case the entry in the sales column would be £80.

(g)   The total boxes – at the end of a period (say a week or a month) the sales day book is totalled and the total values of each column are written in the total boxes.

The sales day book would therefore look as follows for the example above:

SALES DAY BOOK								
Date	Customer	Reference	Invoice number	Total £	VAT £	Product 1 £	Product 2 £	Product 3 £
	A			94	14	80		
			TOTALS	94	14	80		

Activity 1

An analysed sales day book has the following totals for a week.

Date	Invoice no	Customer name	Code	Total £	VAT £	Europe £	Asia £	America £
23/04/X0		Total		63,979	9,529	21,250	15,400	17,800

How would the totals be posted to the main ledger accounts?

1.4 Casting and cross casting

Casting is the way accountants refer to adding a vertical column of figures and cross-casting is the way accountants refer to adding a horizontal row of figures.

It is worth very briefly doing a simple example of this just to show how a valuable check of the accuracy of your additions is provided by these two operations.

 Example

The following table of numbers is similar to the contents of accounting records such as the 'sales day book' or the 'analysed cash book' which you will come across in the next few chapters.

This table might represent the sales of products A to E in three geographical areas. We have deliberately chosen some awkward numbers to demonstrate the process.

You should calculate the totals yourself before looking at the solution.

	A	B	C	D	E	Total
UK	221,863	17,327	14,172	189,221	5,863	
USA	17,155	14,327	8,962	27,625	73,127	
Africa	18,627	33,563	62,815	1,003	57,100	
Total						

Solution

	A	B	C	D	E	Total
UK	221,863	17,327	14,172	189,221	5,863	**448,446**
USA	17,155	14,327	8,962	27,625	73,127	**141,196**
Africa	18,627	33,563	62,815	1,003	57,100	**173,108**
Total	**257,645**	**65,217**	**85,949**	**217,849**	**136,090**	**762,750**

If you managed to add the vertical columns and horizontal rows and then produced the overall total of *762,750* correctly for the overall table you have done very well.

This is a very useful technique and provides an excellent check on the accuracy of your addition.

2 The main and subsidiary ledgers

2.1 Introduction

The main ledger is the place where the double entry takes place in the appropriate ledger accounts. The main ledger contains all the accounts you have become familiar with so far, for example:

Capital

Drawings

Van

Rent

Electricity

Purchases

Bank

etc.

One of these typical accounts is the debtors account but now we will call this the sales ledger control account.

This account contains (for a given period) the **total** value of all the invoices issued to customers and the **total** of all the cash received. It does not contain any detail.

[**Note** that the AAT refers to this ledger as the main ledger. In some businesses it is referred to as the 'general ledger' or the 'nominal ledger'.]

2.2 The sales ledger

However as well as information about our debtors in total we have to keep track of each individual debtor. How much have we invoiced him with? What has he paid? How much does he owe?

We do this in the sales ledger. This ledger is not part of the main ledger and it is **not** part of the double entry. (Remember it is also sometimes called the subsidiary (sales) ledger.)

The sales ledger contains a separate ledger account for each individual debtor. Every individual invoice and cash receipt is posted to an individual's account in the sales ledger.

2.3 Fitting it all together

We have now looked at the three elements of a typical accounting system. We must now see how it all fits together.

Consider three credit sales invoices

Customer	Amount
A	£1,500
B	£2,000
C	£2,500

Step 1

Each invoice is recorded in the sales day book and in the personal account of each debtor in the sales ledger. The entry required for each invoice is a debit in each debtor account to indicate that this is the amount that each one owes us.

Step 2

At the end of the period the sales day book is totalled and the total is entered into the sales ledger control account (SLCA) (total debtors account) in the main ledger.

The full double entry is as we saw in the previous chapter (ignoring VAT at the moment):

Debit   Sales ledger control account

Credit   Sales

Step 3

Now consider the following cheques being received against these debts.

Customer	Amount
A	£1,000
B	£2,000

Each receipt is recorded in the cash book (see later chapter) and in the personal account of each debtor in the sales ledger. The entry for cash received in the individual accounts is a credit entry to indicate that they no longer owe us these amounts.

Step 4

At the end of the period the cash book is totalled and the total is entered into the sales ledger control account (total debtors account) in the main ledger.

The full double entry is:

Debit   Cash account (money in)

Credit   Sales ledger control account

This is illustrated on the next page.

Notes

1   The invoices are entered into the SDB and the cheques are entered into the cash book.

2   The totals from the cash book and SDB are posted to the SLCA.

3   The individual invoices and cash received are posted to the sales ledger.

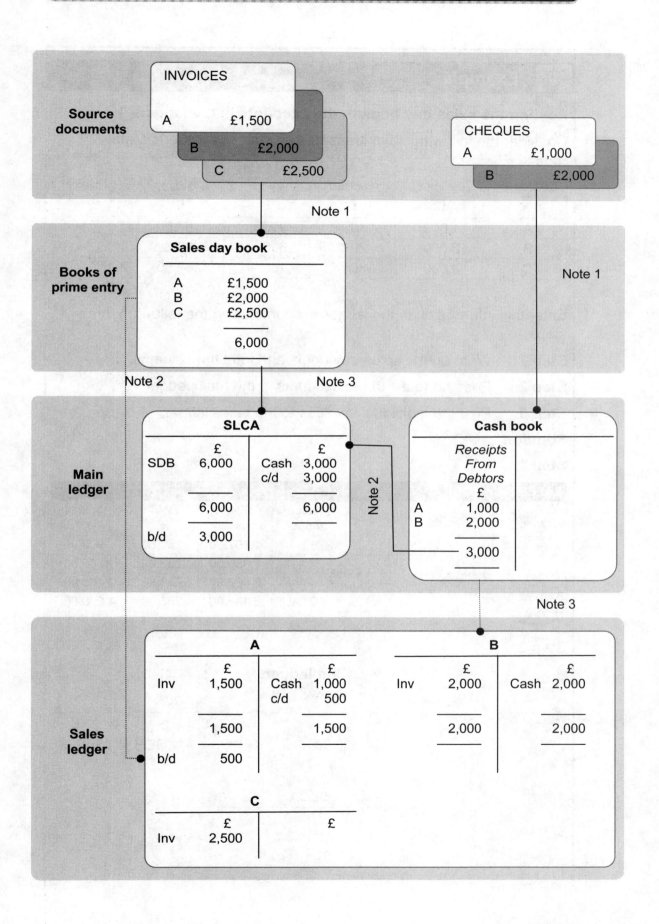

Example

Posting the sales day book to the accounts in the ledgers

Consider the following sales transactions made by Roberts Metals.

Customer	Sales value (ex VAT) £	Trade discount £	Net sales value £	VAT £	Total £
A	1,000	10%	900	157.50	1,057.50
B	2,000	20%	1,600	280.00	1,880.00
C	3,000	30%	2,100	367.50	2,467.50

Enter this information in the ledger accounts using the following three steps.

Step 1 Write up the sales day book, and total the columns.

Step 2 Post the totals to the accounts in the main ledger.

Step 3 Post the individual invoices to the sales ledger.

Solution

Step 1

SALES DAY BOOK

Date	Customer	Reference	Invoice number	Total £	VAT £	Sales £
	A			1,057.50	157.50	900.00
	B			1,880.00	280.00	1,600.00
	C			2,467.50	367.50	2,100.00
			TOTALS	5,405.00	805.00	4,600.00

Step 2

Main ledger

Sales

£		£
	SDB	4,600.00

VAT

£		£
	SDB	805.00

SLCA

	£	£
SDB	5,405.00	

Step 3

Sales ledger

A				B			
	£		£		£		£
SDB	1,057.50			SDB	1,880.00		

C			
	£		£
SDB	2,467.50		

Note to solution

(a) The totals of the SDB are entered in the main ledger.

(b) The individual invoices (total value including VAT) are entered in the individual debtors accounts in the sales ledger. This is the amount that the debtor will pay.

(c) Note that there are no entries for trade discounts either in the SDB or in the ledger accounts.

3 Sales returns

3.1 Introduction

When customers return goods, the accounting system has to record the fact that goods have been returned. If the goods were returned following a cash sale then cash would be repaid to the customer. If goods were returned following a credit sale then the SLCA in the main ledger and the customer's individual account in the sales ledger will need to be credited with the value of the goods returned.

 Example

Returns following a cash sale

X sells £500 of goods to A for cash plus £87.50 VAT.

X subsequently agrees that A can return £200 worth of goods (excluding the VAT).

Record these transactions in the ledger accounts.

Solution

Step 1

First of all we need to set up a new account called the 'sales returns account' in the main ledger. This will be used in addition to the sales account and cash book with which you are familiar.

Step 2

Enter the cash sale in the accounts.

Debit bank account for cash received	£587.50
Credit sales with net amount	£500.00
Credit VAT account with VAT	£87.50

Bank account

	£		£
Sales	587.50		

Sales

	£		£
		Cash book	500.00

Sales returns

	£		£

VAT

	£		£
		Cash book	87.50

Step 3

X will repay A £200 plus VAT of (£200 × 17.5%) = £35. We therefore need to enter the sale return, the cash and the VAT in the accounts.

Debit sales returns account		£200.00
Debit VAT account £200 × 17.5%		£35.00
Credit bank account with cash paid out		£235.00

Bank account

	£		£
Sales	587.50	Sales returns	235.00

Sales

	£		£
		Cash book	500.00

Sales returns

	£		£
Cash book	200.00		

VAT

	£		£
Cash book	35.00	Cash book	87.50

3.2 Sales returns for credit sales

When a credit customer returns goods, he does not receive cash for the return. Instead the seller will issue a credit note to record the fact that goods have been returned. This credit note is sent to the customer and is entered in the seller's books.

Example

X sells goods on credit to A for £500. A returns goods worth £200. X sends a credit note for £200 to A. Enter these transactions in the main ledger of X's books. There is no VAT.

Solution

Step 1

Record the invoice issued for the credit sale for £500:

Debit the SLCA in the main ledger with £500.

Credit the sales account in the main ledger with £500.

SLCA

	£		£
Sales	500.00		

Sales

	£		£
		SLCA	500.00

Step 2

Record the credit note for £200. The return is debited to a 'sales returns account' to reflect the reduction in sales. The SLCA is credited to show that the debtor has been reduced.

SLCA

	£		£
Sales	500.00	Sales returns	200.00

Sales

	£		£
		SLCA	500.00

Sales returns			
	£		£
SLCA	200.00		

3.3 Sales returns with VAT

When a return is made and we include VAT, the VAT has to be accounted for both on the invoice when the sale is made, and on the credit note when the goods are returned. This VAT has to be entered in the books.

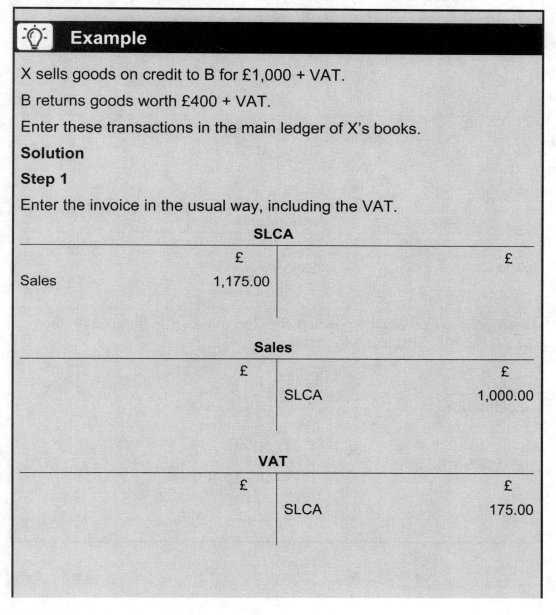

Example

X sells goods on credit to B for £1,000 + VAT.

B returns goods worth £400 + VAT.

Enter these transactions in the main ledger of X's books.

Solution

Step 1

Enter the invoice in the usual way, including the VAT.

SLCA			
	£		£
Sales	1,175.00		

Sales			
	£		£
		SLCA	1,000.00

VAT			
	£		£
		SLCA	175.00

Step 2

Enter the credit note. The VAT on the return will be £400 x 17.5% = £70.
SLCA

SLCA

	£		£
Sales	1,175.00	Sales returns	470.00

Sales

	£		£
		SLCA	1,000.00

VAT

	£		£
SLCA	70.00	SLCA	175.00

Sales returns

	£		£
SLCA	400.00		

The books will reflect the position after the return. The balance on the
SLCA is £705. This is made up as:

	£
Sale	1,000
Sale return	400
	600
VAT 600 × 17.5%	105
	705

4 The sales returns day book

4.1 The sales returns day book

Sales returns are in practice entered in a 'sales returns day book'. This is similar to the sales day book, and the columns are used in the same way. The only difference is that instead of having a column for the invoice number, there is a column for the 'credit note number'. This is because when the goods are received back the business will issue a credit note.

SALES RETURNS DAY BOOK						
Date	Customer	Reference	Credit note number	Total £	VAT £	Sales returns £

Example

A and B are credit customers of Ellis Electricals. The balances on their accounts in the sales ledger are £1,175 and £2,350 because both A and B have made earlier purchases which have not yet been paid.

A returns goods which cost £600 excluding VAT. B returns goods which cost £400 excluding VAT.

Enter the above returns in the sales returns day book and in the main and sales ledgers of Ellis Electricals.

Solution

Step 1

Enter the original sales invoices in the main ledger.

	SLCA		
	£		£
SDB	3,525.00		

SALES

£		£
	SDB	3,000.00

VAT

£		£
	SDB	525.00

Step 2

Write up the sales returns day book.

SALES RETURNS DAY BOOK						
Date	Customer	Reference	Credit note number	Total £	VAT £	Sales returns £
	A			705.00	105.00	600.00
	B			470.00	70.00	400.00
				1,175.00	175.00	1,000.00

Step 3

Enter the SRDB totals in the main ledger accounts.

SLCA

	£		£
SDB	3,525.00	SRDB	1,175.00

Sales

£		£
	SDB	3,000.00

VAT

	£		£
SRDB	175.00	SDB	525.00

Sales returns

	£		£
SRDB	1,000.00		

Step 4

Enter the individual amounts in the sales ledger.

A

	£		£
SDB	1,175.00	SRDB	705.00

B

	£		£
SDB	2,350.00	SRDB	470.00

4.2 Sales returns in sales day book

In some businesses the level of sales returns are fairly low and therefore it is not justified to keep a separate sales returns day book. In these cases any credit notes that are issued for sales returns are recorded as negative amounts in the sales day book.

Activity 2

Given below are the totals of an analysed sales returns day book for a week.

Date	Customer name	Credit note no	Code	Total	VAT	Europe	Asia	America
				£	£	£	£	£
23/04/X0				3,290	490	1,458	650	692

Post these totals to the main ledger accounts.

5 Test your knowledge

 Test your knowledge

Having completed Chapter 6, you should now be able to attempt Practice Activities 21 to 25

6 Summary

The sales day book, analysed sales day book, and the sales returns day book, are fairly straightforward. Remember that they are simply lists of invoices/credit notes which simplify posting entries to the main ledger.

You should make sure that you are familiar with the material in this chapter and fully understand how the various parts of the accounting system relate to each other. You will often be required to enter invoices and credit notes into the books of prime entry and then to post the entries to the main ledger and sales ledger.

KAPLAN PUBLISHING

Answers to chapter activities

Activity 1

The required double entry is as follows:

Debit	Sales ledger control account	£63,979
Credit	VAT	£9,529
	Europe sales	£21,250
	Asia sales	£15,400
	America sales	£17,800

Note carefully that it is the net amount that is credited to each sales account and the gross amount (including VAT) that is debited to the sales ledger control account. The VAT total is credited to the VAT account.

The ledger entries would appear as follows:

Sales ledger control account

	£		£
SDB	63,979		

VAT

	£		£
		SDB	9,529

Europe sales

	£		£
		SDB	21,250

Asia sales

	£		£
		SDB	15,400

America sales

	£			£
		SDB		17,800

Activity 2

Sales returns – Europe account

	£		£
SRDB	1,458		

Sales returns – Asia account

	£		£
SRDB	650		

Sales returns – America account

	£		£
SRDB	692		

VAT account

	£		£
SRDB	490		

Sales ledger control account

	£			£
		SRDB		3,290

Note carefully that it is the net amount that is debited to each returns account and the gross amount to the sales ledger control account. The difference, the VAT, is debited to the VAT account.

KAPLAN PUBLISHING

7

Checking receipts

Introduction

Now that we can account for our sales on both cash and credit terms, the next step in the process would be to account for amounts received in payment. Initially we will look at the receipt of monies in various forms and, in particular, the checking, accounting for and paying in of such receipts.

KNOWLEDGE

1.2 Outline the purpose and content of a range of business documents to include

Remittance advice

SKILLS

3.1 Check the accuracy and validity of receipts against relevant supporting information

3.2 Identify and deal with any discrepancies

CONTENTS

1 Receiving money in a retail business

2 Received money for credit sales

3 Settlement discounts

1 Receiving money in a retail business

1.1 Introduction

Different types of business will receive money in different forms. For example a retail organisation will receive cash, cheques, credit card and debit card payments through the till.

In contrast a totally credit sales based organisation will rarely receive cash and credit/debit card payments but will receive cheques through the post to pay sales invoices which have been sent to customers.

In this section we will start with a look at the checks that should be carried out by a retailer receiving various types of payment through the till.

1.2 Receiving cash

If cash payments are made for goods then the till operator should input the correct price for the goods, check the amount of money offered by the customer, enter this amount in the till or cash register, put the money into the till and pay out to the customer the correct change which will have been calculated by the till.

1.3 Accepting cheques

If a cheque is accepted as payment from an individual rather than a business, then it must be accompanied by a cheque guarantee card.

If a cheque is accepted with a valid cheque guarantee card, this means that the bank will pay the cheque; the cheque is guaranteed. We will go into detail later with regard to ensuring the validity of the cheque itself.

1.4 Cheque guarantee card

- For a £100 cheque guarantee card, this card guarantees that a cheque for up to £100 will be paid by the bank, regardless of the amount of money in that account.

- Only one £100 cheque for each transaction is allowed.

- The cheque must not exceed £100, or the bank can refuse to pay anything.

- The cheque guarantee card is usually the same card as the individual's debit card.

1.5 Checks to carry out on a cheque guarantee card

Look at the following cheque which is supported by a cheque guarantee card, and think of the checks that must be carried out before the cheque is accepted.

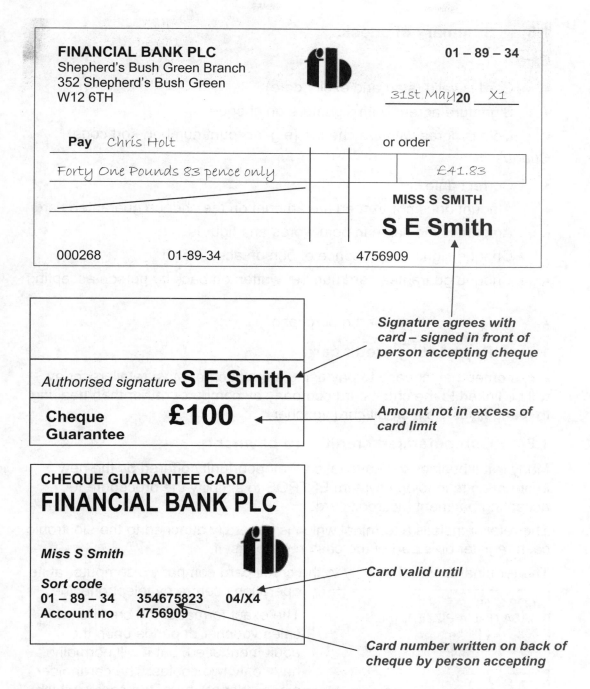

Note: Cheques from companies cannot be guaranteed by a cheque guarantee card.

If the retailer is suspicious in any way he should contact the bank which has issued the card.

1.6 Summary of checks

Card

- Card is valid (start and expiry date)
- Signature agrees with signature on cheque
- Details agree with the cheque (e.g. account number, sort code)

Cheque

- Correct date
- Amount does not exceed the amount on the cheque guarantee card
- Amount is the same in both words and figures
- Cheque signed in presence of person accepting it
- Cheque guarantee card number written on back by person accepting it
- Only one cheque for the purchase

1.7 Payment by credit card

A customer may choose to pay using a credit card. Most retailers today will be linked to the credit card company by computer rather than needing to manually issue a credit card voucher.

1.8 Computerised credit card payments

Many retail businesses have taken the opportunity offered by the new information technology system EFTPOS to simplify the procedure for accepting payment by credit card.

The retailer installs a terminal which is generally attached to the electronic cash register or is part of the cash register itself.

The terminal is linked directly to the credit card company's computer at its operations centre by telephone line.

```
1900 2359
CASA ITALIA PIZZERIA
05/07/X1 21:58
Express: 2554006633579400

TOTAL £15.80

Auth code: 54662
THANK YOU SIGN BELOW
Please debit my account as shown

_____
```

The exact format of the credit card sales voucher depends upon the equipment used, but it will normally have only two copies. The cardholder signs at least one of the copies which is returned to the retailer for the retailer's records. The other copy is for the cardholder's records. Most retailers have introduced the PIN system whereby the customer simply enters their PIN into the credit card machine rather than having to sign the credit card voucher.

KAPLAN PUBLISHING

No banking of the vouchers need be done by the retailer because all transactions are immediately transferred electronically by the terminal via the telephone line.

The terminal automatically performs any authorisation procedures by contacting the computer at the operation centre.

1.9 What is EFTPOS?

Electronic Funds Transfer at Point of Sale (EFTPOS) is a system which uses advanced information technology.

EFTPOS – A national scheme which links terminals in shops and supermarkets with the processing department of banks, building societies and credit card companies.

The system is very flexible because it allows almost any type of credit card or debit card to be accepted by one system.

 Example

- Janet is a 27-year-old nurse from South Wales. She has gone into a petrol filling station on the M3 and filled her car with petrol.

- She wishes to pay by credit card. The filling station is linked up to the EFTPOS system.

- Janet's credit card is a Visa card. The filling station's bank is Lloyds TSB Bank in Gravesend, Kent.

Explain the sequence of transactions.

Solution

- Janet produces her card at the cash desk (point of sale).

- The sales assistant swipes or puts the card into a card reader on a terminal attached to the cash register.

- The sales assistant enters the amount of the purchase into the cash register.

- The information on the magnetic strip on the card is read by the retailer's terminal. A coded message (scrambled for security) is sent by telephone line to the central EFTPOS processing centre. This includes details of the amount. The card details are recorded and the request is sent to Visa for authorisation by telephone line.

- The Visa processing computer checks certain details.

- The customer is asked to enter her PIN number followed by enter which is validated by the credit card company.

- In this case, the Visa processing computer authorises the purchase and updates its records. It notifies the central EFTPOS processing centre of the authorisation.

- The central EFTPOS processing centre transmits the authorisation to the retailer's terminal.

- A two-part credit card sales voucher is printed out and one copy given to Janet.

- The cash register also prints a receipt.

- After authorisation, the central EFTPOS processing centre sends details of the purchase to Lloyds Bank where the money is transferred into the filling station's account.

- The sales assistant gives Janet her card, her copy of the credit card sales voucher and her receipt.

This has all taken a matter of minutes.

1.10   Floor limits

Often credit card companies will set a maximum floor limit on amounts that can be accepted on a credit card for payment e.g. no purchases over £200. However if a customer wishes to use a card for a higher value purchase the company can be contacted for authorisation.

1.11   Checks to be made on the credit card

When accepting payment by credit card, the retailer must check that the card has not reached its expiry date and that the signature on the voucher matches that on the card, or that the PIN number has been accepted. If authorisation is not given for a transaction by the credit card company then the credit card should not be accepted as this will mean that the credit limit has been exceeded or else that the card has been notified as having been stolen.

 Activity 1

A customer wishes to purchase £320 of clothes from a shop using a credit card for payment. The floor limit set by the credit card company is £100.

(a)   Is it possible that the transaction can still go ahead despite the floor limit?

(b)   Briefly explain the reason for your answer.

1.12 Debit cards

Debit cards were introduced in the previous chapter.

- **Debit cards** – The debit card is a method of making payments direct from a bank account without having to write a cheque or produce a cheque guarantee card.

The payments are made by the customer using the EFTPOS technology described above. Payments made appear on the customer's bank statement alongside any other payments made by cheque, standing order, direct debit, etc.

If the payment is not authorised by the bank then the debit card should not be accepted for payment as this may mean that the customer does not have enough funds in their account.

Whatever method is used to pay for retail sales it is vital that the person receiving the payment checks all cheques, guarantee cards and credit/debit cards thoroughly to ensure they are valid. Otherwise the business may not receive payment for the goods sold.

2 Receiving money for credit sales

2.1 Introduction

When a business makes credit sales then it normally receives money from debtors in the post. This will normally be in the form of cheques and it is important that there is strict control of these cheques.

2.2 Remittance lists

All cash received should be listed on a **remittance list** (sometimes known as a **cheques received list).**The list should give details of:

- the customer;
- the invoice numbers to which the payment relates (if known);
- the amount paid; and
- any discount allowed (see later in this chapter).

The list should be totalled and signed.

2.3 Using remittance advices

When a business issues an invoice to a customer, the invoice will often have a detachable slip. This slip is called a **remittance advice.**

This **remittance advice** is a slip returned by the customer when paying an invoice so as to identify what the payment is for. This makes it much easier for the business receiving the cheque to know which outstanding invoices are actually being paid by this cheque.

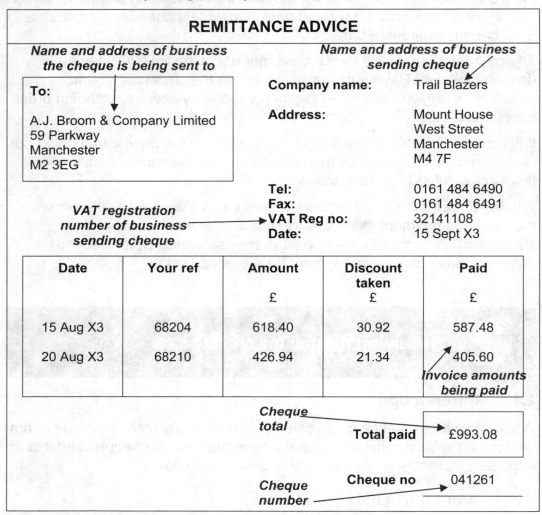

REMITTANCE ADVICE

Name and address of business the cheque is being sent to

To:

A.J. Broom & Company Limited
59 Parkway
Manchester
M2 3EG

VAT registration number of business sending cheque

Name and address of business sending cheque

Company name:	Trail Blazers
Address:	Mount House
	West Street
	Manchester
	M4 7F
Tel:	0161 484 6490
Fax:	0161 484 6491
VAT Reg no:	32141108
Date:	15 Sept X3

Date	Your ref	Amount £	Discount taken £	Paid £
15 Aug X3	68204	618.40	30.92	587.48
20 Aug X3	68210	426.94	21.34	405.60

Invoice amounts being paid

Cheque total

Total paid	£993.08

Cheque number

Cheque no	041261

When receiving cheques from a customer it is vital to ensure that the correct amount has been paid. This can be done by agreeing the amount of the cheque to the details on the remittance advice and to the invoices themselves.

 Activity 2

A remittance advice is a document sent by a supplier to a customer to advise the customer that goods ordered have been sent off to the customer. True/False

Example

This morning the following cheques and supporting remittance advices were received in the post by your organisation, A. J. Broom & Company Ltd.

You are required to check the remittance advice and cheque amounts to the invoices given to ensure that the correct amount has been received.

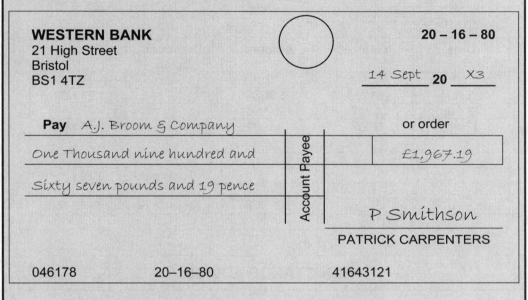

WESTERN BANK
21 High Street
Bristol
BS1 4TZ

20 – 16 – 80

14 Sept 20 X3

Pay A.J. Broom & Company   or order

One Thousand nine hundred and

Sixty seven pounds and 19 pence

Account Payee

£1,967.19

P Smithson

PATRICK CARPENTERS

046178   20–16–80   41643121

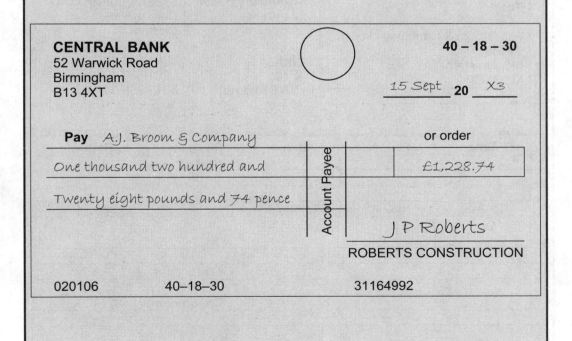

CENTRAL BANK
52 Warwick Road
Birmingham
B13 4XT

40 – 18 – 30

15 Sept 20 X3

Pay A.J. Broom & Company   or order

One thousand two hundred and

Twenty eight pounds and 74 pence

Account Payee

£1,228.74

J P Roberts

ROBERTS CONSTRUCTION

020106   40–18–30   31164992

REMITTANCE ADVICE

To:		Company name:	Patrick Carpenters
		Address:	Simba Industrial Est.
A.J. Broom & Company Limited			Leeds
59 Parkway			
Manchester		Tel:	0714 304 2990
M2 3EG		Fax:	0714 304 2963
		VAT Reg no:	318 4861 27
		Date:	14 Sept 20X3

Date	Your ref	Amount	Discount taken	Paid
		£	£	£
23 Aug	68229	1,614.69	–	1,614.69
23 Aug	3217	(352.50)	–	(352.50)
4 Sept	68237	705.00	–	705.00
			Total paid	£ 1,967.19
			Cheque no	046178

REMITTANCE ADVICE

To:		Company name:	Roberts Construction
		Address:	Chillian Park
A.J. Broom & Company Limited			Oldham
59 Parkway			
Manchester		Tel:	0201 632 497
M2 3EG		Fax:	0201 632 498
		VAT Reg no:	331 4986 91
		Date:	15 Sept 20X3

Date	Your ref	Amount	Discount taken	Paid
		£	£	£
23 Aug	68230	1,288.74	–	1,288.74
			Total paid	£ 1,288.74
			Cheque no	020106

Invoice 68229

A.J. Broom & Company Limited

59 Parkway
Manchester
M2 6EG
Tel: 0161 560 3392
Fax: 0161 560 5322

Patrick Carpenters
Samba Industrial Estate
Leeds

Tax Point:					23 August 20X3	
VAT reg no:					452 4585 48	

Code	Suppply	Description	Quantity	VAT rate %	Unit price £	Amount excl of VAT £
336 BTB	Sale	Roof tiles – black	10	17.50	123.00	1,230.00
667 LL5	Sale	Softwood plank – 20 cm	14	17.50	10.30	144.20
						1,374.20
VAT at 17.5%						240.49
Total amount payable						**1,614.69**

Invoice 68237

A.J. Broom & Company Limited

59 Parkway
Manchester
M2 6EG
Tel: 0161 560 3392
Fax: 0161 560 5322

Patrick Carpenters
Samba Industrial Estate
Leeds

Tax Point:					4 September 20X3	
VAT reg no:					452 4585 48	

Code	Suppply	Description	Quantity	VAT rate %	Unit price £	Amount excl of VAT £
630 CC4	Sale	Oak veneer in Panels	3	17.50	200.00	600.00
VAT at 17.5%						105.00
Total amount payable						**705.00**

Credit note 3217

A.J. Broom & Company Limited

	59 Parkway		
	Manchester		
	M2 6EG		
	Tel: 0161 560 3392		
Patrick Carpenters	Fax: 0161 560 5322		
Samba Industrial Estate	Tax Point:	23 August 20X3	
Leeds	VAT reg no:	452 4585 48	

Code	Suppply	Description	Quantity	VAT rate %	Unit price £	Amount excl of VAT £
950 BB3	Return	Cotswold bricks	1	17.50	300.00	300.00

VAT at 17.5%	52.50
Total amount credited	**352.50**

Invoice 68230

A.J. Broom & Company Limited

	59 Parkway		
	Manchester		
	M2 6EG		
	Tel: 0161 560 3392		
Roberts Construction	Fax: 0161 560 5322		
Chillian Park	Tax Point:	23 August 20X3	
Oldham	VAT reg no:	452 4585 48	

Code	Suppply	Description	Quantity	VAT rate %	Unit price £	Amount excl of VAT £
160 TT7	Sale	Insulation	5	17.50	95.50	477.50
632 BS4	Sale	Brick tiles	20	17.50	33.25	665.00

	1,142.50
Trade discount 4%	45.70
	1,096.80
VAT at 17.5%	191.94
Total amount payable	**1,288.74**

Solution

From Patrick Carpenters

	£
Invoice number 68229	1,614.69
Invoice number 68237	705.00
Credit note 3217	(352.50)
	1,967.19

This agrees with the cheque.

From Roberts Construction

Invoice number 68230	£1,288.74

This does not agree with the cheque as the cheque is made out for £1,228.74. This discrepancy should be brought to the attention of the manager responsible for credit control at Roberts Construction and a polite letter should be written to the customer explaining the error that has been made. Request can be made for payment but if this is a regular customer then the additional amount may simply be added to the next cheque that Roberts Construction sends.

2.4 Cheque received with no accompanying remittance advice

If a cheque arrives in the post from a customer with no remittance advice or other confirmation of which invoices are being paid then it will be necessary to examine the details of this customer's transactions in the sales ledger.

The name of the customer should be fairly obvious from the name of the payer on the cheque – this will be printed by the bank as well as signed by the customer. The individual account for this debtor must then be extracted from the subsidiary ledger in an attempt to match the payment received to invoices and credit notes.

Example

A cheque has been received in the post this morning from A J Holland, a credit customer, for £878.00 but it is not supported by any other documentation.

The individual debtor account for A J Holland has been found in the sales ledger.

A J Holland

	£		£
13/05/X2 Invoice 2256	336.67	20/05/X2 Credit 249	54.09
18/05/X2 Invoice 2271	846.23		
20/05/X2 Invoice 2280	447.69		
25/05/X2 Invoice 2288	147.73		

Solution

By a process of trial and error it can be discovered that the invoices that are being paid off are number 2256, 2280 and 2288 less the credit note. It would appear therefore that the cheque is for the correct amount although there might be some concern as to why invoice 2271 has not been paid, maybe there is some dispute over the amount of this invoice which should be investigated.

Always check figures carefully as such errors are often easy to miss.

2.5 Checking cheques

When cheques are received in the post it is important that they are checked for their validity, particularly in respect of:

- the date; a cheque can become out of date as it is only valid for 6 months from the date of issue.

- The payee's name: should the same as the one shown on the account the cheque is being paid into.

- the words and figures agree; if they disagree the cheque should be return by the bank for amendment or for a new cheque to be issued.

- the cheque is signed.

Example

The following three cheques were received in the post today, 3 June 20X6, by your organisation, L L Traders.

Check each one carefully to ensure that they are valid.

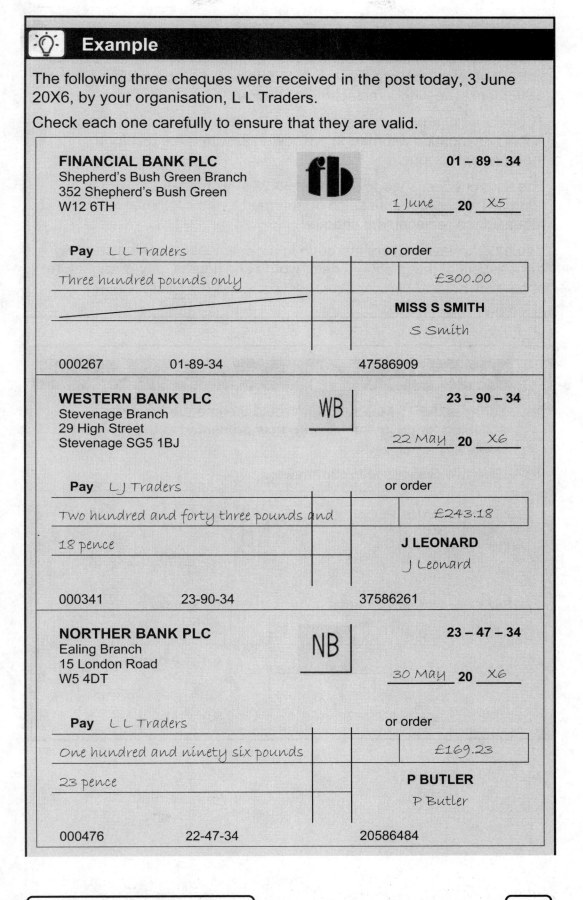

FINANCIAL BANK PLC
Shepherd's Bush Green Branch
352 Shepherd's Bush Green
W12 6TH

01 – 89 – 34

1 June 20 X5

Pay L L Traders   or order

Three hundred pounds only   £300.00

MISS S SMITH
S Smith

000267   01-89-34   47586909

WESTERN BANK PLC
Stevenage Branch
29 High Street
Stevenage SG5 1BJ

23 – 90 – 34

22 May 20 X6

Pay L J Traders   or order

Two hundred and forty three pounds and   £243.18

18 pence

J LEONARD
J Leonard

000341   23-90-34   37586261

NORTHER BANK PLC
Ealing Branch
15 London Road
W5 4DT

23 – 47 – 34

30 May 20 X6

Pay L L Traders   or order

One hundred and ninety six pounds   £169.23

23 pence

P BUTLER
P Butler

000476   22-47-34   20586484

Solution

The first cheque is dated 1 June 20X5 whereas today's date is 3 June 20X6. Therefore this cheque is out of date and must be returned to the customer requesting a replacement cheque.

The second cheque is made out to L J Traders instead of L L Traders. Again this must be returned to the customer with a request for a replacement cheque.

The third cheque is made out for £196.23 in words but £169.23 in figures. This cheque must also be returned to the customer with a request for a replacement cheque.

You must always be very thorough in assessments checking carefully each aspect of the cheque – date, words and figures, payee, signature, etc.

Activity 3

(a)   Today is the 15 March 20X3. Would the cheque below be accepted for payment if it were now presented to the National Bank plc?

(b)   Give two reasons for your answer.

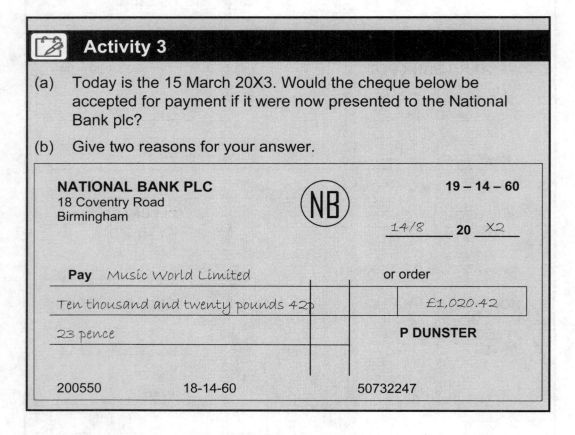

3 Settlement discounts

3.1 Introduction

When a settlement discount is offered to a customer, this will normally be offered as a percentage amount. If a customer takes advantage of the discount they will calculate it themselves, therefore it is important to check that this is correct.

3.2 Checks to make

Where a payment is received after deducting a settlement discount then great care should be taken in checking this receipt.

Step 1   Check back to the original invoice to ensure that the discount is valid, i.e. that the customer has paid within the stated period.

Step 2   Check that the correct percentage discount has been taken and that it has been correctly calculated.

Example

Cheques have been received from two credit customers. Today's date is 3 October 20X3.

Garden Supplies Ltd	£2,168.81
Porter & Co	£963.91

The invoices that these cheques are paying are given below.

You are required to check that the receipt is for the correct amount.

		Invoice 66293
	A.J. Broom & Company Limited	
	59 Parkway	
	Manchester	
	M2 6EG	
	Tel: 0161 560 3392	
Garden Supplies Ltd	Fax: 0161 560 5322	
Grange Hill	Tax Point:	20 September 20X3
Chester	VAT reg no:	452 4585 48

Code	Suppply	Description	Quantity	VAT rate %	Unit price £	Amount excl of VAT £
950 BB3	Sale	Cotswold brocks	2	17.50	300.00	600.00
159 504	Sale	Roof tiles – red	6	17.50	195.50	1,173.00
874 KL5	Sale	Brick tiles	3	17.50	56.65	169.95
						1,942.95
VAT at 17.5%						323.01
Total amount payable						**2,265.96**

5% settlement discount is offered for payments received within 10 days of the invoice date

Invoice 66299

A.J. Broom & Company Limited

	59 Parkway
	Manchester
	M2 6EG
	Tel: 0161 560 3392
	Fax: 0161 560 5322
Porter & Co Tax Point:	26 September 20X3
Cunard Place VAT reg no:	452 4585 48
Manchester	

Code	Suppply	Description	Quantity	VAT rate %	Unit price £	Amount excl of VAT £
262 BPT	Sale	Lined Oak Panels 1m^2	6	17.50	145.00	870.00
VAT at 17.5%						144.63
Total amount payable						**1,014.63**

5% settlement discount is offered for payments received within 10 days of the invoice date

Solution

The invoice to Garden Supplies Ltd is dated 20 September. As today's date is 3 October then the payment has not been received within 10 days of the invoice date which are the stated terms for the settlement discount. Therefore the customer should be politely informed of this fact and a request made for the balance of the invoice to be paid, 5% × £1,942.95 = £97.15.

The invoice to Porter & Co is dated 26 September and therefore is valid in terms of date. However the correct amount of the discount should be £43.50 (5% × £870). The discount that has been taken is £50.73 (5% × £1,014.64). Again the customer must be informed of the error and the balance requested. For such a small amount, £7.23 (£50.73 – £43.50), the credit controller may decide that this amount can be added to the next payment from Porter & Co if they are regular customers.

In assessments you must always check all discount calculations and dates very thoroughly.

Remember that as the VAT has already been calculated on the assumption that the discount has been taken the amount of discount is based on the net of VAT amount.

3.3 Recording any settlement discounts taken

When the settlement discounts have been checked and are valid it is important that the amount of the discount is noted. This should be either on the back of the cheque or on the remittance list. This is necessary because when the primary records are written up for these receipts (see next chapter) the amount of the discount must be recorded.

3.4 Automated payments

It is entirely possible that a customer might pay an amount due with a bank giro credit. A bank giro credit is a method of transferring money into someone else's bank account in any bank in the country. This amount would then appear as a credit in the bank statement. Just as with a cheque receipt this automated receipt must be checked back to the original invoices to ensure that it is for the correct amount and to check for items such as settlement discounts deducted.

4 Test your knowledge

 Test your knowledge

Having completed Chapter 7, you should now be able to attempt Practice Activities 26 and 27.

5   Summary

This chapter has concentrated on all of the important checks that must be made when receiving money from customers to ensure that the correct amounts have been paid and that the payment method is valid. Cash, cheques and credit card payments must be carefully checked by a retailer. A supplier on credit terms has to make a number of checks when cheques are received from a customer. Is the cheque for the correct amount given the invoices that are paid? Is any settlement discount valid and correctly calculated? Are the cheques that have been received correctly made out so that they can be paid into the organisation's bank account?

Answers to chapter activities

 ### Activity 1

(a) Yes

(b) The credit card company can be contacted by phone to authorise use of the card for the purchase.

 ### Activity 2

False. A remittance advice is a slip that the customer can send back to the supplier with his payment to identify what the payment is for.

 ### Activity 3

(a) No

(b) Any two from the following:

  (i) The cheque has not been signed.

  (ii) The cheque is out of date.

  (iii) The words and figures on the cheque are not the same.

The analysed cash receipts book

Introduction

Once we have carried out all relevant checks on our receipts, we need to record these transactions within our accounting records. As we have seen before, however, if we were to do this individually, the accounting records would become cluttered. In this chapter we will look in more detail at the recorded of cash receipts, particularly from credit customers

KNOWLEDGE
1.1 Outline the purpose , format and content of the books of prime entry
1.4 Explain how transactions are entered in the following books of prime entry: cash book
3.3 Outline how the books of prime entry integrate with a double entry bookkeeping system
3.4 Explain how to process financial transactions from the books of prime entry into the double entry bookkeeping system
SKILLS
1.2 Transfer data correctly from the cash book to the ledgers

CONTENTS
1 The analysed cash receipts book
2 Settlement discounts allowed to customers
3 Cash and credit sales contrasted

1 The analysed cash receipts book

1.1 Layout

A proforma analysed cash receipts book is shown below.

CASH RECEIPTS BOOK							
Date	Narrative	Reference	Total £	VAT £	SLCA £	Cash sales £	Discount allowed £
		TOTALS					

Notes

(a) The date column contains the date of the transaction.

(b) The narrative column describes the transactions – typically the name of the customer who is paying. It would also contain the sales ledger code of the debtor.

(c) The reference column contains any other information that may be helpful e.g. 'cash', 'cheque', 'BACS' etc.

(d) The total column contains the total cash received (including any VAT).

(e) The VAT column contains the VAT on the transaction but not if the VAT has already been entered in the sales day book. This is a tricky point and is dealt with later.

(f) The SLCA column contains any cash received that has been received from a debtor. The total received including VAT is entered in this column.

(g) The cash sales and discount allowed columns will be dealt with later.

Example

The following is an example of the main and sales ledgers, including entries from the sales and sale returns day books.

Main ledger

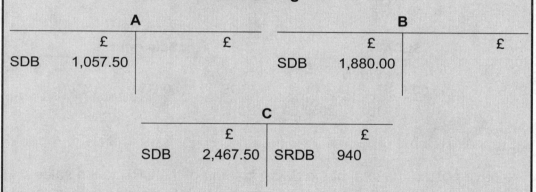

Sales							
£			£				
		SDB	4,600.00				

VAT							
£		£					
SRDB	140.00	SDB	805.00				

SLCA				
£		£		
SDB	5,405.00	SRDB	940.00	

Sale returns			
£		£	
SRDB	800.00		

Sales ledger

A			
£		£	
SDB	1,057.50		

B			
£		£	
SDB	1,880.00		

C			
£		£	
SDB	2,467.50	SRDB	940

The following transactions took place:

   Debtor A pays £1,057.50

   Debtor B pays £1,000.00

Enter this information in the cash receipts book and in the ledger accounts given above.

Solution

The following steps are needed.

Step 1   Enter these transactions in the cash book.

Step 2   Total the cash book and post the totals to the main ledger.

Step 3   Post the individual amounts of cash paid by debtors to the individual accounts in the sales ledger.

Step 1

CASH RECEIPTS BOOK							
Date	Narrative	Reference	Total	VAT	SLCA	Cash sales	Discount allowed
			£	£	£	£	£
	A		1,057.50	See Note 2	1,057.50		
	B		1,000.00	of Step 2	1,000.00		
		TOTALS	2,057.50		2,057.50		

Step 2

We have brought forward the balances from the main ledger in the earlier example and now post the cash received book (CRB) totals to the main ledger.

Main ledger

Sales

£		£
	SDB	4,600.00

VAT

£		£
SRDB	140.00	SDB	805.00

SLCA

£		£
SDB	5,405.00	SRDB	940.00
		CRB	2057.50

Sale returns

£	£
SRDB	800.00	

Note 1

We have posted the total of the SLCA column of the CRB to the sales ledger control account. This is the same as the total column in this example, but in more complex examples it need not be. The entry to the sales ledger control account is a credit entry as this is reducing the amount owed by our debtors.

Note 2

A common confusion is for people to wonder about the VAT – surely some of the money paid by A and B is actually paying the VAT part of the invoice. Yes it is, but we have already accounted for this VAT element when we entered the invoices themselves into the ledger accounts via the sales day book. Look back at Chapter 6 – the total of the invoices in the SDB were debited to the SLCA and the VAT and sales were the corresponding credits. We therefore now post the total cash including VAT to the sales ledger control account but nothing is posted to the VAT account as this has already been done when dealing with the invoices.

Note 3

This is now the full double entry for the cash received completed.

Debit   Bank account (cash receipts book)

Credit   Sales ledger control account

We have credited the sales ledger control account and the entry in the cash receipts book itself is the related debit entry. So there is no need for any further debit entry.

Step 3

We have brought forward the balance from the sales ledger in the earlier example and now post the cash received to the individual sales ledger accounts. Again, as with the sales ledger control account, this is a credit entry in each case as the cash received is reducing the amount owed by each debtor.

A	£		£	B	£		£
b/f	1,057.50	CRB	1,057.50	b/f	1,880.00	CRB	1,000.00

C	£		£
b/f	2,467.50	SRDB	940.00

1.2   Balancing the accounts

Below we reproduce some of the accounts as they have been written up above and we then balance the accounts and bring down the balances.

Main ledger

SLCA

	£		£
SDB	5,405.00	CRB	2,057.50
		SRDB	940.00
		c/d	2,407.50
	5,405.00		5,405.00
b/d	2,407.50		

Sales ledger

A				B			
	£		£		£		£
SDB	1,057.50	CRB	1,057.50	SDB	1,880.00	CRB	1,000.00
						c/d	880.00
	_____		_____		_____		_____
	1,057.50		1,057.50		1,880.00		1,880.00
	_____		_____		_____		_____

C			
	£		£
SDB	2,467.50		940.00
		c/d	1,527.50
	_____		_____
	2,467.50		2,467.50
	_____		_____

Note

The balance on the sales ledger control account in the main ledger (£2,407.50) is the same as the total balances of the individual accounts in the subsidiary sales ledger (£880.00 + £1,527.50 = £2,407.50). We will come back to this important point when we study basic accounting II.

2 Settlement discounts allowed to customers

2.1 Introduction

Settlement discounts are a small but tricky complication when dealing with the analysed sales day book and cash book.

We shall consider the same example as before with only one change – debtor A is offered an additional 5% settlement discount if he pays his invoice within 30 days.

Example

The sales day book with settlement discounts

Consider again the following sales transactions made by Roberts Metals.

Customer	Sales value (ex VAT) £	Trade discount £	Net sales value £	VAT £	Total £
A	1,000	10%	900	149.62	1,049.62
B	2,000	20%	1,600	280.00	1,880.00
C	3,000	30%	2,100	367.50	2,467.50

In addition to the trade discount, customer A has been offered an additional 5% discount if he pays his invoice within 30 days.

Enter this information in the sales day book and ledger accounts.

Solution

The following steps are needed.

Step 1 Write up the sales day book.

Step 2 Post the totals to the accounts in the main ledger.

Step 3 Post the individual invoices to the sales ledger.

The solution is the same as before except that the VAT for customer A has been recalculated to take account of the settlement discount (W1).

SALES DAY BOOK						
Date	Customer	Reference	Invoice number	Total £	VAT £	Sales £
	A			1,049.62	149.62 (W1)	900.00
	B			1,880.00	280.00	1,600.00
	C			2,467.50	367.50	2,100.00
			TOTALS	5,397.12	797.12	4,600.00

Workings

	£
Sales value	1,000.00
Trade discount	100.00
Net sale value	900.00
VAT (900 − 5%)17.5%	149.62
	——————
	1,049.62
	——————

Step 2

Main ledger

Sales				VAT			
£		£		£		£	
		SDB	4,600.00			SDB	797.12

SLCA			
£		£	
SDB	5,397.12		

Sales ledger

A				B			
£		£		£		£	
SDB	1,049.62			SDB	1,880.00		

C			
£		£	
SDB	2,467.50		

As you can see the offering of the settlement discount has had no effect on the entries to the sales day book or the ledgers other than the calculation of the VAT.

Example

The analysed cash receipts book with settlement discounts

Now we will look at the cash receipts book.

Debtor A pays his debt within 30 days and therefore takes the 5% discount and debtor B pays £1,000 on account.

Enter these transactions in the cash receipts book and the ledger accounts.

Solution

Notes

The entries in the cash receipts book are different when a debtor takes a settlement discount because a new column is added to the CRB – the 'discount allowed' column. In addition, a new account is opened in the main ledger – the 'discount allowed ledger account'.

The four steps are now:

Step 1 Calculate the cash that A pays after allowing for the discount.

Step 2 Enter the cash received in the CRB (with the additional column for 'discounts allowed'). Total the columns.

Step 3 Enter the totals in the main ledger (including the 'discount allowed account').

Step 4 Enter the individual cash received from debtors A and B in the sales ledger account.

Step 1

Calculate the cash paid by A.

	£
Sale value after trade discount	900.00
VAT (900 – (5% × 900)) × 17.5%	149.62
Invoice value (as entered in SDB)	1,049.62
Less: 5% settlement discount (900 × 5%)	(45.00)
Cash paid by A	1,004.62

Step 2

Enter cash received in the CRB.

CASH RECEIPTS BOOK

Date	Narrative	Reference	Total	VAT	SLCA	Cash sales	Discount allowed
			£	£	£	£	£
	A		1,004.62		1,004.62		45.00
	B		1,000.00		1,000.00		
		TOTALS	2,004.62		2,004.62		45.00

Note

The CRB does not 'cross-cast', i.e. if you add the totals across (debtors + discounts) this does not equal the total column.

The discount allowed column is known as a 'memorandum column' – it is not really part of the cash book – it is simply there to remind the book-keeper to make an entry in the main ledger as we shall see below.

Step 3 – posting the CRB totals

The CRB totals are posted as follows to the main ledger.

Sales				VAT			
	£		£		£		£
		SDB	4,600.00			SDB	797.12

SLCA				Discount allowed			
	£		£		£		£
SDB	5,397.12	CRB	2,004.62	CRB	45.00		
		CRB	45.00				

Note that the discount allowed figure in the CRB is entered in the SLCA (to acknowledge the fact that discount has been taken) and is debited to the discount allowed account.

This debit is an expense of the business – allowing the discount has cost the business £45.

Step 4 – posting to the sales ledger

A				B			
	£		£		£		£
SDB	1,049.62	CRB	1,004.62	SDB	1,880.00	CRB	1,000.00
		Disc	45.00			c/d	880.00
	1,049.62		1,049.62		1,880.00		1,880.00
				b/d	880.00		

C			
	£		£
SDB	2,467.50		

Note again that the discount is credited to the account of A to show that he has taken the £45 discount which clears his account.

Note also that there is no corresponding debit entry of £45 to a discount account in the sales ledger. The sales ledger is simply there to show the detail in the main ledger SLCA. The double entry for the £45 discount only takes place in the main ledger as we have seen between the SLCA and the discounts allowed account.

3   Cash and credit sales contrasted

3.1   Introduction

We studied cash sales at the very start of double entry bookkeeping and saw that the entries were very simple – debit cash and credit sales. Nothing has happened to change that but it is worth looking at cash and credit sales 'side by side' to appreciate the difference in their treatment, when we consider the sales day book and cash receipts book.

 Example

Linda's Electricals sells goods to three customers.

Customer A buys an electric fire for £100 cash plus VAT of £17.50.

Customer B buys rolls of electrical wiring on credit for £1,000 plus VAT of £175.00.

Customer C buys 100 switches on credit for £200 plus VAT of £35.00. Customer B pays his debt in full.

There are no trade or settlement discounts. Write up the books in the following steps.

Step 1   Enter the cash sale in the analysed cash receipts book in the main ledger.

Step 2   Enter the credit sales in the SDB and cash received in the analysed cash receipts book in the main ledger.

Step 3   Post the totals of the SDB and cash book to the accounts in the main ledger.

Step 4   Post the individual amounts in the SDB and cash book to the sales ledger.

Solution

Step 1

Enter the cash sale in the cash book.

CASH RECEIPTS BOOK

Date	Narrative	Total	VAT	SLCA	Cash sales	Discount allowed
		£	£	£	£	£
	A	1,004.62	17.50		100.00	

This is a very simple entry. At the moment of course it is only half of the double entry (the debit side of the entry). We have yet to do the credit entries (see Step 3).

Step 2

Enter the credit sales into the SDB and the cash received into the analysed cash receipts book (which already has the cash received from A per Step 1).

SALES DAY BOOK

Date	Customer	Reference	Invoice number	Total £	VAT £	Net sales value £
	B			1,175.00	175.00	1,000.00
	C			235.00	35.00	200.00
			TOTALS	1,410.00	210.00	1,200.00

CASH RECEIPTS BOOK

Date	Narrative	Total	VAT	SLCA	Cash sales	Discount allowed
		£	£	£	£	£
	A	117.50	17.50		100.00	
	B	1,175.00		1,175.00		
		1,292.50	17.50	1,175.00	100.00	

Note the different treatment of VAT for a cash and credit sale. For the cash sale, the VAT paid by A is entered in the VAT column of the cash book. For the credit sales of B and C, the VAT is entered in the VAT column of the SDB, and because it has already been 'captured' in the books it is not entered again in the cash book when the debt is paid by B.

In Step 3, we will see how the double entry is completed to ensure that all amounts are correctly treated.

Step 3

Post the SDB totals and cash book totals to the main ledger.

Sales			
£		£	
	SDB	1,200.00	
	CRB	100.00	

VAT			
£		£	
	SDB	210.00	
	CRB	17.50	

SLCA			
£		£	
SDB	1,410.00	CRB	1,175.00

Note 1

The VAT on the three sales are all now correctly credited to the VAT account, either by way of the SDB for credit sales or the CRB for cash sales.

Remember that the CRB is part of the double entry. The total column in the CRB is the debit entry that tells us how much cash has been paid in (£1,292.50), and the entries from the CRB to the other main ledger accounts are the balancing credit entries.

	£
Sales	100.00
VAT	17.50
SLCA	1,175.00
	————
Total credits	1,292.50
	————

Activity 1

Ellis Electricals makes the following credit sales to A and B giving a 20% trade discount plus a 5% settlement discount if customers pay their invoices within 30 days.

	Customer A £	Customer B £
Sales value	1,000	4,000
Trade discount (20%)	200	800
Net sales value	800	3,200
VAT (calculated on the net sales value after allowing for the settlement discount)		
Customer A: (800 – (800 × 5%)) × 17.5%	133	
Customer B: (3,200 – (3,200 × 5%)) × 17.5%		532
Total invoice value	933	3,732

Ellis Electricals also makes a cash sale to C for £300 plus VAT.

Remember that the VAT is calculated as if the settlement discount is taken whether the customer pays within 30 days and takes it or not – there is no going back to recalculate the VAT.

Customer A pays his invoice in full within 30 days and takes the settlement discount. Customer B pays £2,000 on account.

Task

Write up the SDB and the CRB and post the entries to the main and sales ledgers.

4 Test your knowledge

 Test your knowledge

Having completed Chapter 8, you should now be able to attempt Practice Activities 28 and 29.

5 Summary

This has been quite a difficult chapter which has addressed some of the trickier topics in the standards for these Units. There are two points which typically cause trouble and which you should get to grips with.

(a)   Accounting for VAT on cash received from debtors and cash received from cash sales.

(b)   Accounting for discounts allowed in the analysed cash book and main ledger accounts.

If you have any doubt at all about the treatment of these you should go back and study these two points in the chapter.

Answers to chapter activities

 Activity 1

Step 1

Write up the sales day book.

SALES DAY BOOK				
Date	Customer	Total £	VAT £	Sales £
	A	933.00	133.00	800.00
	B	3,732.00	532.00	3,200.00
		4,665.00	665.00	4,000.00

Step 2

Write up the cash receipts book.

CASH RECEIPTS BOOK						
Date	Narrative	Total	VAT	SLCA	Cash sales	Discount allowed
		£	£	£	£	£
	A (W)	893.00		893.00		40.00
	B	2,000.00		2,000.00		
		352.50	52.50		300.00	
		3,245.50	52.50	2,893.00	300.00	40.00

Working

Cash paid by A:

	£
Sale value net of VAT	800
VAT	133
	933
Less: Settlement discount (800 × 5%)	(40)
	893

Step 3

Post the totals to the main ledger.

Sales				VAT			
£		£		£		£	
		SDB	4,000.00			SDB	665.00
		CRB	300.00			CRB	52.50

SLCA				Discount allowed			
£		£		£		£	
SDB	4,665.00	CRB	2,893.00	SDB	40.00		
		CRB	40.00				

Step 4

Post individual amounts for the SDB and CRB to the sales ledger.

A				B			
£		£		£		£	
SDB	933.00	CRB	893.00	SDB	3,732.00		2,000.00
		CRB	40.00				

Debtors' statements

Introduction

In this chapter we consider communication with our debtors. If we are to receive the money owed to us on time it is important to ensure that the customers are fully aware of the amount they owe us and our credit terms.

KNOWLEDGE	CONTENTS
6.4 Describe the usefulness of an aged debtor analysis for monitoring debtors	1 Accounting for credit sales and receipts from customers
6.5 Explain the need to deal with discrepancies quickly and professionally	2 Debtors' statements
	3 Aged debt analysis
SKILLS	
1.3 Produce statements of account to be sent to credit customers	

1 Accounting for credit sales and receipts from customers

1.1 Introduction

Before we consider the preparation of debtors' statements, we will firstly bring together all of the accounting that has taken place for credit sales and receipts from credit customers in one example so that you can see how it all fits together. It is important that you understand how the amount owed by customers is calculated and recorded.

Example

Given below is the sales day book, sales returns day book and cash receipts book for the first month of trading by Nick Brookes.

SALES DAY BOOK						
Date	Invoice No	Customer name	Code	Total	VAT	Net
20X2				£	£	£
03/04	001	Mayer Ltd	SL1	185.65	27.65	158.00
04/04	002	Elizabeth & Co	SL2	257.34	37.34	220.00
07/04	003	Hofen Partners	SL3	129.25	19.25	110.00
10/04	004	Penken Bros	SL4	157.91	22.91	135.00
14/04	005	Mayer Ltd	SL1	206.80	30.80	176.00
18/04	006	Hofen Partners	SL3	122.20	18.20	104.00
21/04	007	Mayer Ltd	SL1	253.80	37.80	216.00
24/04	008	Penken Bros	SL4	167.27	24.27	143.00
26/04	009	Mayer Ltd	SL1	192.70	28.70	164.00
28/04	010	Elizabeth & Co	SL2	233.95	33.95	200.00
28/04	011	Penken Bros	SL4	138.03	20.03	118.00
				2,044.90	300.90	1,744.00

SALES RETURNS DAY BOOK						
Date	CN No	Customer name	Code	Total	VAT	Net
20X2				£	£	£
10/04	CN001	Mayer Ltd	SL1	49.35	7.35	42.00
17/04	CN002	Penken Bros	SL4	39.77	5.77	34.00
				89.12	13.12	76.00

CASH RECEIPTS BOOK						
Date	Narrative	Total	VAT	Debtors	Cash sales	Discount
		£	£	£	£	£
20X2						
07/04	Cash sales	374.23	55.73		318.50	
15/04	Elizabeth & Co	250.74		250.74		6.60
18/04	Mayer Ltd	136.30		136.30		
21/04	Cash sales	566.93	84.43		482.50	
21/04	Penken Bros	115.11		115.11		3.03
28/04	Hofen Partners	129.25		129.25		
		1,572.56	140.16	631.40	801.00	9.63

Solution

First we must post the totals from each of the books of prime entry to the main ledger accounts. As this is the first month of trading there will of course be no opening balances on any of the ledger accounts.

Sales ledger control account

		£			£
30/04	SBD	2,044.90	30/04	SRDB	89.12
			30/04	CRB	631.40
			30/04	CRB – discount	9.63

VAT account

		£			£
30/04	SRDB	13.12	30/04	SDB	300.90
			30/04	CRB	140.16

Sales account

		£			£
			30/04	SDB	1,744.00
			30/04	CRB	801.00

Sales returns account

		£			£
30/04	SRDB	76.00			

Discounts allowed account

		£			£
30/04	CRB	9.63			

Once the entries have been made in total to the main ledger accounts then each individual invoice, credit note, cash receipt and discount must be entered into the individual debtor accounts in the sales ledger.

Mayer Ltd

		£			£
03/04	001	185.65	10/04	CN001	49.35
14/04	005	206.80	18/04	CRB	136.30
21/04	007	253.80			
26/04	009	192.70			

Elizabeth & Co

		£			£
04/04	002	257.34	15/04	CRB	250.74
28/04	010	233.95	15/04	CRB – discount	6.60

Hofen Partners

		£			£
07/04	003	129.25	28/04	CRB	129.25
18/04	006	122.20			

Penken Bros

		£			£
10/04	004	157.91	17/04	CN002	39.77
24/04	008	167.27	21/04	CRB	115.11
28/04	011	138.03	21/04	CRB – discount	3.03

From this you can see how the full accounting system for credit sales works and the information that is accumulated in each of the individual debtor accounts in the sales ledger.

2 Debtors' statements

2.1 Introduction

The sales ledger clerk prepares monthly statements to send to debtors:

- to remind them that certain invoices are due for payment;
- to reconfirm amounts outstanding where credit notes have been issued.

Definition

A statement is a document issued (normally monthly) by a supplier to a customer showing unpaid sales invoices and the amount due in total.

2.2 Layout of statement

Statements can be prepared in a number of different ways. Some also have remittance advices attached to them in order to encourage early payment.

A remittance advice is a blank document that the customer fills out when making a payment to the supplier. It shows the total payment being made and which invoices (less credit notes) the payment is paying off.

2.3 Preparing a debtors' statement

A debtors' statement will normally be prepared from the information in the debtors' individual account in the sales ledger. Different businesses will use different formats but the basics that must be shown are all invoices, credit notes, payments received and discounts for the period together with usually a running total of the balance.

2.4 Procedure for preparing a debtors' statement

When preparing a statement for a credit customer, it is important that all details are correct, therefore a logical and accurate approach is required.

Step 1 Find the customer's account in the filing system for the sales ledger.

Step 2 Work through the account by date order listing each transaction in turn on the statement – invoices as a debit and credit notes, payments and discounts as credits.

Step 3 Return to the start of the statement and calculate the balance at each transaction date to appear in the balance column.

Example

Given below are the sales ledger accounts for two of Nick Brookes' customers. We will start by balancing each account to show the total amount due by each customer.

		Mayer Ltd			SL01
		£			£
03/04	001	185.65	10/04	CN001	49.35
14/04	005	206.80	18/04	CRB	136.30
21/04	007	253.80			
26/04	008	192.70		Balance c/d	653.30
		_____			_____
		838.95			838.95
		_____			_____
Balance b/d		653.30			

		Penken Bros			SL04
		£			£
10/04	004	157.91	17/04	CN002	39.77
24/04	008	167.27	21/04	CRB	115.11
28/04	011	138.03	21/04	CRB – discount	3.03
				Balance c/d	305.30
		_____			_____
		463.21			463.21
		_____			_____
Balance b/d		305.30			

We can now use this information to prepare statements for these two customers as at the end of April 20X2.

Solution

	NICK BROOKES
	225 School Lane
	Weymouth
To: Mayer Ltd	Dorset WE36 5NR
	Tel: 0149 29381
	Fax: 0149 29382
	Date: 30/04/X2

STATEMENT

Date	Transaction	Debit £	Credit £	Balance £
03/04	INV001	185.65		185.65
10/04	CN001		49.35	136.30
14/04	INV005	206.80		343.10
18/04	Payment		136.30	206.80
21/04	INV007	253.80		460.60
26/04	INV008	192.70		653.30

**May we remind you that our credit terms are 30 days
With 3% discount for payment within 14 days**

	NICK BROOKES
	225 School Lane
	Weymouth
To: Penken Bros	Dorset WE36 5NR
	Tel: 0149 29381
	Fax: 0149 29382
	Date: 30/04/X2

STATEMENT

Date	Transaction	Debit £	Credit £	Balance £
10/04	INV004	157.91		157.91
17/04	CN002		39.77	118.14
21/04	Payment		115.11	
21/04	Discount		3.03	0.00
24/04	INV008	167.27		167.27
28/04	INV011	138.03		305.30

**May we remind you that our credit terms are 30 days
With 3% discount for payment within 14 days**

These are documents that are being sent to customers, therefore it is extremely important that it is completely accurate. Always check your figures and additions.

Activity 1

You are to prepare a statement to be sent out to one customer, Jack Johnson, for the month of May 20X6. At the start of May this customer did not owe your business, Thames Traders, any money. The sales ledger account for Jack for the month of May is given below.

Jack Johnson

Date		£	Date		£
03 May	Invoice 1848	38.79	08 May	Credit note 446	12.40
07 May	Invoice 1863	50.70	15 May	Cash receipt	77.09
10 May	Invoice 1870	80.52	24 May	Credit note 458	16.50
18 May	Invoice 1881	42.40			
23 May	Invoice 1892	61.20			
30 May	Invoice 1904	27.65			

You are required to prepare a statement for Jack on the blank statement given below.

Thames Traders

To: Date:

STATEMENT

Date	Transaction	Debit £	Credit £	Balance £

May we remind you that our credit terms are 30 days

3 Aged debt analysis

3.1 Introduction

An aged debt analysis shows the age of invoices making up each customer's balance. This can be used to identify debtors who need chasing and a suitable letter can then be written to the customer.

For this assessment you do not need to be able to prepare an aged debt analysis, only to be able to use one to identify any debtors who may be a problem.

3.2 What an aged debt analysis looks like

An aged debt analysis takes the total debt due from a customer and splits it into the amount of invoices that are dated within the current month, the amounts that are normally more than 30 days old and amounts that are more than 60 days old.

The layouts will differ from business to business but in general terms a typical aged debt analysis may look like this:

Customer	Total	Current	> 30 days	> 60 days
	£	£	£	£
H Hardy	689.46	368.46	321.00	–
L Farmer	442.79	379.60	–	63.19
K Knight	317.68	–	169.46	148.22

3.3 How to use an aged debt analysis

The aged debt analysis can be used to indicate any customers who may be a problem in terms of credit control by giving an indication of their payment patterns.

Example

Given below is a typical extract from an aged debt analysis. What might the figures indicate about each of the debtors?

	Total	Current	> 30 days	> 60 days
	£	£	£	£
H Hardy	689.46	368.46	321.00	–
L Farmer	442.79	379.60	–	63.19
K Knight	317.68	–	169.46	148.22

Solution

H Hardy – It would appear that this customer tends to take more than 30 days of credit – this may be acceptable to your business or it may be felt that a reminder that credit terms are 30 days may be appropriate.

L Farmer– The vast amount of this debt is current but £63.19 is from more than 60 days old – there may be a dispute about this invoice and the customer would normally be contacted in order to determine what the problem is.

K Knight – This is a worrying picture as there have been no sales to the customer in the current period but older amounts are still owing – this may be due to the fact that your organisation has stopped sales to this customer until payment is received for the older debts or it may be that the customer has not wished to make any further purchases – this should be investigated.

3.4 Communication with customers

If there is a problem with a customer's balance then it will be normal practice to write a polite letter to the customer requesting payment and enquiring if there is any problem with the amounts shown in the statement. If there are no problems or disputed invoices but payment is still not received within a reasonable time then this initial letter should be followed by a letter with a firmer tone requesting payment. This may include a statement that the matter will be put into the hands of your business's solicitors if payment if not received. However, this will be a matter of policy within each business.

 Example

You are the credit controller for GoGo Limited, a wholesaler of discount children's clothing. You have been reviewing the aged debtors' listing. The following customer is causing you concern:

	Total £	Current £	30+ days £	60+ days £
Candy Limited	556.78	0	0	556.78

You must write a letter to this customer to ask for payment.

Solution

> **GoGo Limited**
> 225 Western Road
> Anytown
> Anyshire AN1 2RN
>
> Creditors' Ledger Clerk   23 August 20X4
> Candy Limited
> 53 High Street Anytown
> Anyshire AN1 6BN
>
> Dear Sir
>
> **Outstanding balance**
>
> According to our records your company has an outstanding balance of £556.78.
>
> Our normal credit terms are 30 days. As this debt is now over 60 days old we would be very grateful if you could send us your payment immediately.
>
> If you have any queries please do not hesitate to contact me. Yours faithfully
>
> AN Smith
> Credit Controller

Do not be tempted to write a letter that sounds angry or threatening. Polite efficiency is what is required.

 Activity 2

The following is an extract from an aged debt analysis report prepared on 1 June.

Name	Balance	Up to 1 month	Up to 3 months	Over 3 months
	£	£	£	£
West & Co	4,860	3,400	1,460	0
Star Limited	2,719	0	0	2,719
Norwood Limited	3,116	1,200	1,900	16
Just Electric	1,391	1,320	0	71

(a) With which one of the four accounts might you be most concerned?

(b) Explain briefly the reason for your answer.

4 Test your knowledge

Test your knowledge

Having completed Chapter 9, you should now be able to attempt Practice Activities 30 and 31.

5 Summary

In this chapter all of the accounting entries for sales invoices, credit notes and receipts from debtors were brought together. We also saw how to produce a statement to be sent to a customer from the customer's account in the sales ledger.

We have also introduced an aged debt analysis. You do not need to be able to produce one but you do need to be able to use it to determine any customers who appear to be causing problems with debt collection. It is important when communicating with customers that you deal effectively but politely at all times.

Answers to chapter activities

 Activity 1

Thames Traders

To: Jack Johnson

Date: 31 May 20X6:

STATEMENT

Date	Transaction	Debit £	Credit £	Balance £
03 May	Inv 1848	38.79		38.79
07 May	Inv 1863	50.70		89.49
08 May	CN 446		12.40	77.09
10 May	Inv 1870	80.52		157.61
15 May	Payment		77.09	80.52
18 May	Inv 1881	42.40		122.92
23 May	Inv 1892	61.20		184.12
24 May	CN 458		16.50	167.62
30 May	Inv 1904	27.65		195.27

May we remind you that our credit terms are 30 days

 Activity 2

(a)   Star Limited

(b)   The balance has been outstanding for over three months with no sales since.

Consolidation

Introduction

The following example comprises six tasks and will bring together all the techniques studied in this book so far.

1	Approach

1.1 Tasks explained

Task 1 Application of the DEAD/CLIC mnemonic is tested within this task.

Task 2 The double entry techniques studied to date are tested within this task, as are how to post the books of prime entry. The task will also test your understanding of the relationship between the main and sales ledgers.

Task 3 The importance of balancing the ledger accounts is tested within this task

Task 4 The transfer skills needed to show the ledger balances correctly on the initial trial balance are tested within this task.

Task 5 Again, this task tests the application of the DEAD/CLIC mnemonic to enter balances onto the initial trial balance, and the completion of the trial balance itself.

 Activity 1

Mark Spencer is the owner of a retail business called De-Groot King

You are employed by the business as a bookkeeper

The business uses a manual accounting system

Double entry takes place in the main ledger. Individual debtor accounts are kept in the sales ledger as memorandum accounts.

Assume today's date is 30 June 20X9, unless you are told otherwise

Balances at the start of the date on 30 June 20X9

Credit customers

McConnell & Co	11,200
Twelve Towers	3,720
Booth Ltd	28,456
Invigor8	50,400

Cash overdraft	12,267
Sales	455,600
Sales returns	9,000
Sales ledger control	242,094
Discount allowed	1,800
VAT (credit balance)	25,680

Task 1

Enter the opening balances above into the 'T' accounts given.

Transactions

The following transactions took place on 30 June 20X9 and have been entered into the daybooks below:

Sales day book					
Date	Details	Inv. No.	Total £	VAT £	Net £
30/06/X9	McConnell & Co	879	36,660	5,460	31,200
30/06/X9	Twelve Towers	880	2,115	315	1,800
30/06/X9	Booth Ltd	881	10,575	1,575	9,000
30/06/X9	Invigor8	882	4,230	630	3,600
			53,580	7,980	45,600

Sales returns day book

Date	Details	Credit No.	Total £	VAT £	Net £
30/06/X9	Twelve Towers	C16	705	105	600
30/06/X9	Invigor8	C17	141	21	120
			846	126	720

Cash receipts book

Date	Details	Total £	SLCA £	VAT £	Cash sales £	Discount allowed £
30/06/X9	Invigor8	13,200	13,200			342
30/06/X9	Cash sale	1,175		175	1,000	
		14,375	13,200	175	1,000	342

Task 2

From the daybooks and cash book shown, make the relevant entries into the accounts in the main ledger and the sales ledger.

Task 3

Balance the accounts showing clearly the balances carried down at 30 June and brought down at 1 July.

Task 4

List the balances you have calculated in Task 3 in the trial balance.

Sales ledger

McConnell & Company

Date	Details	£	Date	Detail	£

Twelve Towers

Date	Details	£	Date	Detail	£

Booth Ltd

Date	Details	£	Date	Detail	£

Invigor8

Date	Details	£	Date	Detail	£

Main ledger

Cashbook

Date	Details	£	Date	Detail	£

Sales

Date	Details	£	Date	Detail	£

Sales returns

Date	Details	£	Date	Detail	£

Sales ledger control

Date	Details	£	Date	Detail	£

Discount allowed

Date	Details	£	Date	Detail	£

VAT					
Date	Details	£	Date	Detail	£

Other balances

Plant & machinery	34,200
Motor vehicles	42,970
Stock	8,700
Petty cash control	277
Capital	7,890
Loan from bank	30,000
Discount received	360
Purchases	185,950
Purchases returns	4,200
Purchases ledger control	54,324
Motor expenses	1,940
Wages	38,900
Rent	2,750
Heat & light	5,420
Stationery	630
Telephone	1,860
Insurance	9,750
Miscellaneous expenses	4,080

Task 5

List the remaining balances shown above in the trial balance and total each column.

Trial balance

	Dr £	Cr £
Cashbook		
Sales		
Sales returns		
Sales ledger control		
Discount allowed		
VAT		
Plant & machinery		
Motor vehicles		
Stock		
Petty cash control		
Capital		
Loan from bank		
Discount received		
Purchases		
Purchases returns		
Purchases ledger control		
Motor expenses		
Wages		
Rent		
Heat & light		
Stationery		
Telephone		
Insurance		
Miscellaneous expenses		
Totals		

2 Test your knowledge

Test your knowledge

Having completed Chapter 10, you should also complete Practice Activity 32

3 Summary

This question has tested all of the techniques learned to date. It is important that these tasks can be completed confidently.

Answers to chapter activity

 Activity 1

Sales ledger

		McConnell & Company			
Date	**Details**	**£**	**Date**	**Detail**	**£**
30/6/X9	Bal b/d	11,200	30/6/X9	Bal c/d	47,860
30/6/X9	SDB	36,660			
		47,860			**47,860**
1/7/X9	Bal b/d	47,860			

		Twelve Towers			
Date	**Details**	**£**	**Date**	**Detail**	**£**
30/6/X9	Bal b/d	3,720	30/6/X9	SRDB	705
30/6/X9	SDB	2,115	30/6/X9	Bal c/d	5,130
		5,835			**5,835**
1/7/X9	Bal b/d	5,130			

		Booth Ltd			
Date	**Details**	**£**	**Date**	**Detail**	**£**
30/6/X9	Bal b/d	28,456	30/6/X9	Bal c/d	39,031
30/6/X9	SDB	10,575			
		39,031			**39,031**
1/7/X9	Bal b/d	39,031			

Invigor8

Date	Details	£	Date	Detail	£
30/6/X9	Bal b/d	50,400	30/6/X9	SRDB	141
30/6/X9	SDB	4,230	30/6/X9	Cashbook	13,200
			30/6/X9	Discount	342
			30/6/X9	Bal c/d	40,947
		54,630			**54,630**
1/7/X9	Bal b/d	40,947			

Cashbook

Date	Details	£	Date	Detail	£
30/6/X9	Invigor8	13,200	30/6/X9	Bal b/d	12,267
30/6/X9	Cash sale	1,175	30/6/X9	Bal c/d	2,108
		14,375			**14,375**
1/7/X9	Bal b/d	2,108			

Sales

Date	Details	£	Date	Detail	£
			30/6/X9	Bal b/d	455,600
			30/6/X9	SDB	45,600
30/6/X9	Bal c/d	502,200	30/6/X9	Cashbook	1,000
		502,200			**502,200**
			1/7/X9	Bal b/d	502,200

Sales returns

Date	Details	£	Date	Detail	£
30/6/X9	Bal b/d	9,000	30/6/X9	Bal c/d	9,720
30/6/X9	SRDB	720			
		9,720			**9,720**
1/7/X9	Bal b/d	9,720			

Sales ledger control

Date	Details	£	Date	Detail	£
30/6/X9	Bal b/d	242,094	30/6/X9	SRDB	846
30/6/X9	SDB	53,580	30/6/X9	Cashbook	13,200
			30/6/X9	Discount	342
			30/6/X9	Bal c/d	281,286
		295,674			**295,674**
1/7/X9	Bal b/d	281,286			

Discount allowed

Date	Details	£	Date	Detail	£
30/6/X9	Bal b/d	1,800			
30/6/X9	Cashbook	342	30/6/X9	Bal c/d	2,142
		2,142			**2,142**
1/7/X9	Bal b/d	2,142			

VAT

Date	Details	£	Date	Detail	£
30/6/X9	SRDB	126	30/6/X9	Bal b/d	25,680
			30/6/X9	SDB	7,980
30/6/X9	Bal c/d	33,709	30/6/X9	Cashbook	175
		33,835			**33,835**
			1/7/X9	Bal b/d	33,709

Trial balance

	Dr £	Cr £
Cashbook	2,108	
Sales		502,200
Sales returns	9,720	
Sales ledger control	281,286	
Discount allowed	2,142	
VAT		33,709
Plant & machinery	34,200	
Motor vehicles	42,970	
Stock	8,700	
Petty cash control	277	
Capital		7,890
Loan from bank		30,000
Discount received		360
Purchases	185,950	
Purchases returns		4,200
Purchases ledger control		54,324
Motor expenses	1,940	
Wages	38,900	
Rent	2,750	
Heat & light	5,420	
Stationery	630	
Telephone	1,860	
Insurance	9,750	
Miscellaneous expenses	4,080	
Totals	**632,683**	**632,683**

KAPLAN PUBLISHING

Credit purchases: Documents

Introduction

Now that we have covered the detail with regard to sales, we can apply the same principles to the transactions involved with purchases.

SKILLS	CONTENTS
4.1 Check the accuracy of supplier invoices and credit notes against purchase orders, goods received and delivery notes	**1** Summary of a credit purchase
	2 Ordering goods and services
5.1 Code supplier invoices and credit notes	**3** Receipt of the goods
	4 The purchase invoice
	5 Credit notes

1 Summary of a credit purchase

The main document flows for a credit purchase are illustrated below. The various documents are described in the paragraphs that follow.

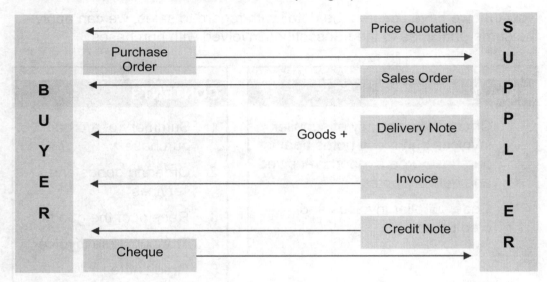

2 Ordering goods and services

2.1 Introduction

There are a variety of different methods of placing an order with a supplier.

(a) **Telephone**

If an order is made by telephone then it is important that the details are confirmed with the supplier in writing. This may be by the supplier sending your organisation an order confirmation or alternatively by you following up the telephone order with a written confirmation of the details.

(b) **In writing**

If an order is to be made in writing then again you would expect an order confirmation to be sent back to you by the supplier confirming all of the details of the order, for example, price, discounts and delivery details.

(c) **Fax**

An order could be made with a supplier by sending a fax. This is similar to sending an order in writing, only that it is received sooner by the supplier. However again you would expect to receive an order confirmation from the supplier.

(d) **Internet**

These days it is also possible to order many goods over the internet as there are many websites that allow you to purchase goods directly online. This should only be considered if it is a procedure that is allowed by your organisation's policy manual and this course of action should be authorised by the appropriate person before any order is placed. It is advisable to only order goods from reputable, well-known organisations but if the organisation is unknown then try to find one that at least has a telephone number that will allow you to verify their authenticity. A copy of the order placed over the internet should be printed out to act as a purchase order and be filed accordingly.

In all instances of ordering, a copy of the order or order confirmation should be filed so that it can be compared with the actual goods when they arrive and eventually with the purchase invoice.

2.2 An internal purchasing system

When a department needs goods and services from outside suppliers it may make an internal request using a purchase requisition.

A purchase requisition is an internal document by which a department requests purchases from an outside supplier.

When the purchasing department of a business receives a purchase requisition then it will start the procedures of the purchasing system.

This will normally start with price enquiries being made of a number of different suppliers in order to identify the supplier who will provide the goods at the best price and with the best terms. The suppliers will then send a price quotation in order for the purchasing department to be able to compare prices and terms.

A typical quotation is shown below. Note that this is exactly the same as the quotation received in the examples in Chapter 4 where we studied the sales order systems. The purchasing system is the 'mirror image' of the sales system and the documents are the same. We are simply looking at these systems from the point of view of the customer rather than the supplier.

City Woods Suppliers

192 Old Kent Road
London
SE1 8QT

*Name and address of
business quoting price*

Tel: 020 7248 7009 – Fax: 020 728 7890

QUOTATION

TO: Alpha Limited
        Mountjoy Street
        London W12 6RS

*Name and address of
customer*

Date: 14 Sept 20X3

Today's date

Thank you for your telephone enquiry of 10 September. We are pleased to
quote the following price:

Chipboard sheeting 6' × 4' Code CB0351 £23.00 per unit, excluding VAT

*Details of
goods*

J Kramer

*Authorisation
signature*

*Price being
quoted*

Sales Manager

When the supplier has been chosen then a purchase order will be sent out
to that supplier.

2.3   Purchase order

🔍 Definition

A purchase order is a document sent to a supplier confirming an order
for goods or services.

Each purchase order must be authorised by the relevant department head
or supervisor before being sent to the supplier. Each department head has
an **authorisation limit**. Orders above that value must be authorised by a
director, e.g. managing director.

Only approved suppliers (shown on an official list) should be used.

Purchase orders should be sequentially numbered and carefully controlled
and filed in numerical order for later use.

An example purchase order is shown below:

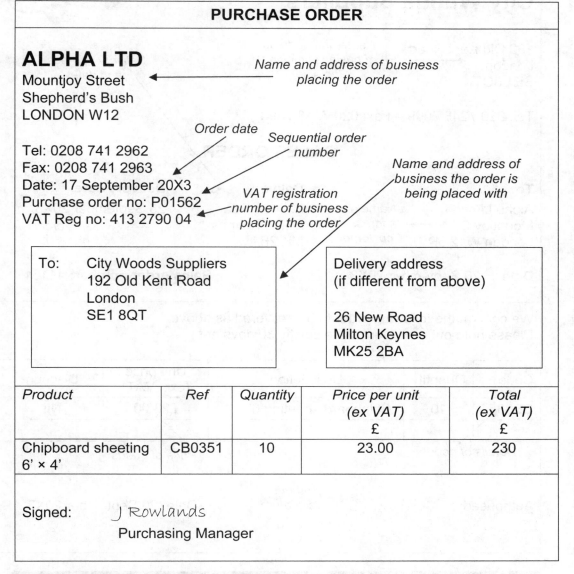

PURCHASE ORDER

ALPHA LTD
Mountjoy Street   *Name and address of business*
Shepherd's Bush   *placing the order*
LONDON W12

                         Order date   *Sequential order*
Tel: 0208 741 2962   *number*
Fax: 0208 741 2963   *Name and address of*
Date: 17 September 20X3   *business the order is*
Purchase order no: P01562   *VAT registration*   *being placed with*
VAT Reg no: 413 2790 04   *number of business*
                            placing the order

To:	City Woods Suppliers		Delivery address
	192 Old Kent Road		(if different from above)
	London		
	SE1 8QT		26 New Road
			Milton Keynes
			MK25 2BA

Product	Ref	Quantity	Price per unit (ex VAT) £	Total (ex VAT) £
Chipboard sheeting 6' × 4'	CB0351	10	23.00	230

Signed: *J Rowlands*
            Purchasing Manager

2.4 Confirming sales orders

To avoid misunderstandings, a supplier will normally confirm a customer's order by completing a sales order, even if the customer has already sent a written **purchase order**.

A sales order is a document confirming:

* quantity/type of goods or service;
* date of supply;
* location of supply;
* price and terms.

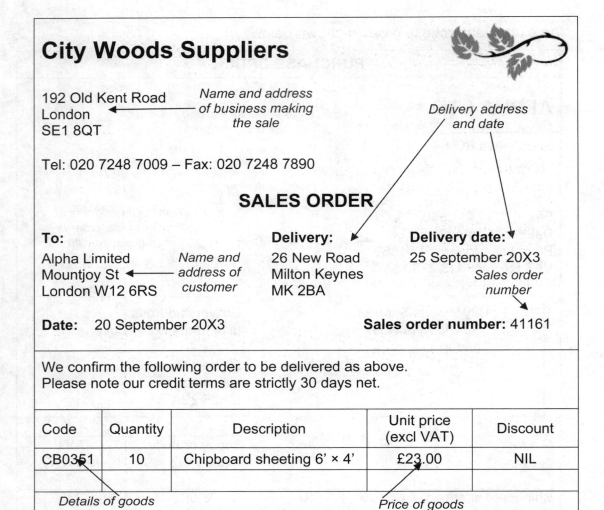

City Woods Suppliers

192 Old Kent Road
London
SE1 8QT

Name and address
of business making
the sale

Delivery address
and date

Tel: 020 7248 7009 – Fax: 020 7248 7890

SALES ORDER

To:
Alpha Limited
Mountjoy St
London W12 6RS

Name and
address of
customer

Delivery:
26 New Road
Milton Keynes
MK 2BA

Delivery date:
25 September 20X3

Sales order
number

Date: 20 September 20X3

Sales order number: 41161

We confirm the following order to be delivered as above.
Please note our credit terms are strictly 30 days net.

Code	Quantity	Description	Unit price (excl VAT)	Discount
CB0351	10	Chipboard sheeting 6' × 4'	£23.00	NIL

Details of goods

Price of goods

Authorised: *P. Anders*

Authorised
signature

Date: 20 September 20X3

3   Receipt of the goods

3.1   Introduction

Once the order has been placed with the supplier then the next stage will be for the goods to be received.

3.2   Delivery note

When the supplier sends the goods they will normally be accompanied by a delivery note.

Definition

A delivery note is a document that accompanies the goods when they are delivered by the supplier.

The delivery note details the goods that have been delivered to your organisation. When the goods are received by the business they must be checked by the stores or warehouse to ensure that the goods that are detailed on the delivery note are indeed the goods that have been delivered. The goods must also be checked to ensure that they are in good condition. The person in your organisation who has checked the goods will then sign the delivery note.

There will normally be three parts to a delivery note:

Part one – This is kept by your organisation in order to compare to the purchase order to ensure that the goods that have been delivered were ordered and then to the purchase invoice when it is received.

Part two – Returned to the supplier as evidence that you have received the goods detailed on the delivery note.

Part three – Kept by the delivery organisation as evidence that they have delivered the goods and that your organisation has received them.

City Woods Suppliers

192 Old Kent Road
London
SE1 8QT

Tel: 020 7248 7009 – Fax: 020 7248 7890

DN 005673

DELIVERY NOTE

To:	Delivery:	Delivery date:
Alpha Limited	26 New Road	25 September 20X3
Mountjoy St	Milton Keynes	
London W12 6RS	MK 2BA	

Date: 25 September 20X3

Sales order number: 41161

We confirm the following order to be delivered as above.

Product	Code	Quantity
Chipboard 6' × 4'	CB0351	10

Received in good condition: *A Patel*

4 The purchase invoice

4.1 Introduction

The final stage in the purchasing system will normally be the receipt of the purchase invoice from the supplier detailing the cost of the goods purchased and the payment terms.

A typical invoice is shown below.

City Woods Suppliers

192 Old Kent Road
London
SE1 8QT

Tel: 020 7248 7009 – Fax: 020 7248 7890

Invoice no: 1005673
Tax point: 25 September 20X3
VAT reg no: 618 2201 63
Delivery note: DN005673
Account no: AL6215

INVOICE

To:

Alpha Limited
Mountjoy St
London W12 6RS

Delivery:

26 New Road
Milton Keynes
MK 2BA

Delivery date:

25 September 20X3

Date: 25 September 20X3

Sales order number: 41161

We confirm the following order to be delivered as above.

Product	Code	Quantity	Price per unit £	Total £
Chipboard 6' × 4'	CB0351	10	23.00	230.00
			VAT	40.25
			Total	270.25

4.2   Checks on purchase invoices

Once the purchase invoice arrives then a number of checks need to be made on it before it can be passed for payment.

4.3   Order and receipt of goods

Firstly the purchase invoice must be checked to the purchase order and to the delivery note. This is to ensure that not only is this an invoice for goods that were ordered but also for goods that were received. In particular check the description and the quantity of the goods.

For example suppose that the purchase order for goods shows that 100 packs were ordered and the delivery note shows that 100 packs were received. If when the invoice arrives it is for 120 packs then the supplier should be politely informed of the error and a credit note requested.

4.4 Calculations

All of the calculations on the invoice should also be checked to ensure that they are correct. This will include the following:

- all pricing calculations;
- any trade discount or bulk discount calculations;
- the VAT calculations remembering any cash discounts that may be offered;
- the total addition of the invoice.

4.5 Trade discounts

Remember that trade discounts are a definite amount that is deducted from the list price of the goods for the supplies to some customers. As well as checking the actual calculation of the trade discount on the face of the invoice, the supplier's file or the price quotation should be checked to ensure that the correct percentage of trade discount has been deducted.

Even if no trade discount appears on the purchase invoice, the supplier's file or price quotation must still be checked as it may be that a trade discount should have been deducted but has been inadvertently forgotten by the supplier.

4.6 Bulk discounts

A bulk discount is similar to a trade discount in that it is deducted from the list price on the invoice. However, a bulk discount is given by a supplier for orders above a certain size. As with a trade discount the calculation of any bulk discount must be checked to the supplier's file to ensure that the correct discount has been given.

4.7 Settlement or cash discounts

Settlement or cash discounts are offered to customers in order to encourage early payment of invoices. The details of the settlement discount will normally be shown at the bottom of the purchase invoice and it is up to the customer to decide whether to pay the invoice early enough to benefit from the settlement discount or whether to delay payment and ignore the settlement discount.

Again the supplier's file should be checked to ensure that the correct percentage of settlement discount according to the correct terms has been offered.

If there is no settlement discount offered the supplier's details must still be checked to ensure that the settlement discount has not been forgotten by the supplier.

A trade discount or a bulk discount is a definite reduction in price from the list price whereas a cash or settlement discount is only a reduction in price if the organisation decides to take advantage of it by paying earlier.

4.8   VAT calculations and cash discounts

You will remember from an earlier chapter that when a cash or settlement discount is offered then the VAT calculation is based upon the assumption that the customer will take the settlement discount and pay the discounted price for the goods.

 Example

An invoice has a list price of goods of £400.00 with a trade discount of 10% then deducted. A settlement discount of 5% is also offered for payment within 10 days. The goods are charged to VAT at a rate of 17.5%.

How much should the VAT charge on the invoice be and what would be the invoice total?

Solution

	£
List price	400.00
Less: Trade discount 10%	40.00
	360.00
VAT (17.5% × (360 × 95%))	59.85
Invoice total	419.85

 Activity 1

A business receives an invoice for £2,400 (exclusive of VAT) from a supplier offering a 5% cash discount. What should be the total of the invoice inclusive of VAT at 17.5%

Example

Given below are two invoices; they must be thoroughly checked to ensure that they are correct.

Invoice 7761B

J Hardy Construction
Poplar Works,
Poplar Street
Oldham OL4 6QB

Barrett & Company

Ewe House, Parkside, Oldham.

Tel: 0161 560 3392
Fax: 0161 560 5322
Tax point:　　 28 August 20X3
VAT reg no:　　 268 9104 07

Code	Supply	Description	Quantity	VAT rate %	Unit price £	Amount (£) exclusive of VAT
734 226	Sale	Insular Bricks	40	17.50	16.25	650.00
874 KL5	Sale	Brick Tiles	15	17.50	43.12	664.80
Total						1,296.80
VAT at 17.5%						226.94
Total amount payable						1,523.74

A settlement discount of 5% is offered for payment within 20 days of the invoice date.

| | | | | | | **Invoice 68553** |

A.J. Broom & Company Limited
59 Parkway, Manchester M2 6EG

J Hardy Construction
Poplar Works,
Poplar Street
Oldham OL4 6QB

Tel: 0161 560 3392
Fax: 0161 560 5322
Tax point: 23 August 20X3
VAT reg no: 417 1066 22

Code	Supply	Description	Quantity	VAT rate %	Unit price £	Amount (£) exclusive of VAT
950 BB3	Sale	Cotswold Bricks	3	17.50	300.00	900.00
159 504	Sale	Roof Tiles – Red	5	17.50	195.50	977.50
874 KL5	Sale	Brick Tiles	1	17.50	56.65	56.65
Total						1,934.15
Less: Trade discount 2%						28.68
						1,905.47
VAT at 17.5%						333.45
Total amount payable						**2,238.92**

Solution

Invoice from Barrett & Co

• the calculation of the brick tiles total is incorrect – it should be 15 × £43.12 = £646.80;

• the VAT has been incorrectly calculated as it has been taken on the invoice total instead of on the figure that would be due if the cash discount were taken. The VAT should be 95% × 17.5% × £1,296.80 = £215.59.

Invoice from A J Broom & Co

• the trade discount of 2% has been incorrectly calculated and this means that the VAT is also incorrect. The supplier should be notified of these errors and a credit note requested.

In assessments you should thoroughly check every figure and every calculation on a purchase invoice just as you would in practice.

Activity 2

When passing a purchase invoice for payment, what two aspects need to be checked, other than calculations?

4.9   Invoices for services

Invoices or bills can also be received for services such as rent, electricity, cleaning, etc. There will be no delivery note, however the accuracy of the invoice can be checked and it should be sent to the appropriate person to be authorised. This person should be able to assess whether the service has in fact been received and was required.

5   Credit notes

5.1   Introduction

A credit note is simply the reverse of an invoice. It is sent by a supplier to a customer either to correct an error on a previous invoice or because the customer has returned some goods that do not therefore need to be paid for. Exactly the same checks should be made on credit notes as on invoices. The reason for the credit note and the amount that has been credited should be checked, so should all of the calculations and the VAT.

If Alpha Ltd returned two panels of wood, the credit note would be as follows.

City Woods Suppliers

192 Old Kent Road ← *Name and address of issuer of credit note*
London
SE1 8QT

Tel: 020 7248 7009 – Fax: 020 7248 7890

VAT registration number of supplier

Returns inwards note reference

Sequential credit note number

Credit note no: CN 02542
Tax point: 30 September 20X3
VAT reg no: 618 2201 63
Return inwards note no: 01531
Invoice no: 1005673
Account no: AL 6215

Date of credit note

CREDIT NOTE

Credit to: *Name and address of customer*
Alpha Limited
Mountjoy St
London W12 6RS

Customer's account code

Date: 30 September 20X3

Description	Code	Quantity	VAT rate %	Unit price £	Amount exclusive of VAT £
Chipboard 6' × 4'	CB0351	2	17.5	23.00	46.00
			Goods returned total		46.00
					46.00
VAT at 17.5%				*VAT charged*	8.05
Total amount of credit				*Total amount of credit*	**54.05**

Rate of VAT on goods returned

Activity 3

State the document appropriate to each of the following stages for purchasing and paying for goods.

(a)   Notification to purchasing manager of need to order.

(b)   Request to supplier to supply goods.

(c)   Form accompanying goods sent by supplier.

5.2 The importance of checking documents

Every purchase invoice or credit note received by an organisation, whether it is for goods or services, must be thoroughly checked and approved before it is entered into the accounting records. The checks must ensure that the invoice is for goods or services actually ordered and received, and also ensure that the invoice or credit note is accurately made up, including checks on all calculations and VAT.

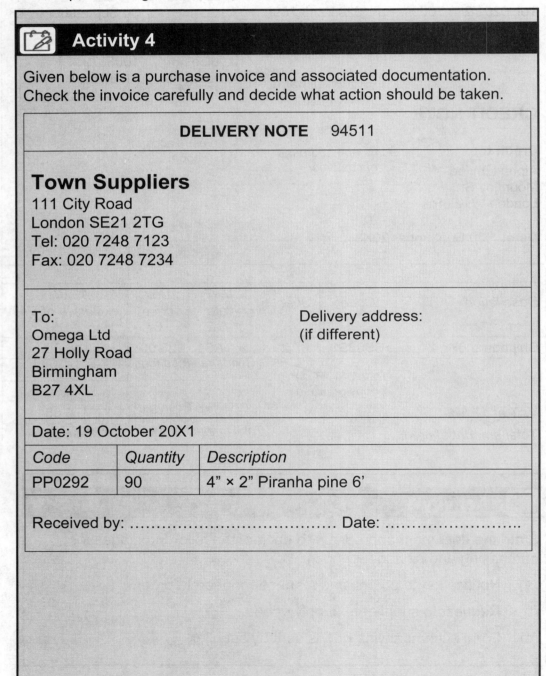

Activity 4

Given below is a purchase invoice and associated documentation. Check the invoice carefully and decide what action should be taken.

DELIVERY NOTE 94511

Town Suppliers
111 City Road
London SE21 2TG
Tel: 020 7248 7123
Fax: 020 7248 7234

To:
Omega Ltd
27 Holly Road
Birmingham
B27 4XL

Delivery address:
(if different)

Date: 19 October 20X1

Code	Quantity	Description
PP0292	90	4" × 2" Piranha pine 6'

Received by: .... Date: ....

PURCHASE ORDER	263

Omega Ltd
27 Holly Road
Birmingham
B27 4XL

To: Town Suppliers   Date: 6 October 20X1
11 City Road
London SE21 2TG

PLEASE SUPPLY TO THE ABOVE ADDRESS

Code	Quantity	Description	Unit price (exclusive of VAT) £
PP0292	100	6' Piranha pine (4" × 2")	3.50

Received by: …………………………………. Date: ………………………..

INVOICE	94511

Town Suppliers
111 City Road
London SE21 2TG
Tel: 020 7248 7123
Fax: 020 7248 7234

To:
Omega Ltd
27 Holly Road
Birmingham
B27 4XL

Tax point: 19 October 20X1

VAT Reg No: 234 4610 23

Code	Quantity	Amount exclusive of VAT £	VAT rate %	VAT net £
PP0292	100	350.00	17.5	61.25
		————		
	Total	350.00		
	VAT	61.25		
		————		
		411.25		
		————		

6 Test your knowledge

 Test your knowledge

Having completed Chapter 11, you should now be able to attempt
Practice Activities 33 and 34.

7 Summary

In this chapter the documentation that is used in the purchases system is firstly considered. The different methods of ordering goods and services are covered, as well as the documents that are required when goods are received: the delivery note, the purchase invoice and possibly any credit notes. The most important aspect of the chapter, however, are the thorough and accurate checks that must be made on all purchase invoices and credit notes received from suppliers. The invoices and credit notes must be checked to supporting documentation such as the delivery note, purchase order, returns note, etc. All of the calculations on the invoice or credit note should be checked as well as the percentage of trade, bulk and settlement discounts that have been stated on the invoice or credit note.

Activity 1

£2,799

Note: This answer is arrived at as follows:

	£
Goods/services	2,400
VAT @ 17.5% × 2,400 × 95%	399
	2,799

 Activity 2

(i) That the goods or services invoiced are as ordered.

(ii) That the goods or services invoiced have been received in good condition or carried out properly.

 Activity 3

(a) Purchase requisition

(b) Purchase order

(c) Delivery note

 Activity 4

The delivery note shows that only 90 units were delivered, not the 100 units that were ordered and invoiced.

You should write to the supplier requesting a credit note for the 10 missing units. Once the supplier has agreed the situation, the invoice can then be passed for payment.

KAPLAN PUBLISHING

Credit purchases – Discounts and VAT 12

Introduction

In this chapter we move on from considering the accounting entries for sales and look here at the equivalent accounting entries for purchases.

KNOWLEDGE
1.4 Explain how transactions are entered in the following books of prime entry: purchases and purchases returns day books

SKILLS
4.2 Check agreed trade, bulk and settlement discounts where appropriate

CONTENTS
1 Discounts and VAT
2 Credit purchases – double entry

1 Discounts and VAT

1.1 Introduction

We studied discounts and VAT when studying sales. The calculation of VAT and discounts are **exactly** the same when considering purchases. Remember that it is the seller who offers the discounts and it is the seller who charges the VAT, so the fact that we are now studying purchases does not change how these things are calculated.

The purchaser will receive a 'sales invoice' from the seller. This will have details of discounts and VAT exactly as we saw before when studying sales. The purchaser will call this a 'purchase invoice' and enter it in the books accordingly as we shall see.

We shall not therefore go through all the details of VAT and discounts but will simply revise this with a short example.

Example

Carl buys £1,000 of goods from Susan on credit. Susan sends a sales invoice with the goods offering a 5% discount if Carl pays within 30 days. Carl pays within 30 days.

Calculate:

(a)   the VAT;

(b)   the total value of the invoice; and

(c)   the amount that Carl will pay.

Solution

(a)   VAT = (£1,000 – (5% × £1,000)) × 17.5% = £166.25

(b)   **Total value of invoice**

	£
Goods	1,000.00
VAT	166.25
Invoice value	1,166.25

(c)   **Amount Carl will pay**

	£
Goods	1,000.00
Less settlement discount	50.00
	950.00
VAT	166.25
	1,116.25

Note: Remember that if Carl does not pay within 30 days the VAT is not recalculated.

2   Credit purchases – double entry

2.1   Basic double entry

The basic double entry for credit purchases with VAT is as follows:

Debit   Purchases account with the net amount

Debit   VAT account with the VAT

Credit   Creditors account with the gross amount

Purchases have been debited with the net amount as the VAT is not a cost to the business. Instead the VAT is an amount that can be set off against the amount of VAT due to HM Revenue and Customs and therefore the VAT is a debit entry in the VAT account. The creditors account is credited with the gross amount as this is the amount that must be paid to the supplier.

As with debtors and the sales ledger control account we will now be calling the creditors account the purchases ledger control account (PLCA).

Work through the following examples to practise the double entry for credit purchases.

Example 1

B sells goods on credit to Y for £500 plus VAT. Y pays B the full amount due. Record these transactions in the accounts of Y.

Solution

Step 1   Calculate the VAT on the purchase and enter the transaction in the PLCA, purchases and VAT accounts.

Calculation of VAT

	£
Net value of sale	500.00
VAT at 17.5%	87.50
	———
Gross value of purchase	587.50
	———

PLCA

	£		£
		Purchases and VAT	587.50

Purchases

	£		£
PLCA	500.00		

VAT

	£		£
PLCA	87.50		

Step 2   Enter £587.50 paid by Y in the PLCA and the bank account.

PLCA

	£		£
Bank	587.50	Purchases and VAT	587.50

Purchases

	£		£
PLCA	500.00		

VAT

	£		£
PLCA	87.50		

Bank

	£		£
		PLCA	587.50

Example 2

B sells £1,000 of goods to Y net of VAT on credit. He gives Y a deduction of 20% trade discount from the £1,000 net value. Y pays his account in full. Enter these amounts in the accounts of Y.

Solution

Step 1   Calculate the value of the sale net of discount and the VAT thereon.

	£
Sales value	1,000
Less: 20% discount	200
Net value	800
VAT at 17.5%	140
Total invoice value	940

Step 2   Enter the invoice in the PLCA, purchases and VAT accounts.

PLCA

	£		£
		Purchases and VAT	940

Purchases

	£		£
PLCA	800		

VAT

	£		£
PLCA	140		

Note 1 Note that the trade discount does not feature at all in the accounts. The invoice value is expressed after deduction of the trade discount and it is this invoiced amount that is entered in the accounts.

Step 3 Enter the cash paid by Y.

PLCA

	£		£
Bank	940	Purchases and VAT	940

Purchases

	£		£
PLCA	800		

VAT

	£		£
PLCA	140		

Bank

	£		£
		PLCA	940

Example 3

C sells £2,000 of goods net of VAT to Z on credit. He offers Z a 5% settlement discount if Z pays within 30 days. Z pays his account within 30 days and takes the settlement discount. Enter these transactions in the accounts of Z.

Solution

Step 1   Calculate the VAT on the purchase.

	£
Invoice value net of VAT	2,000.00
VAT = 17.5% × (2,000 – (5% × 2,000))	332.50
Invoice value	2,332.50

Step 2   Enter the invoice in the accounts of Z.

PLCA

£		£
	Purchases and VAT	2,332.50

Purchases

	£		£
PLCA	2,000.00		

VAT

	£		£
PLCA	332.50		

Step 3   Calculate the amount paid by Z.

	£
Invoice value net of VAT	2,000.00
Less: settlement discount = 5% × 2,000	(100.00)
VAT (as per the invoice)	332.50
Amount paid by Z	2,232.50

Step 4   Enter this amount in the accounts.

PLCA

	£		£
Bank	2,232.50	Purchases and VAT	2,332.50
Discount received	100.00		

Purchases

	£		£
PLCA	2,000.00		

VAT

	£		£
PLCA	332.50		

Bank

	£		£
		PLCA	2,232.50

Discount received

	£		£
		PLCA	100.00

Note   Because Z takes the settlement discount, he pays C £100 less than the invoice value. In order to clear the PLCA we have to debit that account with the £100 and credit a discount received account with £100. This £100 is income (reduction of an expense) of the business as the business is paying less than the face value of the invoice.

3 Test your knowledge

 Test your knowledge

Having completed Chapter 12, you should now be able to attempt Practice Activities 35 to 37.

4 Summary

The topics covered in this chapter will have been familiar to you as you have already studied the similar topics for sales.

Make sure you understand the point about VAT when there is a settlement discount offered. You must also understand the double entry for settlement discounts.

KAPLAN PUBLISHING

The purchases day book – main and subsidiary ledgers

Introduction

Just as we did for sales on credit we will now consider how purchases on credit are recorded in the books of prime entry and the ledger accounts.

KNOWLEDGE

1.1 Outline the purpose, content and format of the books of prime entry

3.3 Outline how the books of prime entry integrate with a double entry bookkeeping system

3.4 Explain how to process financial transactions from the books of prime entry into the double entry bookkeeping system

SKILLS

5.2 Enter supplier invoices and credit notes into the books of prime entry

1.1 Transfer data correctly from the daybooks to the ledgers

CONTENTS

1 Accounting for credit purchases

2 The analysed purchases day book

3 Purchases returns – cash suppliers

4 Purchases returns – credit suppliers

5 Purchases returns day book

1 Accounting for credit purchases

1.1 Introduction

When we studied accounting for sales in the earlier chapters of this book, we dealt with the three parts of the accounting records as they affected sales.

In the case of purchases, the parts are exactly the same except that instead of a 'sales day book' we have the 'purchases day book', and instead of the sales ledger we have the purchases ledger. The third part, namely the main ledger, is exactly the same and contains all the main ledger accounts with which you are familiar. Remember that, as for sales, the double entry goes through the main ledger, and the purchases ledger is just a memorandum ledger that holds the details of the individual creditor's accounts (it is sometimes called the subsidiary (purchases) ledger).

Below we will illustrate how these parts fit together with a diagram.

1.2 Fitting it all together

Consider these three credit purchases invoices

Supplier	Amount
X	£4,000
Y	£5,000
Z	£6,000

Step 1

Each invoice is recorded in the purchases day book by the purchaser.

Step 2

At the end of the period the purchases day book is totalled and the total is entered into the purchases ledger control account in the nominal ledger. The individual entries are recorded in the individual creditor accounts in the purchases ledger.

Now consider these cheques being paid to the creditors.

Customer	Amount
X	£2,000
Y	£3,000

Step 1

Each payment is recorded in the cash book.

Step 2

At the end of the period the cash book is totalled and the total is entered into the purchases ledger control account in the nominal ledger. The individual entries are recorded in the individual creditor accounts in the purchases ledger.

This is illustrated below.

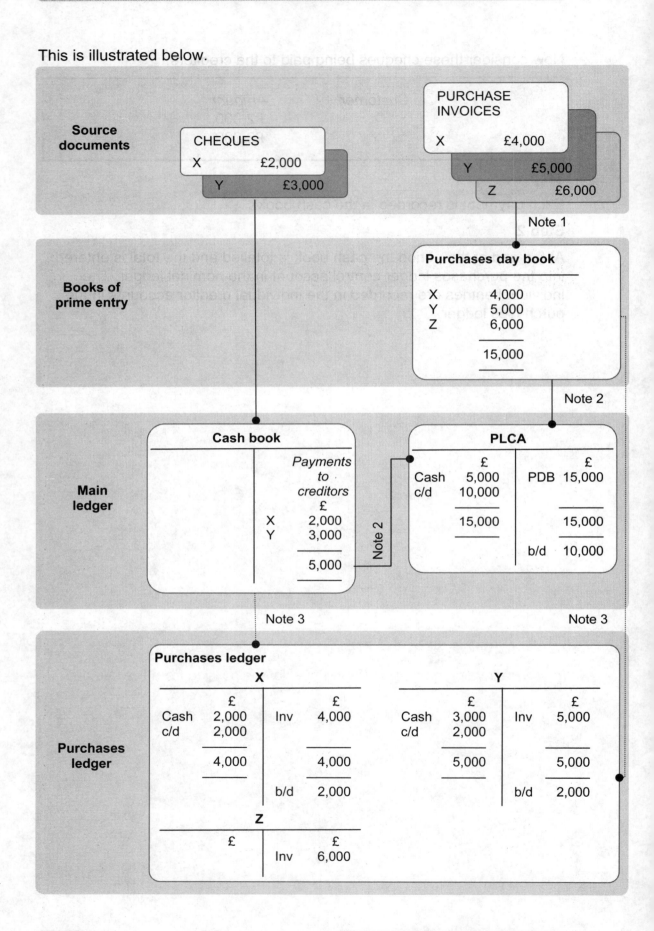

Notes

1   The invoices are entered into the PDB and the cheques are entered into the cash book.

2   The totals from the cash book and PDB are posted to the PLCA.

3   The individual invoices and cash received are posted to the purchases ledger.

2   The analysed purchases day book

2.1   Layout

The purchases day book is usually analysed with 'analysis columns' showing how the total value of each supplier's invoice is made up.

PURCHASES DAY BOOK								
Date	Supplier	Reference	Invoice number	Total £	VAT £	Product 1 £	Product 2 £	Product 3 £
			TOTALS					

(a)   The date and supplier columns are self explanatory.

(b)   The reference number is the number of the supplier's account in the purchases ledger.

(c)   The invoice number is the number of the invoice from the supplier.

(d)   The total column is the value of the goods purchased:

 •   after deducting any trade discount that may have been offered;

 •   including VAT;

 •   and including (i.e. not deducting) any settlement discount that may be offered to the purchaser (we shall not complicate things at this stage by considering this further).

Example

Customer B receives an invoice as follows from supplier X:

	£
50 units at £6 per unit	300
Less: 20% trade discount	60
	240
VAT @ 17.5% (£240 × 17.5%)	42
	282
Total invoice value	282

The £282 would be entered in the 'total' column.

(e) The VAT column – this column is the value of the VAT on the invoice – in this case £42.

(f) Product 1, 2, etc columns – these are columns that analyse the net purchases value (i.e. the total value after deducting VAT) into groupings that are of interest to the business.

In this introductory section we shall not complicate things by considering more than one type of product so that there will only be one column for purchases.

In this case the entry in the purchases column would be £240.

(g) The total boxes – at the end of a period (say a week or a month) the purchases day book is totalled and the total values of each column are written in the total boxes.

The purchases day book would therefore look as follows for the example above:

PURCHASES DAY BOOK

Date	Supplier	Reference	Invoice number	Total £	VAT £	Product 1 £	Product 2 £	Product 3 £
	X			282	42	240		
			TOTALS	282	42	240		

Note: In the pages that follow we shall concentrate on the basic entries in the purchases day book using only the supplier, total, VAT and one purchases column. This will enable us to concentrate on the simple double entry.

Example

Posting the purchases day book to the accounts in the ledgers

Consider the following purchase invoices received from suppliers by Roberts Metals.

Customer	Purchases value (ex VAT)	Trade discount	Net purchases value	VAT	Total
	£	£	£	£	£
X	500	10%	450	78.75	528.75
Y	1,750	20%	1,400	245.00	1,645.00
Z	5,000	30%	3,500	612.50	4,112.50

The following three steps are needed to enter this information in the ledger accounts.

Step 1 Write up the purchases day book, and total the columns.

Step 2 Post the totals to the accounts in the main ledger.

Step 3 Post the individual invoices to the purchases ledger.

Solution

Step 1

PURCHASES DAY BOOK

Date	Supplier	Reference	Invoice number	Total £	VAT £	Sales £
	X			528.75	78.75	450.00
	Y			1,645.00	245.00	1,400.00
	Z			4,112.50	612.50	3,500.00
			TOTALS	6,286.25	936.25	5,350.00

Step 2

Main ledger

Purchases				VAT			
	£		£		£		£
PDB	5,350.00			PDB	936.25		

PLCA

£		£	
	PDB	6,286.25	

Step 3

Purchases ledger

X

£		£	
	PDB	528.75	

Y

£		£	
	PDB	1,645.00	

Z

£		£	
	PDB	4,112.50	

Note to solution

(a)   The totals of the PDB are entered in the main ledger.

(b)   The individual invoices (total value including VAT) are entered in the individual creditor accounts in the purchases ledger. This is the amount that will be paid to the creditor.

(c)   Note that there are no entries for trade discounts either in the PDB or in the ledger accounts.

📝 Activity 1

Date	Invoice no	Supplier	Code	Total	VAT	Dept 1	Dept 2	Dept 3
				£	£	£	£	£
		Total		88,125	13,125	20,000	15,000	40,000

How would the totals be posted to the main ledger accounts?

3 Purchases returns – cash suppliers

3.1 Introduction

When a business buys and then returns goods to a supplier, the accounting system has to record the fact that goods have been returned. If the goods were returned following a cash purchase then cash would be repaid by the supplier to the customer who had bought the goods. If goods were returned following a credit purchase then the PLCA in the main ledger will need to be debited and the individual supplier's account in the purchases ledger will need to be debited with the value of the goods returned (we shall see the other entries required below).

 Example

Returns following a cash purchase

Y buys £1,000 of goods from B for cash plus £175 VAT.

B subsequently agrees that Y can return £500 worth of goods (excluding VAT).

Record these transactions in the ledger accounts of Y.

Solution

Step 1

First of all we need to set up a new account called the 'purchases returns account' in the main ledger.

Step 2

Enter the cash purchases in the accounts of Y.

Credit cash book for cash paid	£1,175.00
Debit purchases with expense	£1,000.00
Debit VAT account with VAT	£175.00

Cash book

£		£
	Purchases and VAT	1,175.00

Purchases

	£		£
Cash book	1,000.00		

Purchases returns

	£		£

VAT

	£		£
Cash book	175.00		

Step 3

B will repay Y £500 plus VAT of £87.50. We therefore need to enter the purchases returns, the cash and the VAT in the accounts.

Cash book

	£		£
Purchases return + VAT	587.50	Purchases and VAT	1,175.00

Purchases

	£		£
Cash book	1,000.00		

Purchases returns

	£		£
		Cash book	500.00

VAT

	£		£
Cash book	175.00	Cash book	87.50

4 Purchases returns – credit suppliers

4.1 Introduction

When a credit customer returns goods, he does not receive cash for the return; the seller will issue a credit note to record the fact that goods have been returned. This credit note is sent to the customer and is entered in the customer's books.

4.2 Purchases returns with VAT

When a return is made we include VAT; the VAT was accounted for on the invoice when the purchase was made, and now has to be accounted for on the credit note when the goods are returned. This VAT has to be entered in the books.

Example

D buys goods from Z for £800 + VAT (= £940).

D returns goods worth £200 + VAT.

Enter these transactions in the main ledger of D's books.

Solution

Step 1

Enter the invoice in the usual way, including the VAT.

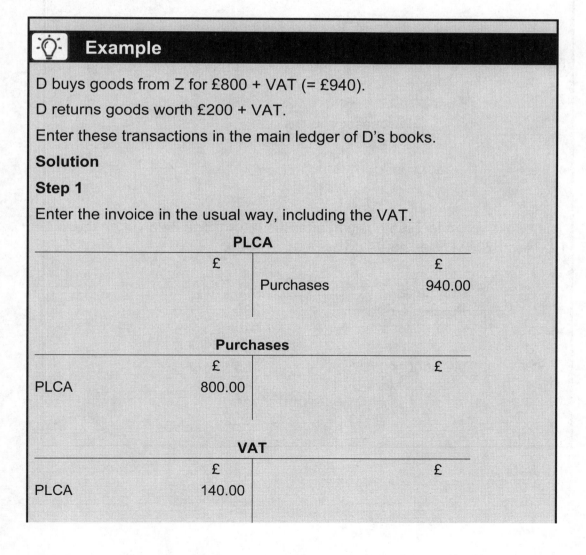

PLCA			
	£		£
		Purchases	940.00

Purchases			
	£		£
PLCA	800.00		

VAT			
	£		£
PLCA	140.00		

Step 2

Enter the credit note. The VAT on the return will be £200 × 17.5% = £35. This gives a total credit note of £235.

PLCA

	£		£
Purchases returns + VAT	235.00	Purchases	940.00

Purchases

	£		£
PLCA	800.00		

VAT

	£		£
PLCA	140.00	PLCA	35.00

Purchases returns

	£		£
		PLCA	200.00

The books will reflect the position after the return. The balance on the PLCA is £705. This is made up as:

	£
Purchase	800
Purchase return	200
	600
VAT 600 × 17.5%	105
	705

5 The purchases returns day book

5.1 Introduction

Purchases returns are in practice entered in a 'purchases returns day book'. This is similar to the purchases day book, and the columns are used in the same way. The only difference is that instead of having a column for the invoice number, there is a column for the 'credit note number'. This is because when the goods are sent back the business will receive a credit note from the supplier.

PURCHASES RETURNS DAY BOOK						
Date	Supplier	Reference	Credit note number	Total £	VAT £	Purchases returns £

Example

John bought goods for £750 + VAT from X and £1,000 + VAT from Y.

John returns goods which cost £200 excluding VAT to X, and goods which cost £400 excluding VAT to Y.

Enter the above purchases and returns in the main and purchases ledger of John, using a purchases returns day book.

Solution

Step 1

Enter the original purchases invoices in the main ledger.

PLCA

	£			£
		PDB		2,056.25

Purchases

	£		£
PDB	1,750.00		

VAT

	£		£
PDB	306.25		

Step 2

Write up the purchases returns day book.

PURCHASES RETURNS DAY BOOK						
Date	Supplier	Reference	Credit note number	Total £	VAT £	Purchases returns £
	X			235.00	35.00	200.00
	Y			470.00	70.00	400.00
				705.00	105.00	600.00

Step 3

Enter the PRDB totals in the main ledger accounts.

PLCA

	£		£
PRDB	705.00	PDB	2,056.25

Purchases

	£		£
PDB	1,750.00		

VAT

	£		£
PDB	306.25	PRDB	105.00

Purchases returns

	£		£
		PRDB	600.00

Step 4

Enter the individual amounts in the purchases ledger. The amounts will be debited to the individual creditor accounts as the return is reducing the amount that is owed to the creditor.

	X		
	£		£
PRDB	235.00	PDB (£750 + VAT)	881.25

	Y		
	£		£
PRDB	470.00	PDB (£1,000 + VAT)	1,175.00

5.2 Purchases returns in purchases day book

In some businesses the level of purchases returns are fairly low and therefore it is not justified to keep a separate purchases returns day book. In these cases any credit notes that are received for purchases returns are recorded as negative amounts in the purchases day book. If this is the case then you will be told that this is the policy of the business. Care should be taken, however, when adding up the columns in the purchases day book as any credit notes must be deducted rather than added in.

Activity 2

Given below are the totals of an analysed purchases returns day book for a week.

Date	Supplier	Credit note no	Code	Total	VAT	Dept 1	Dept 2	Dept 3
				£	£	£	£	£
23/04/X0				9,400	1,400	1,000	2,000	5,000

Post these totals to the main ledger accounts.

6 Test your knowledge

Test your knowledge

Having completed Chapter 13, you should now attempt Practice Activities 38 to 42.

7 Summary

The purchases day book and the purchases returns day book are simple devices for grouping together purchases invoices for goods purchased and credit notes for goods returned. The topics you need to practise are:

(a) posting the total of these day books to the main ledger accounts; and

(b) posting the individual invoices and credit notes to the creditors accounts in the purchases ledger.

It is also useful if you understand how the accounts fit together as shown in the diagram in Section 1.2 of this chapter.

Answers to chapter activities

✍ Activity 1

The required double entry is as follows:

Debit	VAT	£13,125
	Department 1 purchases	£20,000
	Department 2 purchases	£15,000
	Department 2 purchases	£40,000
Credit	Purchases ledger control account	£88,125

Note carefully that it is the net amount that is debited to each purchases account and the gross amount (including VAT) that is credited to the purchases ledger control account. The VAT total is debited to the VAT account.

The ledger entries would appear as follows:

Purchases ledger control account

	£		£
		PDB	88,125

VAT

	£		£
PDB	13,125		

Department 1 purchases

	£		£
PDB	20,000		

Department 2 purchases

	£		£
PDB	15,000		

Department 3 purchases

	£		£
PDB	40,000		

Activity 2

Purchases returns – Department 1 account

	£		£
		PRDB	1,000

Purchases returns – Department 2 account

	£		£
		PRDB	2,000

Purchases returns – Department 3 account

	£		£
		PRDB	5,000

VAT account

	£		£
		PRDB	1,400

Purchases ledger control account

	£		£
PRDB	9,400		

Note carefully that it is the net amount that is credited to each returns account and the gross amount to the purchases ledger control account. The difference, the VAT, is credited to the VAT account.

Making payments

Introduction

Once the invoice for purchases has been received then payment must be made for the goods or services. In this chapter we will consider the different methods of payment, the most appropriate methods of payment, the timing of payments and how the payment procedure works.

KNOWLEDGE

1.2 Outline the purpose and content of a range of business documents to include:

Remittance advice

1.3 Identify when authorisation is required

SKILLS

6.1 Reconcile supplier statements

6.2 Calculate the payments due to suppliers from relevant documentation

6.3 Prepare remittance advices to accompany payments to suppliers

CONTENTS

1 Payments by cheque

2 Transferring money by different methods

3 Payments to credit suppliers

4 Payment by invoice

5 Payment of suppliers' statements

6 Payment on a set date

7 Authorisation of invoices

8 Cheque requisitions

9 Capital and revenue expenditure

1 Payments by cheque

1.1 Introduction

Most of the payments that a business will make will be by cheque. This may be by writing a cheque for cash purchases or sending a cheque to a credit supplier. The detailed legal requirements relating to cheques were covered in an earlier chapter and therefore we will only cover these requirements briefly.

1.2 Writing a cheque

When a cheque is written out by a business it is important that it is correctly drawn up. The main factors to consider are:

- The cheque must be dated with the date on which it is written – a cheque is only valid for six months after the date on the cheque and most suppliers would not accept a post-dated cheque so care should be taken when writing the date onto the cheque.

- The payee's name must be correct – the supplier's name will be on the purchase invoice and this should be correctly reproduced on the cheque otherwise the supplier will not be able to pay the cheque into his bank account.

- The amount of the cheque in words and figures must agree with each other – if there is a difference then the cheque cannot be paid into the supplier's account and will be returned by the bank to your business.

- The cheque must be signed by the appropriate cheque signatory within the business – in many businesses it will be the organisation's policy that cheques, particularly if they exceed a certain limit, must be signed by more than one cheque signatory.

- If any alterations are made to the cheque then these must be initialled by the cheque signatory.

1.3 Stopped cheques

If a cheque is written by your business and sent out to a supplier it can be stopped at any point in time right up until the bank pays it. In order to stop a cheque your business must write to the bank and give clear details of the payee's name, the cheque's number and the amount payable.

Activity 1

You are writing out a cheque for £374 as payment for goods. As you write out the cheque you do not notice that you have dated it 1 June 20X1. Today's date is 1 June 20X2.

Will payment of the cheque by the drawer's bank be affected by the incorrect date? Yes/No

Having noticed the error, is it acceptable for you to alter the cheque to the correct date? Yes/No

2 Transferring money by different methods

2.1 Introduction

A bank customer can transfer money from his account to another person's account by a number of other methods which do not involve writing cheques.

These methods have been previously covered.

2.2 The appropriate method of payment

There are a number of methods available to businesses of making payments – by cheque, standing order, direct debit, bank giro credit, BACS, CHAPS. The organisation will normally have policies regarding which method of payment is to be used for different types of payment.

Most credit suppliers are likely to require payment by cheque or by direct bank giro credit.

Many organisations such as gas, telephone and electricity providers will encourage customers to pay by direct debit. This means that once the direct debit has been set up then this will automatically be taken from your bank account on the agreed day with no action necessary for your business.

Any fixed periodic payments however might be more appropriately made by standing order, which is for a fixed amount on a fixed periodic date.

Often the wages and salaries payments of a business will be one of the largest and most regular of payments that must be made. The most common method of making the regular wages and salaries payments to employees is using the BACS system.

3 Payments to credit suppliers

3.1 Authorised documentation

A business must make a payment only if there is authorised documentation to show that the payment is genuine. Authorised documentation might include:

- an invoice which has been signed or stamped by a responsible official;
- a cheque requisition form;
- a memo from a responsible official.

Cheques are normally prepared by the cashier. The cashier should ensure that the amount of the cheque agrees to the authorised documentation.

3.2 Methods of scheduling payments

Different businesses will have different policies for determining the timing of payments to credit suppliers. Some of the most common methods are:

- to pay each invoice that arrives at the latest possible date according to the credit terms;
- to pay a number of invoices at the same time when the supplier's statement is received;
- to make payments on a set day, such as every Friday, and to pay all of those invoices that will have exceeded their credit terms by the following Friday.

4 Payment by invoice

4.1 Introduction

When each invoice is received it is looked at and the latest date on which it can be paid according to the credit terms of the supplier will be determined. The invoice will then be scheduled for payment on this date.

4.2 Invoices and cash discounts

When the cashier is dealing with writing a cheque for payment of an invoice, then the invoice should already be marked as authorised by the appropriate person in the organisation, having checked it against appropriate documentation such as the purchase order and delivery note. The only remaining task is to deal with any cash or settlement discounts.

Firstly it must be checked that it is company policy to take cash discounts. If this is the case then it must be determined whether there is time to make the payment on time and claim the discount. Finally the amount of the cash discount and the net amount that is to be paid should be calculated.

Example

An invoice shows the following details:

Date: 3 June 20X6

	£
List price of goods	4,000.00
Trade discount 5%	200.00
	3,800.00
VAT	638.40
Invoice total	4,438.40

A settlement discount of 4% is offered for payment received within 10 days of the invoice date.

Suppose that today's date is 7 June.

Solution

Today is 7 June and in order to claim the settlement discount the payment must arrive with the supplier by 13 June. Provided that the payment is made in the next few days and posted to the supplier immediately then the settlement discount can be claimed.

The amount of the discount should then be calculated and deducted from the invoice total. This final amount is the amount for which the cheque should be drawn.

	£
Net of VAT amount	3,800.00
Settlement discount (3,800 × 4%)	(152.00)
	3,648.00
Add:VAT	638.40
Cheque amount	4,286.40

You should always check that the VAT has been correctly calculated on the basis of the assumption that the settlement discount will in fact be taken.

The settlement discount is calculated as the stated percentage of the net invoice amount. The VAT per the invoice is then added to find the final total payment.

 Activity 2

A company has recently purchased supplies from International Toiletries Ltd for £250, less 20% trade discount, plus 17.5% VAT. International allow 2.5% cash discount for payment within seven days of the receipt of their invoice.

(a)   State which of the following total amounts is due for payment by the company if they take advantage of the cash discount.

   A   £237.66

   B   £227.65

   C   £229.12

(b)   What would be the VAT inclusive total shown on the original invoice?

 Activity 3

You have received the following invoices from suppliers who offer settlement discounts. You must calculate the discount offered and decide whether or not you can take the discount if you send a cheque today. Today is 21 June 20X9.

	Supplier	Invoice date	Net invoice amount	Discount terms	
(a)	ABC Fencing	20 May 20X9	£239.50	2.5%	30 days
(b)	Brown & Black	15 June 20X9	£458.63	1.5%	28 days
(c)	Peter's Wood Products	10 June 20X9	£168.00	2.0%	14 days
(d)	S J Lever	15 May 20X9	£391.48	2.0%	30 days
(e)	A J Bennett	1 June 20X9	£56.91	2.5%	14 days

5 Payment of suppliers' statements

5.1 Introduction

A supplier's statement can also be used to request a cheque to be drawn. It will have the same form as the customer's statement that we considered in an earlier chapter. The supplier's statement could be used when the intention is to pay a number of invoices to this supplier with just one cheque.

5.2 Checking suppliers' statements

Before any payments are made it is important to check that the supplier's statement is correct. Each invoice and credit note should be checked either to the original documentation or to the supplier's account in the purchases ledger.

When the accuracy of the statement has been ascertained then it must be determined exactly which invoices from the statement are to be paid.

Example

Given below is a statement from a supplier together with that supplier's account from the purchases ledger.

To:	Scott Brothers	Nemo Limited
	34 Festival Way	Date: 31 August 20X3
	Oldham	
	OL2 3BD	

STATEMENT

Date	Transaction	Total £	Current £	30+ £	60+ £
12 May 20X3	Invoice 2569	92.35			92.35
13 June 20X3	CN 2659	(23.60)			(23.60)
09 July 20X3	Invoice 2701	102.69		102.69	
18 July 20X3	Invoice 2753	133.81		133.81	
02 Aug 20X3	Invoice 2889	56.50	56.50		
10 Aug 20X3	Invoice 2901	230.20	230.20		
28 Aug 20X3	Invoice 3114	243.24	243.24		
	TOTALS	835.19	529.94	236.50	68.75

May we remind you our credit terms are 30 days

Nemo Ltd

		£			£
13 June	CN 2659	23.60	12 May Invoice 2569		92.35
			09 July Invoice 2701		102.69
			18 July Invoice 2753		133.81
			02 Aug Invoice 2889		56.50
			10 Aug Invoice 2901		203.20
			28 Aug Invoice 3114		243.24

To check that the supplier's statement is correct prior to paying any amounts, the statement should be carefully checked to the supplier's account in the purchases ledger.

Solution

The invoice dated 10 August is in the purchases ledger at a total of £203.20 whereas it appears on the supplier's statement as £230.20.

The purchase invoice itself should be accessed from the filing system to determine whether the amount is £203.20 or £230.20. If the supplier's statement is incorrect then a polite telephone call should be made or letter sent to the supplier, Nemo Ltd, explaining the problem.

5.3 Which invoices to pay

Once the supplier's statement has been checked for accuracy then it has to be decided which invoices shall be paid. Most organisations will have a policy regarding the payment of supplier's invoices or, alternatively, a fairly senior figure in the business will decide each month which invoices are to be paid.

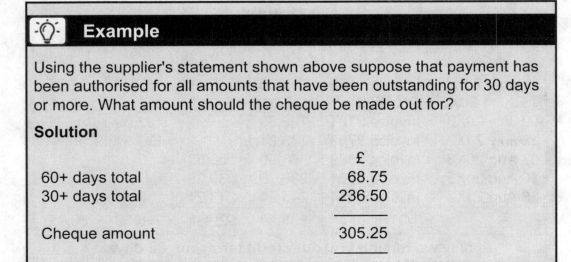

Example

Using the supplier's statement shown above suppose that payment has been authorised for all amounts that have been outstanding for 30 days or more. What amount should the cheque be made out for?

Solution

	£
60+ days total	68.75
30+ days total	236.50
	———
Cheque amount	305.25
	———

5.4   Remittance advices

Some suppliers will attach a remittance advice to the bottom of their statement so that the customer can indicate which invoices less credit notes are being paid with this cheque.

 Example

Given below is a supplier's statement from Bart & Partners. Attached to it is the remittance advice. The policy of the business is to pay all of the January and February invoices less credit notes.

Complete the remittance advice on the basis that the payment was made by cheque number 047732 on 4 April 20X2.

 Example (continued)

Bart & Partners
Spring House
Park Estate
Oldham OL2 3CF

To: Fells Brothers
Simpfield House
Oldham
OL1 3XJ

Date: 31 August 20X3

STATEMENT

Date	Transaction	Total £	Current £	30+ £	60+ £
15 Jan 20X2	INV 12611	308.50			308.50
01 Feb 20X2	CN 04779	(112.60)		(112.60)	
20 Feb 20X2	INV 12683	419.80		419.80	
02 Mar 20X2	INV 12710	384.20	384.20		
14 Mar 20X2	INV 12748	116.88	116.88		
		1,116.78	501.08	307.20	308.50
May we remind you our credit terms are 30 days					

REMITTANCE ADVICE

To:

Company name:

Address:

Date:

Date	Our ref	Amount £	Discount taken £	Paid £
15 Jan 20X2	INV 12611	308.50		
01 Feb 20X2	CN 04779	(112.60)		
20 Feb 20X2	INV 12683	419.80		
02 Mar 20X2	INV 12710	384.20		
14 Mar 20X2	INV 12748	116.88		

Total paid
Cheque no

Solution

REMITTANCE ADVICE

To: Bart & Partners
Spring House
Park Estate
Oldham
OL2 3CF

Company name: Fells Brothers

Address: Simpfield House
Oldham OL1 3XJ

Date: 4 April 20X2

Date	Our ref	Amount £	Discount taken £	Paid £
15 Jan 20X2	INV 12611	308.50		308.50
01 Feb 20X2	CN 04779	(112.60)		(112.60)
20 Feb 20X2	INV 12683	419.80		419.80
02 Mar 20X2	INV 12710	384.20		
14 Mar 20X2	INV 12748	116.88		

Total paid £615.70

Cheque no 047732

6 Payment on a set date

6.1 Introduction

The problem with paying each invoice on the last possible date that it can be paid is that this means that someone in the organisation is tied up with invoice payments every day. However, the other alternative of paying when the supplier's statement is received means that in many cases the opportunity to take advantage of any settlement discount offered is lost.

6.2 Alternative method

Therefore an alternative method is to set a day each week/fortnight for payment of invoices. On that day all invoices that would have exceeded their credit limit or lost the chance of the settlement discount by the next payment date would be paid.

 Example

Your business has the policy of paying invoices each Friday and on that day to pay all invoices that would either exceed their settlement discount period or that would be exceeding their credit period by the following Friday.

Today is Friday 7 May. The following invoices are in the pile of unpaid invoices. Indicate which invoices would be paid today and why.

Supplier	Date	Amount £	Settlement terms
K Fielden	30 Apr	376.90	2% discount for payment within 14 days
Giles Associates	12 Apr	269.46	Net 30 days
Penfold Ltd	05 May	316.58	3% discount for payment within 14 days
Yalders Partners	06 May	146.37	4% discount for payment within 10 days

Solution

K Fielden	30 Apr	376.90	2% discount for payment within 14 days

– in order to take the discount the payment must be received by the supplier by 14 May. As next Friday will be 14 May it is too late to make the payment then so, if the discount is to be taken, payment must be made today.

Giles Associates   12 Apr   269.46   Net 30 days

– as April has 30 days the payment must be received by 12 May. Therefore payment must be made today in order to remain within the stated credit terms.

Penfold Ltd   5 May   316.58   3% discount for payment within 14 days

– in order to take the discount the payment must be received by the supplier by 19 May. Next Friday will be 14 May which should give enough time for the cheque to be drawn and sent to the supplier to arrive by 19 May.

Yalders Partners   6 May   146.37   4% discount for payment within 10 days

– in order to take the discount the payment must be received by the supplier by 16 May. As next Friday is the 14 May, making 16 May the Sunday, it would seem unlikely that if payment were put off until next week, it would reach the supplier in time. Therefore if the discount is to be taken it should be paid today.

7 Authorisation of invoices

7.1 Introduction

In an earlier chapter we saw how all purchase invoices should be thoroughly checked to ensure that they are for goods or services that have been received by the business, that the goods and services have been charged at the correct rate and that all discounts and calculations are correct.

7.2 Authorisation stamp

At this point in the checking process the invoice was stamped with an authorisation stamp or grid stamp which showed that the invoice had been checked and also coded the invoice for the information required for entering it into the accounting records. A typical authorisation stamp at this stage in the process is shown following.

Purchase order no	436129
Invoice no	388649
Cheque no	
Account code	PL70
Checked	J Wilmber
Date	03/05/X4
ML account	006

7.3 Authorisation for payment

As we have seen, different organisations will have different methods of determining precisely when invoices will be paid. The only invoices that will be paid are ones that have already been checked and the authorisation stamp completed. The next stage, however, is for today's list of invoices to be paid to be authorised by the appropriate person within the organisation.

In a small organisation the appropriate person may be the cashier who will write out the cheques. Provided the cashier knows that the invoice has been checked and coded then he/she will determine which invoices need paying and will write out the cheque. At this stage the cheque number is the final entry on the authorisation stamp to show that the cheque has been paid and to ensure that it is not paid a second time in error.

In a larger organisation it may be that a more senior member of the management team must review the invoices due for payment before they are paid. In this case there may be an additional entry on the authorisation stamp for the signature of the manager or he may just initial the stamp itself to indicate to the cashier that payment is to be made.

8 Cheque requisitions

8.1 Introduction

In some instances a payment will need to be made but there is no invoice or bill as yet. Such payments can be made but must be requested by a completed and authorised cheque requisition form.

8.2 Cheque requisition

 Definition

A cheque requisition is a request for a cheque for payment to a third party where there is no invoice or bill to support this payment.

The cheque requisition is a request for a cheque for a certain amount for a payment that does not work its way naturally through the purchase invoice system.

Once a cheque requisition has been completed it must be authorised by an appropriate senior person within the organisation and then the cheque can be issued.

 Example

The managing director's company car is in the garage for a service. At 4 o'clock the garage telephones to say that the car is ready to be collected and the cost of the service has been £342.60. It is necessary to give the garage a cheque for this amount upon collection of the car.

A cheque requisition form must be completed.

Solution

CHEQUE REQUISITION FORM

CHEQUE DETAILS

Date .... 3 June 20X6 ....

Payee .... Ricky's Garage ....

Amount £ .... 342.60 ....

Reason .... Service of MD's car .... Account code ...... ML03 ....

Invoice no. (attached/to follow) ....

Receipt (attached/to follow) ....

Required by (Print)......M..PLUMMER... ....

       Signature ..M..Plummer..................................

Authorised by:..........J Swain

9 Capital and revenue expenditure

9.1 Introduction

Most payments that are made by a business are for day-to-day expenses. These may be for:

- goods for resale;
- materials to be used in production;
- general expenses.

9.2 Revenue expenditure

These types of everyday expenses for the general running of the business are known as revenue expenditure. The other type of expenditure that a business might incur is capital expenditure.

9.3 Capital expenditure

Capital expenditure is payments for fixed assets. Fixed assets are long term assets for use in the business rather than for items that are either to be sold or to be used in the short term within the business. Typical items of capital expenditure are land and buildings, plant and machinery, office equipment, salesmen's cars, delivery vehicles or fixtures and fittings.

9.4 Payments for capital expenditure

In most cases the appropriate method of payment for a fixed asset will be by payment of a cheque. The procedure is exactly the same as for payments to credit suppliers for goods. The payment must be authorised and the cheque must be correctly prepared.

10 Test your knowledge

Test your knowledge

Having completed Chapter 14, you should be able to attempt Practice Activity 43.

11 Summary

In this chapter we considered the authorisation of the actual payments to be made to suppliers for goods, services and expenses. Remember that the invoices have already been checked for their accuracy and therefore the key to authorisation of payments is which invoices are to be paid. This will often depend upon the method of payment of invoices that it is the policy of the organisation to use. In some businesses all invoices are checked upon arrival to determine the latest date on which they can be paid in order to either validly claim a settlement discount or stay within the supplier's stated credit terms.

An alternative is to wait until the statement is received from the supplier at the end of the month. Once the statement has been checked to ensure that it is correct, it will be determined which invoices minus credit notes are to be paid. The statement may be accompanied by a remittance advice which should be completed in order to show which invoices less credit notes are being paid.

The problem with waiting until the supplier's statement is received is that many settlement discounts that are offered are lost due to the payment only being made every month. Therefore an alternative is for the business to set a day each week or possibly every two weeks on which invoices are paid in order either to take advantage of the settlement discount or to ensure that the payment does not exceed the stated credit terms.

Prior to the payment of the invoice it must be authorised. In many small organisations the process of checking the invoice to ensure that the goods or services have been received and the checking of all of the details of the invoice for accuracy is all that is required for authorisation. In other organisations more senior managers might be required to authorise the invoices due to be paid.

In some instances a cheque will be required although there is no invoice or bill to support it. In this case a cheque requisition form must be completed and authorised by an appropriate senior person within the organisation before the cheque is issued.

Payments may not only be made for revenue expenditure items but also for capital expenditure on fixed assets.

Answers to chapter activities

Activity 1

(a)   Yes (since the cheque is more than six months old).

(b)   Yes, provided that you initial the date change.

Activity 2

(a)   Option C

   (£250 × 80% × 97.5% × 1.175) = £229.12

(b)   £

   Supplies (£250 less 20% discount)   200.00
   VAT (£200 × 17.5% × 0.975)   34.12
                                                   ─────────
   Total   234.12
                                                   ─────────

Activity 3

	Discount	Can take discount?
(a)	£5.99	No
(b)	£6.88	Yes
(c)	£3.36	Yes
(d)	£7.83	No
(e)	£1.42	No

The analysed cash payments book

Introduction

In this chapter we will consider how cash payments for cash purchases and to credit suppliers are recorded in the cash payments book and in the ledger accounts.

KNOWLEDGE

1.1 Outline the purpose, content and format of the books of prime entry

1.4 Explain how transactions are entered in the following books of prime entry: cash book

3.3 Outline how the books of prime entry integrate with a double entry bookkeeping system

3.4 Explain how to process financial transactions from the books of prime entry into the double entry bookkeeping system

SKILLS

1.2 Transfer data correctly from the cashbook to the ledgers

CONTENTS

1 The analysed cash payments book

2 Settlement discount received from suppliers

1 The analysed cash payments book

1.1 Layout

A proforma analysed cash payments book is shown below

CASH PAYMENTS BOOK

Date	Narrative	Reference	Total £	VAT £	PLCA £	Cash purchases £	Admin £	Rent and rates £	Discount received £
		TOTALS							

Notes

(a) The date column contains the date of the transaction.

(b) The narrative column describes the transactions.

(c) The total column contains the total cash paid (including any VAT).

(d) The VAT column contains the VAT on the transaction but not if the VAT has already been entered in the purchases day book. This is a tricky point but is in principle exactly the same as the treatment of VAT that we studied for the cash receipts book.

(e) The PLCA column contains any cash paid that has been paid to a supplier. The total paid including VAT is entered in this column.

(f) The cash purchases column contains cash paid for purchases that are not bought on credit.

(g) We saw with the analysed cash receipts book that nearly all receipts come from debtors or cash sales. In the case of payments, there is a great variety of suppliers who are paid through the cash book; rent and rates, telephone, electricity, marketing, etc. The business will have a separate column for the categories of expense that it wishes to analyse.

(h) The discount received column is a memorandum column that contains details of any cash/settlement discounts received. These discounts will need to be entered into the ledger accounts as we shall see.

1.2 Main ledger payments not entered in the PDB

The PDB is often used only for invoices from suppliers of purchases, i.e. goods for resale. Invoices for rent, electricity, telephone, etc will typically not be entered in the PDB. They will be paid by cheque, and the double entry will be made directly between the cash payments book and the relevant expense account in the main ledger.

One reason for this is that the purchases day book (like the sales day book) is used because the business will typically have a large number of similar transactions (e.g. purchases of goods for resale). To simplify the accounting these are all listed in the PDB and posted in total to the main ledger. Payment of rent or telephone only happens once every three months so there is no need to group these together; they are easily dealt with on an individual basis.

 Example

Parma Products buys goods for resale from two suppliers on credit. The business buys £1,000 + VAT of goods from X and £3,000 + VAT of goods from Y. Parma receives an invoice and pays £500 + VAT rent to their landlord. Parma also pays X's invoice in full. Enter these transactions in the accounts of Parma Products. The rent invoice is not entered in the PDB.

Solution

Step 1 Enter the invoices for goods in the PDB

SALES DAY BOOK						
Date	Supplier	Reference	Invoice number	Total £	VAT £	Purchases £
	X			1,175	175	1,000
	Y			3,525	525	3,000
			TOTALS	4,700	700	4,000

Step 2 Enter the totals of the PDB in the main ledger.

Purchases

	£		£
PDB	4,000.00		

VAT

	£		£
PDB	700.00		

PLCA

	£		£
		PDB	4,700.00

Step 3 Enter the cash paid in the analysed cash payments book.

CASH PAYMENTS BOOK

Date	Narrative	Reference	Total	VAT	PLCA	Rent	Discount received
			£	£	£	£	£
	X		1,175.00		1,175.00		
	Rent		587.50	87.50		500.00	
	TOTALS		1,762.50	87.50	1,175.00	500.00	

Note that the VAT on the payment to the supplier has already been accounted for in the main ledger via the entries in the PDB. However, the rent invoice was not entered in the PDB and so the VAT has to be entered in the VAT column of the cash book from where it will be posted to the VAT account (see Step 4).

Step 4 Post the cash paid totals from the cash book to the main ledger.

Purchases

	£		£
PDB	4,000.00		

VAT

	£		£
PDB	700.00		
CPB	87.50		

PLCA

	£		£
CPB	1,175.00	PDB	4,700.00

Rent

	£		£
CPB	500.00		

Note 1: All the VAT paid is now debited to the VAT account. You must make sure that you understand how some is posted via the PDB and some via the cash book.

Note 2: All of the entries made from the cash payments book are debit entries. The credit entry is the total of the cash payments (£1,762.50) since the cash payments book is part of the double entry.

Step 5 Enter the amounts in the purchases ledger.

X

	£		£
CPB	1,175.00	PDB	1,175.00

Y

	£		£
		PDB	3,525.00

The entries to the purchases ledger from the cash payments book are debit entries in the individual creditor accounts as the payment means that less is owed to the creditor.

2 Settlement discounts received from suppliers

2.1 Introduction

Settlement discounts are a tricky complication when dealing with the analysed purchases day book and cash book.

 Example

Consider a business run by Francis which buys goods costing £2,000 + VAT from Z. Z offers a 5% settlement discount if Francis pays within 30 days. Francis pays within 30 days.

Enter these new transactions in the books of Francis.

Solution

Step 1 Calculate the value of the invoice.

	£
Cost of goods	2,000.00
VAT (2,000 – (5% × 2,000)) × 17.5%	332.50
Total invoice value	2,332.50

Step 2 Enter the invoice from Z in the purchases day book.

PURCHASES DAY BOOK						
Date	Supplier	Reference	Invoice number	Total £	VAT £	Purchases £
	Z			2,332.50	332.50	2,000.00
			TOTALS	2,332.50	332.50	2,000.00

Step 3 Enter the totals of the purchases day book in the main ledger.

Purchases			
	£		£
PDB	2,000.00		

VAT

	£		£
PDB	332.50		

PLCA

	£		£
		PDB	2,332.50

Step 4   Calculate the cash paid by Francis.

	£
Cost of goods	2,000.00
5% settlement discount	(100.00)
	1,900.00
VAT (2,000 − (5% × 2,000)) × 17.5%	332.50
Total cash paid	2,232.50

Step 5   Enter the cash paid in the analysed cash payments book.

CASH PAYMENTS BOOK

Date	Narrative	Reference	Total	VAT	PLCA	Rent	Discount received
			£	£	£	£	£
	Z		2,232.50		2,232.50		100.00
		TOTALS	2,232.50		2,232.50		100.00

Note: Remember that the discount received column is a 'memorandum' account. The cash book only cross-casts if you ignore the discount received column.

Step 6   Post the cash payments book totals to the main ledger.

Purchases

	£		£
PDB	2,000.00		

VAT		
	£	£
PDB	332.50	

PLCA			
	£		£
CPB	2,232.50	PDB	2,332.50
Discount received	100.00		

Discount received			
	£		£
		PLCA	100.00

📝 Activity 1

FFP makes the following payments in respect of various credit invoices and other items:

- Payment of £4,230 on 23/7/X4 to N Hudson for credit purchases. A settlement discount of £130 was taken. This was paid by cheque (cheque number 1003). The purchases ledger reference code is P4153.

- On 24/7/X4, £2,350 to G Farr in respect of credit purchases by cheque (cheque number 1004). The purchases ledger reference code is P4778.

- On 28/7/X4, purchase of stock, not on credit, of £940 including VAT of £140 (cheque number 1005).

- On 30/7/X4, payment of a salary by cheque of £2,500, using cheque number 1006. (There is no VAT on wages and salaries.)

Task 1   Enter these transactions in the cash payments book and total the columns.

Task 2   Post the totals to the main ledger.

Task 3   Post the payments to N Hudson and G Farr to the purchases ledger. The opening balances are N Hudson £10,327.00 and G Farr £8,263.00.

     KAPLAN PUBLISHING

3 Test your knowledge

Test your knowledge

Having completed Chapter 15, you should now be able to attempt Practice Activities 44 and 45.

4 Summary

The two main areas covered in this chapter which cause problems are: (a) the treatment of VAT in the cash payments book; and (b) the treatment of discount received.

Regarding VAT, remember that if an invoice has been entered in the purchases day book, the VAT will have been captured in the PDB and posted to the VAT account from there. If, however, an invoice is not entered in the purchases day book, the VAT has to be entered in the VAT column of the cash book and posted to the VAT account from there.

Regarding discounts, remember that the discount column in the cash book is simply a memorandum column. The double entry for discount received is entered in the main ledger as: debit PLCA; credit discount received. Remember also that in the subsidiary purchases ledger, the discount received is entered in the suppliers account but there is no corresponding double entry in the discount received account (it has already been posted from the PLCA).

Answers to chapter activities

Activity 1

Task 1

ANALYSED CASH PAYMENTS BOOK

Date	Cheque number	Payee/ account number	Total £	PLCA £	VAT £	Wages and salaries £	Purchases £	Discount received £
23/7/X4	1003	N Hudson, P4153	4,230	4,230				130
24/7/X4	1004	G Farr, P4778	2,350	2,350				
28/7/X4	1005	Purchases	940		140		800	
30/7/X4	1006	Salary	2,500			2,500		
			10,020	6,580	140	2,500	800	130

Task 2

Purchases ledger control account   **2001**

Date	Details	Folio	£	Date	Details	Folio	£
31/7/X4	Bank	CPB	6,580				
31/7/X4	Discounts received	CPB	130				

VAT account   **3215**

Date	Details	Folio	£	Date	Details	Folio	£
31/7/X4	Bank	CPB	140				

Wages and salaries account   **4100**

Date	Details	Folio	£	Date	Details	Folio	£
31/7/X4	Bank	CPB	2,500				

Purchases account   4200

Date	Details	Folio	£	Date	Details	Folio	£
31/7/X4	Bank	CPB	800				

Discount received account   1000

Date	Details	Folio	£	Date	Details	Folio	£
				31/7/X4	PLC	CPB	130

Purchases ledger

N Hudson account   P4153

Date	Details	Folio	£	Date	Details	Folio	£
23/7/X4	Bank	CPB	4,230		b/f		10,327
23/7/X4	Discounts received	CPB	130				

G Farr account   P4778

Date	Details	Folio	£	Date	Details	Folio	£
24/7/X4	Bank	CPB	2,350		b/f		8,263

The cashbook

Introduction

As we have studied the two aspects of a business, sales and purchases, we have seen the two sides of the cash book; the cash receipts book and the cash payments book. However, the cashbook actually combines both these sides, and this chapter will look at how we use this book within the double entry system.

KNOWLEDGE
1.1 Outline the purpose, content and format of the books of prime entry
1.4 Explain how transactions are entered in the following books of prime entry: cash book
3.3 Outline how the books of prime entry integrate with a double entry bookkeeping system
3.4 Explain how to process financial transactions from the books of prime entry into the double entry system
SKILLS
1.2 Transfer data correctly from the cash book to the ledgers

CONTENTS
1 The cashbook

1 The cashbook

1.1 Cashbook as part of the main ledger

The basic accounting I assessment often shows the cashbook as a ledger account format. This means that the cashbook actually forms a part of the main ledger, with the entries being one side of the double entry required within the main ledger. The requirement will be to complete the other side of the entry within the main ledger, and to update the individual accounts in the subsidiary ledger.

Example 1

Date	Detail	Disc Allow	Bank £	Date	Detail	Bank £
30/6/X9	Bal b/d		16,173	30/6/X9	Plant & machinery	25,500
30/6/X9	Debtor	342	13,200	30/6/X9	Loan repayment	1,500
				30/6/X9	Motor expenses	1,440
				30/6/X9	Bal c/d	933
		342	**29,373**			**29,373**

We need to appreciate that the bank account has already been completed with one side of the entries, and the other side of the entry is all that is required in order to complete the double entry postings.

It is also important to note that the discount column is still to be treated as a memorandum column, requiring both the debit and the credit entries.

Postings to main ledger (ignoring VAT)

Account	Amount	Dr or Cr
SLCA	13,200	Cr
Plant and machinery	25,500	Dr
Loan	1,500	Dr
Motor expenses	1,440	Dr
SLCA	342	Cr
Discount allowed	342	Dr

Postings to the sales ledger

Account	Amount	Dr or Cr
Debtor account	13,200	Cr
Debtor account	342	Cr

Activity 1

Date	Detail	Bank £	Date	Detail	VAT £	Bank £
30/6/X9	Bal b/d	24,067	30/6/X9	Motor vehicles		20,000
30/6/X9	Bal c/d	2,903	30/6/X9	Motor expenses	70	470
			30/6/X9	Creditor		6,500
		26,970			**70**	**26,970**
			1/7/X9	Bal b/d		2,903

What are the postings to the main and purchases ledgers?

Example 2

Sometimes within the assessment, you are only asked to record the transactions for one half of the cashbook.

Cashbook – debit side

Details	Discount £	Bank £
Balance b/f		2,568
Edwards Ltd	36	3,864

(a) Record the TWO transactions within the sales ledger.

(b) Record the THREE transactions within the main ledger.

Solution

It is important to appreciate that the above is still the cashbook as a ledger account, but only one half is required. Therefore, the entries will be the same as previously shown.

(a)   Sales ledger

Details	Amount £	Debit / Credit
Edwards Ltd	3,864	Credit
Edwards Ltd	36	Credit

(b)   Main ledger

Details	Amount £	Debit / Credit
Sales ledger control account	3,864	Credit
Discounts allowed	36	Debit
Sales ledger control account	36	Credit

KAPLAN PUBLISHING

Activity 2

Cashbook – credit side

Details	VAT £	Bank £
Motor expenses	56	376
Wages		4,785

(a) Record the THREE transactions within the main ledger.

Details	Amount £	Debit / Credit

2 Test your knowledge

Test your knowledge

Having completed Chapter 16, you should now be able to attempt Practice Activities 46 to 48.

3 Summary

We have dealt with both sides of the cashbook in an earlier chapter, but the basic accounting I exam often shows the cashbook as part of the main ledger, leaving us with only one side of the entries to complete.

Answers to chapter activities

Activity 1

Postings to main ledger

Account	Amount	Dr or Cr
Motor vehicle	20,000	Dr
Motor expenses	400	Dr
VAT	70	Dr
PLCA	6,500	Dr

Postings to the purchases ledger

Account	Amount	Dr or Cr
Creditor account	6,500	Dr

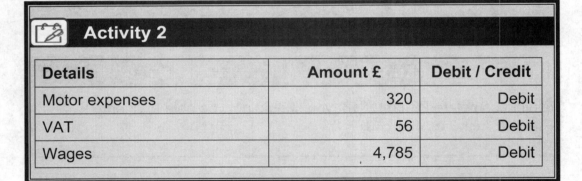 Activity 2

Details	Amount £	Debit / Credit
Motor expenses	320	Debit
VAT	56	Debit
Wages	4,785	Debit

KAPLAN PUBLISHING

Consolidation

Introduction

The following example will bring together all the techniques we have learned with regard to the purchases of a business. It comprises six tasks, and the approach to take is the same as that used for the consolidation question within chapter 10.

 Activity 1

Shauna Holly is the owner of a retail business called Sweet Somethings

You are employed by the business as a bookkeeper

The business uses a manual accounting system

Double entry takes place in the main ledger. Individual accounts of sales and purchase ledger are kept in subsidiary ledgers as memorandum accounts.

Assume today's date is 30 June 20X9, unless you are told otherwise

Balances at the start of the date on 30 June 20X9

Credit suppliers

	Creative Supplies	5,600
	Decorates	1,860
	Mr Flour	14,228
	Roses & Ribbons	25,200
Motor vehicles		19,350
Purchases		171,800
Purchases returns		600
Purchases ledger control		81,047
Discount received		900
Stationery		2,000
Loan from bank		15,750
VAT (credit balance)		12,840

Task 1

Enter the opening balances above into the 'T' accounts given.

Transactions

The following transactions took place on 30 June 20X9 and have been entered into the daybooks below:

Purchases day book

Date	Details	Inv. No.	Total £	VAT £	Net £
30/06/X9	Creative supplies	196	18,330	2,730	15,600
30/06/X9	Decorates	972	1,058	158	900
30/06/X9	Mr Flour	N73	5,287	787	4,500
30/06/X9	Roses & Ribbons	34G	2,115	315	1,800
			26,790	3,990	22,800

Purchases returns day book

Date	Details	Credit No.	Total £	VAT £	Net £
30/06/X9	Creative supplies	98	352	52	300
30/06/X9	Roses & Ribbons	56N	71	11	60
			423	63	360

Cash book

Date	Detail	Bank £	Date	Details	VAT £	Bank £
30/6/X9	Bal b/d	28,100	30/6/X9	Motor vehicles		12,750
				Loan repayment		750
				Stationery	107	720
				Bal c/d		13,880
		28,100			107	28,100

Task 2

From the daybooks and cash book shown, make the relevant entries into the accounts in the main ledger and the purchases ledger.

Task 3

Balance the accounts showing clearly the balances carried down at 30 June and brought down at 1 July.

Task 4

List the balances you have calculated in Task 3 in the trial balance.

Purchases ledger

Creative supplies					
Date	Details	£	Date	Detail	£

Decorates					
Date	Details	£	Date	Detail	£

Mr Flour

Date	Details	£	Date	Detail	£

Roses & Ribbons

Date	Details	£	Date	Detail	£

Main ledger

Motor vehicles

Date	Details	£	Date	Detail	£

Purchases

Date	Details	£	Date	Detail	£

Purchases returns

Date	Details	£	Date	Detail	£

Purchases ledger control

Date	Details	£	Date	Detail	£

Discount received

Date	Details	£	Date	Detail	£

Stationery

Date	Details	£	Date	Detail	£

Loan from bank

Date	Details	£	Date	Detail	£

KAPLAN PUBLISHING

VAT					
Date	Details	£	Date	Detail	£

Other balances

Plant & machinery	17,020
Stock	10,150
Petty cash control	456
Sales ledger control	158,162
Capital	6,669
Sales	327,550
Sales returns	2,100
Discount allowed	180
Wages	19,400
Rent	4,575
Heat & light	3,900
Rates	315
Telephone	933
Insurance	4,875
Miscellaneous expenses	2,040

Task 5

List the remaining balances shown above in the trial balance and total each column.

Trial balance

	Dr £	Cr £
Plant & machinery		
Motor vehicles		
Bank		
Stock		
Petty cash control		
Sales ledger control		
Purchases ledger control		
Capital		
VAT		
Loan from bank		
Sales		
Sales returns		
Discount allowed		
Purchases		
Purchase returns		
Discount received		
Wages		
Rent		
Heat & light		
Rates		
Stationery		
Telephone		
Insurance		
Miscellaneous expenses		
Totals		

KAPLAN PUBLISHING

2 Test your knowledge

Test your knowledge

Having completed Chapter 17, you should now be able to attempt Practice Activity 49.

3 Summary

This question has tested all of the techniques learned to date. It is important that these tasks can be completed confidently.

Answers to chapter activity

 Activity 1

Purchases ledger

Creative supplies

Date	Details	£	Date	Detail	£
30/6/X9	PRDB	352	30/6/X9	Bal b/d	5,600
30/6/X9	Bal c/d	23,578	30/6/X9	PDB	18,330
		23,930			**23,930**
			1/7/X9	Bal b/d	23,578

Decorates

Date	Details	£	Date	Detail	£
30/6/X9	Bal c/d	2,918	30/6/X9	Bal b/d	1,860
			30/6/X9	PDB	1,058
		2,918			**2,918**
			1/7/X9	Bal b/d	2,918

Mr Flour

Date	Details	£	Date	Detail	£
30/6/X9	Bal c/d	19,515	30/6/X9	Bal b/d	14,228
			30/6/X9	PDB	5,287
		19,515			**19,515**
			1/7/X9	Bal b/d	19,515

Roses & Ribbons

Date	Details	£	Date	Detail	£
30/6/X9	PDB	71	30/6/X9	Bal b/d	25,200
30/6/X9	Bal c/d	27,244	30/6/X9	PDB	2,115
		27,315			**27,315**
			1/7/X9	Bal b/d	27,244

Main ledger

Motor vehicles					
Date	**Details**	**£**	**Date**	**Detail**	**£**
30/6/X9	Bal b/d	19,350			
30/6/X9	Cashbook	12,750	30/6/X9	Bal c/d	32,100
		32,100			**32,100**
1/7/X9	Bal b/d	32,100			

Purchases					
Date	**Details**	**£**	**Date**	**Detail**	**£**
30/6/X9	Bal b/d	171,800	30/6/X9	Bal c/d	194,600
30/6/X9	PDB	22,800			
		194,600			**194,600**
1/7/X9	Bal b/d	194,600			

Purchases returns					
Date	**Details**	**£**	**Date**	**Detail**	**£**
30/6/X9	Bal c/d	960	30/6/X9	Bal b/d	600
			30/6/X9	PRDB	360
		960			**960**
			1/7/X9	Bal b/d	960

Purchases ledger control					
Date	**Details**	**£**	**Date**	**Detail**	**£**
30/6/X9	PRDB	423	30/6/X9	Bal b/d	81,047
30/6/X9	Bal c/d	107,414	30/6/X9	PDB	26,790
		107,837			**107,837**
			1/7/X9	Bal b/d	107,414

Discount received

Date	Details	£	Date	Detail	£
30/6/X9	Bal c/d	900	30/6/X9	Bal b/d	900
		900			**900**
			1/7/X9	Bal b/d	900

Stationery

Date	Details	£	Date	Detail	£
30/6/X9	Bal b/d	2,000	30/6/X9	Bal c/d	2,613
30/6/X9	Cashbook	613			
		2,613			**2,613**
1/7/X9	Bal b/d	2,613			

Loan from bank

Date	Details	£	Date	Detail	£
30/6/X9	Cashbook	750	30/6/X9	Bal b/d	15,750
30/6/X9	Bal c/d	15,000			
		15,750			**15,750**
			1/7/X9	Bal b/d	15,000

VAT

Date	Details	£	Date	Detail	£
30/6/X9	PDB	3,990	30/6/X9	Bal b/d	12,840
30/6/X9	Cashbook	107	30/6/X9	PRDB	63
30/6/X9	Bal c/d	8,806			
		12,903			**12,903**
			1/7/X9	Bal b/d	8,806

Trial balance

	Dr £	Cr £
Plant & machinery	17,020	
Motor vehicles	32,100	
Bank	13,880	
Stock	10,150	
Petty cash control	456	
Sales ledger control	158,162	
Purchases ledger control		107,414
Capital		6,669
VAT		8,806
Loan from bank		15,000
Sales		327,550
Sales returns	2,100	
Discount allowed	180	
Purchases	194,600	
Purchases returns		960
Discount received		900
Wages	19,400	
Rent	4,575	
Heat & light	3,900	
Rates	315	
Stationery	2,613	
Telephone	933	
Insurance	4,875	
Miscellaneous expenses	2,040	
Totals	**467,299**	**467,299**

Petty cash

18

Introduction

As well as making payments from the business bank account by cheque or other methods, most businesses will also carry a certain amount of cash on the premises known as petty cash. The purpose of this cash is in order to make small business payments for which writing a cheque would not be appropriate, such as payment in the local shop for tea, coffee and milk for the staff kitchen. In this chapter we will consider how a petty cash system will work, the documentation required and how petty cash payments are accounted for.

KNOWLEDGE	CONTENTS
1.2 Outline the purpose and content of a range of business documents to include Petty cash voucher	1 Petty cash 2 Maintaining petty cash records 3 Posting the petty cash book
SKILLS	
1.3 Transfer data correctly from the petty cash book to the ledgers.	

1 Petty cash

 Definition

Petty cash is the small amount of cash that most businesses will hold in order to make small cash payments.

1.1 Petty cash box

Cash being held on business premises is obviously a security risk. Therefore it is important that the petty cash is secure. It will normally be kept in a locked petty cash box and usually this itself will be held in the safe. Only the person responsible for the petty cash should have access to the petty cash box.

1.2 Payment of petty cash

Petty cash will usually be paid out to employees who have already incurred a small cash expense on behalf of the business, such as buying coffee and milk in the local shop or paying for a train fare that the business is to reimburse. It is obviously important that payments are only made out of the petty cash box for valid business expenses that have been incurred. For this reason petty cash should only ever be given to an employee on receipt by the petty cashier of an authorised petty cash voucher and, where appropriate, VAT receipt.

 Definition

A petty cash voucher is an internal document that details the business expenditure that an employee has incurred out of his own money.

This voucher must be authorised before any amounts can be paid to that employee out of the petty cash box.

A typical petty cash voucher is shown below:

Signature of person authorising voucher

Details of expenditure

PETTY CASH VOUCHER				
Authorised by F R Clarke	Received by L Kent	*Signature of claimant*	No	4173
Date	Description		Amount	
4 April 20X1	Train Fare		12	50
Total			12	50

Sequential voucher number

Total paid to employee

2 Maintaining petty cash records

2.1 Introduction

The petty cash vouchers are recorded in their own book of prime entry which is known as the petty cash book. The petty cash book, similar to the cash receipts book and the cash payments book, is not only a primary record but is normally also kept as part of the main ledger double entry system.

2.2 Layout of the petty cash book

The petty cash book is normally set out as a large ledger account with a small receipts side and a larger analysed payments side. A typical petty cash book is set out below.

Receipts			Payments								
Date	Narrative	Total	Date	Narrative	Voucher no	Total £	Postage £	Cleaning £	Tea & Coffee £	Sundry £	VAT £
1 Nov	Bal b/f	35.50									
1 Nov	Cheque 394	114.50	1 Nov	ASDA	58	23.50			23.50		
			2 Nov	Post Office Ltd	59	29.50	29.50				
			2 Nov	Cleaning materials	60	14.76		12.56			2.20
			3 Nov	Postage	61	16.19	16.19				
			3 Nov	ASDA	62	10.35		8.81			1.54
			4 Nov	Newspapers	63	18.90				18.90	
			5 Nov	ASDA	64	11.85				10.09	1.76

2.3 Receipts side of the petty cash book

The receipts side of the petty cash book only requires one column, as the only receipt into the petty cash box is the regular payment into the petty cash box of cash drawn out of the bank account.

2.4 Payments side of the petty cash book

Payments out of the petty cash box will be for a variety of different types of expense and an analysis column is required for each type of expense in the same way as the cash payments book is analysed. Note that a column is also required for VAT, as if a petty cash expense includes VAT this must also be analysed out. Remember that any VAT included in a petty cash expense must be shown separately on the petty cash voucher.

Any VAT shown on the petty cash voucher must be analysed out into the VAT column and the net amount shown in the expense analysis column.

2.5 Writing up the petty cash book

When cash is originally paid into the petty cash book then this will be recorded on the receipts side (debit side) of the petty cash book.

Each petty cash voucher will then in turn be written up in the petty cash book on the payments side.

KAPLAN PUBLISHING

Petty cash vouchers are pre-numbered to ensure that none are mislaid and they will be written into the petty cash book in number order with each item of expenditure being recorded in the correct analysis column.

 Example

A business has just started to run a petty cash system with an amount of £100. £100 is withdrawn from the bank account and paid into the petty cash box on *3 April 20X1*.

During the first week the following authorised petty cash vouchers were paid. These transactions will now be recorded in the petty cash book.

PETTY CASH VOUCHER

Authorised by T Smedley	Received by P Lannall	No	0001	
Date	Description		Amount	
3 April 20X1	Tea/coffee/milk		4	73
	Total		4	73

PETTY CASH VOUCHER

Authorised by T Smedley	Received by R Sellers	No	0002	
Date	Description		Amount	
3 April 20X1	Train fare		14	90
	Total		14	90

PETTY CASH VOUCHER			
Authorised by T Smedley	*Received by* F Dorne	*No*	0003
Date	*Description*	*Amount*	
4 April 20X1	Stationery	4	00
	VAT	0	70
	Total	4	70

PETTY CASH VOUCHER			
Authorised by T Smedley	*Received by* P Dent	*No*	0004
Date	*Description*	*Amount*	
5 April 20X1	Postage costs	16	35
	Total	16	35

PETTY CASH VOUCHER			
Authorised by T Smedley	*Received by* H Polly	*No*	0005
Date	*Description*	*Amount*	
7 April 20X1	Train fare	15	30
	Total	15	30

PETTY CASH VOUCHER			
Authorised by T Smedley	Received by P Lannall	No	0006
Date	Description	Amount	
8 April 20X1	Milk/biscuits	3	85
	Total	3	85

Solution

Petty cash book

Receipts			Payments								
Date	Narrative	Total	Date	Narrative	Voucher no	Total	Postage	Travel	Tea & coffee	Sundry	VAT
20X1		£	20X1			£	£	£	£	£	£
03/04	Cash	100.00	03/04	Tea/coffee	0001	4.73			4.73		
			03/04	Train fare	0002	14.90		14.90			
			04/04	Stationery	0003	4.70				4.00	0.70
			05/04	Postage	0004	16.35	16.35				
			07/04	Train fare	0005	15.30		15.30			
			08/04	Milk/biscuits	0006	3.85			3.85		

3 Posting the petty cash book

3.1 Introduction

Now that we have seen how the petty cash book is written up we must next post the totals of the petty cash book to the main ledger accounts.

Remember that the petty cash book is part of the main ledger double entry system. Therefore the receipt of cash is the debit entry in the petty cash account and the only related credit entry is the cash coming out of the bank account and therefore recorded in the cash payments book.

The total of the payments is effectively the credit entry in the petty cash account and therefore the only postings that are required are the related debit entries to the relevant expense accounts.

3.2 Posting the petty cash receipt

The receipt into the petty cash box has come from cash being withdrawn from the bank account. This will have been done by writing out a cheque for cash and withdrawing this from the bank. Therefore the cheque should be recorded in the cash payments book as a payment when the cash payments book is written up.

The receipt of the cash into the petty cash box is recorded in the receipts side of the petty cash book, debit side.

As both the petty cash book and the cash payments book are normally part of the main ledger double entry system, the double entry has been completed. The debit is the entry into the petty cash book and the credit entry is the entry in the cash payments book.

3.3 Posting the petty cash payments

The petty cash book is part of the main ledger double entry system so the total column in the petty cash payments side is the credit entry to the petty cash account.

All that is required is therefore the debit entries to match this. These debit entries are taken from the totals of each of the analysis columns.

The total from each analysis column is debited to the relevant main ledger account.

Example

The petty cash book written up in an earlier example is given again below. This is to be posted to the main ledger accounts.

Petty cash book

Receipts			Payments							
Date	Narrative	Total	Date	Narrative	Voucher no	Total	Postage	Travel	Tea & coffee	Sundry	VAT
20X1		£	20X1			£	£	£	£	£	£
03/04	Cash	100.00	03/04	Tea/coffee	0001	4.73			4.73		
			03/04	Train fare	0002	14.90		14.90			
			04/04	Stationery	0003	4.70				4.00	0.70
			05/04	Postage	0004	16.35	16.35				
			07/04	Train fare	0005	15.30		15.30			
			08/04	Milk/biscuits	0006	3.85			3.85		

Solution

Step 1 Each of the columns in the petty cash payments side must be totalled.

The accuracy of your totalling should be checked by ensuring that all of the analysis column totals add back to the total of the 'total' column in the petty cash book payments side.

Petty cash book

Receipts			Payments								
Date	Narrative	Total	Date	Narrative	Voucher no	Total	Postage	Travel	Tea & coffee	Sundry	VAT
20X1		£	20X1			£	£	£	£	£	£
03/04	Cash	100.00	03/04	Tea/coffee	0001	4.73			4.73		
			03/04	Train fare	0002	14.90		14.90			
			04/04	Stationery	0003	4.70				4.00	0.70
			05/04	Postage	0004	16.35	16.35				
			07/04	Train fare	0005	15.30		15.30			
			08/04	Milk/biscuits	0006	3.85			3.85		
						59.83	16.35	30.20	8.58	4.00	0.70

Check the totals:

	£
Postage	16.35
Travel	30.20
Tea and coffee	8.58
Sundry	4.00
VAT	0.70
	59.83

Step 2 Each of the analysis column totals must now be entered into the main ledger accounts as debit entries.

VAT account

	£		£
Petty cash book (PCB)	0.70		

The entry has come from the petty cash book and this is the reference – this is now shortened to PCB.

Postage account

	£		£
PCB	16.35		

Travel account

	£		£
PCB	30.20		

Tea and coffee account

	£		£
PCB	8.58		

Sundry expenses account

	£		£
PCB	4.00		

Activity 1

Summary of petty cash vouchers in hand at 31 October 20X7

Date	Description	Total	VAT included
		£	£
1/10	Envelopes (Administration)	19.72	2.93
4/10	Cleaner (Administration)	8.75	
6/10	Food for staff lunch (Marketing)	17.13	
6/10	Taxi fares (Marketing)	16.23	
6/10	Rail fares (Marketing)	43.75	
10/10	Postage (Administration)	4.60	
15/10	Tea and coffee (Production)	4.39	
17/10	Light bulbs and refuse sacks (Distribution)	8.47	1.26
20/10	Flowers for reception (Administration)	21.23	
26/10	Cleaner (Administration)	8.75	

(a) Write up the payments side of the petty cash book for October 20X7 from the information given.

You should allocate a sequential voucher number to each entry in the petty cash book. The last voucher number to be allocated in September was 6578.

Use the blank petty cash book provided.

(b)	Total each of the columns in the petty cash book and cross-cast them.

(c)	Post the totals to the main ledger accounts given.

PETTY CASH BOOK – PAYMENTS

Date	Voucher no	Total	Production	Distribu-tion	Marketing	Administration	VAT
		£	£	£	£	£	£

Production expenses account

£	£

Distribution expenses account

£	£

Marketing expenses account

£	£

Administration expenses account

£	£

VAT account			
	£		£

4 Test your knowledge

Test your knowledge

Having completed Chapter 18, you should now be able to attempt Practice Activities 50 to 54.

5 Summary

In this chapter we have considered some aspects of the petty cash system. Cash is paid into the petty cash box in order to meet the requirements for actual cash in a business's life. This will normally be in the form of reimbursing employees for business expenses that they have incurred on their own behalf. In order to be reimbursed for the expense, the employee must fill out a petty cash voucher which will normally be accompanied by a receipt for the expense and must then be authorised. At this point the employee can be paid the cash out of the petty cash box.

All petty cash is recorded in the petty cash book which is normally both a book of prime entry and part of the main ledger. The cash paid into the petty cash box is recorded as a receipt in the petty cash book and as a payment in the cash payments book, an amount of cash being taken out of the bank account. The payments of petty cash vouchers are recorded as payments in the petty cash book and are analysed as to the type of payment. These payments are then recorded as debit entries in the appropriate expense account.

Answers to chapter activity

Activity 1

(a), (b)

Date	Voucher no	Total £		Production £		Distribution £		Marketing £		Administration £		VAT £	
01/10/X7	6579	19	72							16	79	2	93
04/10/X7	6580	8	75							8	75		
06/10/X7	6581	17	13					17	13				
06/10/X7	6582	16	23					16	23				
06/10/X7	6583	43	75					43	75				
10/10/X7	6584	4	60							4	60		
15/10/X7	6585	4	39	4	39								
17/10/X7	6586	8	47			7	21					1	26
20/10/X7	6587	21	23							21	23		
26/10/X7	6588	8	75							8	75		
		153	02	4	39	7	21	77	11	60	12	4	19

(c)

Production expenses account

	£		£
PCB	4.39		

Distribution expenses account

	£		£
PCB	7.21		

Marketing expenses account

	£		£
PCB	77.11		

Administration expenses account			
	£		£
PCB	60.12		

VAT account			
	£		£
PCB	4.19		

WORKBOOK

QUESTIONS

Practice Activities Questions

1 Double entry bookkeeping – introduction

 Activity 1

Bertie Wooster started a business as an antique dealer on 1 July 20X9.

Required

Show the accounting equation which results from each of the following transactions made during Bertie's first two weeks of trading.

(a) Started the business with £5,000 in cash as opening capital.

(b) Bought an Edwardian desk for £500 cash.

(c) Bought five art deco table lamps for £200 each, on credit from Roderick Spode.

(d) Sold the desk for £750 cash.

(e) Sold four of the table lamps for £300 each on credit to his Uncle Tom.

(f) Paid rent of £250 cash.

(g) Drew £100 in cash out of the business for living expenses.

(h) Earned £50 for writing a magazine article, but had not yet been paid for it.

(i) Paid Roderick Spode £500 on account.

(j) Received £1,200 from Uncle Tom in full settlement of the amount due.

(k) Bought a van for use in the business for £4,000 cash.

(l) Received a telephone bill for £150 but did not pay it yet.

Note: Each transaction follows on from the one before.

Activity 2

On 1 January 20X9 Esmond Haddock inherited £3,000 from an aunt and decided to open his own sports equipment shop. During January the following transactions took place.

01 January   Paid the £3,000 into a bank account.

02 January   Paid one month's rent of £100 for the shop premises.

10 January   Bought stock of sports equipment for £1,000 cash.

14 January   Paid £50 for display equipment.

30 January   Drew out £150 for his own use.

31 January   Bought sports equipment on credit for £1,500.

During the month he sold for £830 half of the equipment he purchased on 10 January. £800 was received in cash and £30 was owed to him by one customer.

Required

Show the accounting equation of the business at 31 January 20X9.

Note: Profit will be the balancing figure.

2   Ledger accounting

 Activity 3

Z, the owner of a consultancy firm, has the following transactions:

(a)   Pays £4,000 into the bank as capital.

(b)   Buys a computer for £1,000.

(c)   Pays rent of £400.

(d)   Earns £800 for consultancy services.

Write up the ledger accounts for the above.

Activity 4

A makes the following cash transactions:

(a)   Pays £5,000 into the **bank** as **capital**.

(b)   Buys goods for £800.

(c)   Pays **rent** of £500.

(d)   Buys a **van** for £2,000.

(e)   Sells some of the goods for £600.

(f)   Sells some more of the goods for £700.

(g)   Buys goods for £1,000.

(h)   Buys **stationery** for £200.

(i)   Takes £500 out of the bank as **drawings**.

Write up the ledger accounts for the above. In addition to the accounts highlighted in bold above you will also need accounts for **sales** and **purchases.**

 Activity 5

B makes the following cash transactions:

(a)   Pays £4,000 into the bank as capital.

(b)   Buys goods for £700.

(c)   Buys champagne to entertain the staff for £300.

(d)   Purchases three computers for £3,000.

(e)   Sells goods for £1,500.

(f)   Draws £500 cash.

(g)   Purchases goods for £1,200.

(h)   Pays telephone bill of £600.

(i)   Receives telephone bill rebate of £200.

(j)   Buys stationery for £157.

Write up the ledger accounts for the above.

Activity 6

C makes the following transactions:

(a)   Pays £2,000 into the bank as capital.

(b)   Purchases goods for £1,000 on credit.

(c)   Buys a van costing £900 and pays with cash.

(d)   Sells goods for £2,500 on credit.

(e)   Receives £3,000 cash for consultancy services.

(f)   Purchases goods for £1,000 cash.

(g)   Buys stationery for £260 cash.

(h)   Sells goods for £800 cash.

(i)   Purchases goods for £200 cash.

(j)   Receives £100 cash for returned stationery.

Write up the ledger accounts for the above.

 Activity 7

A sells books to B for £1,000 on credit.

A also sells books to C for £90 credit.

B pays £500 and C pays £90.

Write up these transactions in the sales ledger accounts of A, using individual debtor accounts for each customer.

 Activity 8

X purchases £600 of goods from Y and £750 of goods from Z on credit.

X pays Y £300 and Z £500.

Write up these transactions in the purchases ledger accounts of X, using individual creditor accounts for each supplier.

3 Drafting an initial Trial Balance

Activity 9

The following cash book has been written up for the month of May 20X9. There was no opening balance.

Bank

	£		£
Capital	10,000	Computer	1,000
Sales	2,000	Telephone	567
Sales	3,000	Rent	1,500
Sales	2,000	Rates	125
		Stationery	247
		Petrol	49
		Purchases	2,500
		Drawings	500
		Petrol	42

Bring down the balance on the account.

Activity 10

The following bank account has been written up during May 20X9. There was no brought forward balance.

Bank

	£		£
Capital	5,000	Purchases	850
Sales	1,000	Fixtures	560
Sales	876	Van	1,500
Rent rebate	560	Rent	1,300
Sales	1,370	Rates	360
		Telephone	220
		Stationery	120
		Petrol	48
		Car repairs	167

Bring down the balance on the account.

Activity 11

The following bank account has been written up during June 20X9.

Bank

	£		£
Balance b/f	23,700	Drawings	4,000
Sales	2,300	Rent	570
Sales	1,700	Purchases	6,000
Debtors	4,700	Rates	500
		Salaries	3,600
		Car expenses	460
		Petrol	49
		Petrol	38
		Electricity	210
		Stationery	89

Bring down the balance on the account.

Activity 12

The following are the balances on the accounts of XYZ at 31 August 20X9:

	£
Sales	41,770
Purchases	34,680
Debtors	6,790
Creditors	5,650
General expenses	12,760
Loan	10,000
Plant and machinery at cost	5,000
Motor van at cost	6,000
Drawings	2,000
Rent and rates	6,700
Insurance	4,000
Bank overdraft	510
Capital	20,000

Prepare XYZ's Trial Balance as at 31 August 20X9.

Activity 13

Tony makes the following transactions during the month of July 20X9:

(a)   Purchases good on credit for £1,000.

(b)   Pays cash for rent of £500.

(c)   Makes sales on credit for £1,500.

(d)   Buys a computer for £900 cash.

(e)   Pays cash for wages of £1,000.

(f)   Receives cash from a credit customer of £400.

(g)   Pays £300 cash to a credit supplier.

(h)   Pays £200 cash for a telephone bill.

(i)   Receives £50 cash refund for overcharge on telephone bill.

(j)   Makes cash purchases of £400.

(k)   Makes cash sales of £2,000.

Write up the ledger accounts for these transactions, balance the accounts off and extract Tony's Trial Balance at 31 July 20X9.

4 **Credit sales: documents**

 Activity 14

You have been given details of goods that have been returned to Keyboard Supplies. The return has been checked and authorised and you are now to prepare the credit note.

Return from: H H Music   Ref no: SL 09
                  Tenant House   Trade discount 15%
                  Perley TN7 8ER

Goods returned: 1 Bento keyboard   Code B3060   Unit price (before
                                                      VAT and
                                                      discount) £126.00

Reason for return: Goods not ordered

Today's date is 17 April 20X1 and the last credit note to have been issued was CN 0336.

Required

Prepare the credit note on the blank credit note given below

CREDIT NOTE	
	Keyboard Supplies
Credit note to:	Trench Park Estate
	Fieldham
	Sussex TN21 4AF
	Tel: 01829 654545
As above	Fax: 01829 654646
	Credit note no:
	Tax point:
	VAT reg no: 466 1128 30
	Purchase order no:

Code	Description	Quantity	VAT rate %	Unit price £	Amount excl of VAT £

VAT at 17.5%
Total amount

Activity 15

You work in the accounts department of Keyboard Supplies, a supplier of a wide range of electronic keyboards to a variety of music shops on credit. Given below are three purchase orders for goods which are due to be despatched today.

You also have an extract from the customer master file:

Customer	Sales ledger code	Trade discount	Settlement discount
F T Music Supplies	SL23	15%	–
Musicolor Ltd	SL06	10%	3% – 10 days
Newford Music	SL18	20%	3% – 10 days

Today's date is 17 April 20X1 and the last sales invoice to be sent out was invoice number 06112. Normal credit terms are 30 days although some customers are offered a settlement discount. The business is registered for VAT and all of the goods are standard rated.

Required

Complete the sales invoices for these sales on the blank invoices supplied.

PURCHASE ORDER			
Musicolour Ltd 23 High Street Nutford Sussex TN11 4TZ Tel: 01826 434111 Fax: 01826 434112 Date: 12 April 20X1 Purchase order no: 04318		**To:**	**Keyboard Supplies** Trench Park Estate Fieldham Sussex TN21 4AF
Delivery addres (If different from above)		**Invoice address** (If different from above)	
Code	Quantity	Description	Unit price (exclusive of VAT and discounts) £
Z4600	2	Zanni Keyboard	185.00
A4802	3	Atol Keyboard	130.00

PURCHASE ORDER

Newford Music
32/34 Main Street
Welland
Sussex TN4 6BD
Tel: 01760 437711
Fax: 01760 436204
Date: 10 April 20X1
Purchase order no: 47115

To: **Keyboard Supplies**
Trench Park Estate
Fieldham
Sussex TN21 4AF

Delivery addres
(If different from above)

Invoice address
(If different from above)

Code	Quantity	Description	Unit price (exclusive of VAT and discounts) £
Z4406	4	Zanni Keyboard	165.00

PURCHASE ORDER

FT Music Supplies
The Barn
Nutford
Sussex TN11 7AJ
Tel: 01826 431799
Fax: 01826 431800
Date: 13 April 20X1
Purchase order no: 71143

To: **Keyboard Supplies**
Trench Park Estate
Fieldham
Sussex TN21 4AF

Delivery addres
(If different from above)

Invoice address
(If different from above)

Code	Quantity	Description	Unit price (exclusive of VAT and discounts) £
B2010	2	Bento Keyboard	148.00
G4706	3	Garland Keyboard	96.00

INVOICE

Keyboard Supplies

Invoice to:

Trench Park Estate
Fieldham
Sussex TN21 4AF
Tel: 01829 654545
Fax: 01829 654646

Deliver to:

Invoice no:
Tax point:
VAT reg no: 466 1128 30
Your reference:
Purchase order no:

Code	Description	Quantity	VAT rate %	Unit price £	Amount excl of VAT £

Trade discount   %

VAT at 17.5%
Total amount payable

INVOICE

Keyboard Supplies

Invoice to:

Trench Park Estate
Fieldham
Sussex TN21 4AF
Tel: 01829 654545
Fax: 01829 654646

Deliver to:

Invoice no:
Tax point:
VAT reg no: 466 1128 30
Your reference:
Purchase order no:

Code	Description	Quantity	VAT rate %	Unit price £	Amount excl of VAT £

Trade discount   %

VAT at 17.5%
Total amount payable

INVOICE
Keyboard Supplies

Invoice to:
Trench Park Estate
Fieldham
Sussex TN21 4AF
Tel: 01829 654545
Fax: 01829 654646

Deliver to:

Invoice no:
Tax point:
VAT reg no: 466 1128 30
Your reference:
Purchase order no:

Code	Description	Quantity	VAT rate %	Unit price £	Amount excl of VAT £

Trade discount   %

VAT at 17.5%

Total amount payable

 ## Activity 16

The purchase order has been received from a customer, M.P. Katz & Co Ltd. M Krupps Cardboard has raised an invoice to send to the customer and both the purchase order and the invoice are shown below.

PURCHASE ORDER

Purchase order to:
M Krupps Cardboard
Hayward Lane
Manor Estate
Stockport
SK7 4AD

M.P. Katz & Company Limited
64 Royce Road
Manchester
M15 5XA
Tel: 0161 560 3392
Fax: 0161 560 5322

Purchase order no: PO02543

Please supply 400 cardboard boxes product code CB1354.
Purchase price: £40 per 100, plus VAT
Discount: less 10% trade discount, as agreed

INVOICE

Invoice to:
M Krupps Cardboard
Hayward Lane
Manor Estate
Stockport
SK7 4AD

M.P. Katz & Company Limited
64 Royce Road
Manchester
M15 5XA
Tel: 0161 560 3392
Fax: 0161 560 5322

Deliver to:
As above

Invoice no:	69472
Tax point:	29 January 20X9
VAT reg no:	625 9911 58
Order no:	PO02543
Delivery note no:	68553
Account no:	SL07

Code	Description	Quantity	VAT rate %	Unit price £	Amount excl of VAT £
CB1354	Cardboard boxes	400	17.5	0.40	160.00
Trade discount 20%					32.00
					128.00
VAT at 17.5%					22.40
Total amount payable					150.40

You have been asked to determine whether the invoice has been correctly prepared.

(i)   Has the correct pricing been used on the invoice?

(ii)   Has the correct discount been applied?

(iii)   What should the correct amount of VAT charged be?

(iv)   What should the correct total amount payable be?

Activity 17

ABC Ltd uses codes within the accounting system. An extract from the general ledger coding list is given below:

General Ledger Account	Code number
Equipment	10
Debtors (SLCA)	20
Electricity	30
Purchases	40
Sales	50

Required

(a) Why are the general ledger codes numbered in steps of 10, rather than 1,2,3,4?

(b) Give 3 examples of the use of code numbers in an accounting system, other than general ledger accounts codes.

(c) Are the following statements true or false?

	TRUE/FALSE
General ledger codes help when barcoding an item of stock	
General ledger codes help when filing a financial document	
General ledger codes help trace relevant accounts quickly and easily	
General ledger codes help find the total amount owing to a supplier	

5 Credit sales – discounts and VAT

 Activity 18

Calculate the VAT on the following sales:

(a) A sale for £140.00 plus VAT.

(b) A sale for £560.00 plus VAT.

(c) A sale for £780.00 including VAT.

(d) A sale for £970.00 including VAT.

Activity 19

Calculate the VAT on the following sales:

(a) A sale for £280.00 plus VAT where a settlement discount of 2% is offered.

(b) A sale for £480.00 plus VAT where a settlement discount of 3% is offered.

(c) A sale for £800.00 plus VAT where a settlement discount of 5% is offered but not taken.

(d) A sale of £650.00 plus VAT where a settlement discount of 4% is offered but not taken.

 Activity 20

A sells £600 of goods to B. VAT has to be added and A offers B a settlement discount of 3%. Calculate the amount that B will pay A if:

(a) B takes the settlement discount; and

(b) B does not take the settlement discount.

 Activity 21

A sells £700 of goods to C net of VAT. A offers C a settlement discount of 5%. Enter the sale and payment for the sale in the main ledger accounts assuming:

(a) C takes the settlement discount; and

(b) C does not take the settlement discount.

6 The sales day book – main and subsidiary ledgers

 Activity 22

You work in the accounts department of D F Engineering and one of your tasks is to write up the day books. In your organisation there is no separate sales returns day book and therefore any credit notes are entered as negative amounts in the sales day book.

Given below are the details of the sales invoices and credit notes that have been issued this week. D F Engineering does not offer trade or settlement discounts but is registered for VAT and all sales are of standard rated goods.

Invoices sent out:

		Code	£	Invoice number
20X1				
1 May	Fraser & Co	SL14	128.68 plus VAT	03466
	Letterhead Ltd	SL03	257.90 plus VAT	03467
2 May	Jeliteen Traders	SL15	96.58 plus VAT	03468
3 May	Harper Bros	SL22	268.15 plus VAT	03469
	Juniper Ltd	SL17	105.38 plus VAT	03470
4 May	H G Frank	SL30	294.67 plus VAT	03471
5 May	Keller Assocs	SL07	110.58 plus VAT	03472

Credit notes sent out:

		Code	£	Credit note number
20X1				
2 May	Garner & Co	SL12	68.70 plus VAT	0746
4 May	Hill Traders	SL26	117.68 plus VAT	0747

Required

Write up the sales day book given for the week ending 5 May 20X1 and total all of the columns.

Date	Invoice no	Customer name	Code	Total £	VAT £	Net £

Activity 23

You work in the accounts department of Keyboard Supplies, a supplier of a wide range of electronic keyboards to a variety of music shops on credit. Given below are three sales invoices that you have just sent out to customers and these are to be written up into the sales day book given below.

Sales of four different types of keyboard are made and the sales are analysed into each of these four types and coded as follows:

Atol keyboards	01
Bento keyboards	02
Garland keyboards	03
Zanni keyboards	04

Required

Write up the analysed sales day book and total each of the columns.

INVOICE

Invoice to:
BZS Music
42 Westhill
Nutford TN11 3PQ

Keyboard Supplies
Trench Park Estate
Fieldham
Sussex TN21 4AF
Tel: 01829 654545
Fax: 01829 654646

Deliver to:
As above

Invoice no:	06116
Tax point:	18 April 20X1
VAT reg no:	466 1128 30
Purchase order no:	77121

Code	Description	Quantity	VAT rate %	Unit price £	Amount excl of VAT £
B4012	Bento Keyboard	3	17.5	180.00	540.00
Z2060	Zanni Keyboard	6	17.5	164.00	984.00
					1,524.00
Trade discount 20%					304.80
					1,219.20
VAT at 17.5%					206.95
Total amount payable					1,426.15

Deduct discount of 3% if paid within 10 days, net 30 days

INVOICE

Keyboard Supplies

Invoice to:
M T Retail
Fraser House
Perley TN7 8QT

Trench Park Estate
Fieldham
Sussex TN21 4AF
Tel: 01829 654545
Fax: 01829 654646

Deliver to:
As above

Invoice no:	06117
Tax point:	18 April 20X1
VAT reg no:	466 1128 30
Purchase order no:	PO4648

Code	Description	Quantity	VAT rate %	Unit price £	Amount excl of VAT £
A6060	Atol Keyboard	1	17.5	210.00	210.00
Z4080	Zanni Keyboard	1	17.5	325.00	325.00
					535.00

VAT at 17.5% 93.62

Total amount payable 628.62

Net 30 days

INVOICE

Keyboard Supplies

Invoice to:
Hammer & Co
1 Acre Street
Nutford TN11 6HA

Trench Park Estate
Fieldham
Sussex TN21 4AF
Tel: 01829 654545
Fax: 01829 654646

Deliver to:
As above

Invoice no:	06118
Tax point:	18 April 20X1
VAT reg no:	466 1128 30
Purchase order no:	7486

Code	Description	Quantity	VAT rate %	Unit price £	Amount excl of VAT £
G4326	Garland Keyboard	3	17.5	98.00	294.00
B2040	Bento Keyboard	5	17.5	115.00	575.00
					869.00

VAT at 17.5% 147.51

Total amount payable 1,016.51

Deduct discount of 3% if paid within 10 days, net 30 days

Sales day book									
Date	Invoice no	Customer name	Code	Total £	VAT £	01 £	02 £	03 £	04 £

Activity 24

Graham Haddow runs a buildings maintenance and decorating business and sends out invoices for the work that he has done. He analyses his sales between the maintenance work and decorating work. You are given three sales invoices that he sent out last week.

Required

Enter the sales invoice details into the analysed sales day book given and total all of the columns.

INVOICE

Graham Haddow

Invoice to:
Portman & Co
Portman House
Tonbridge TN1 4LL

59 East Street
Medford
MF6 7TL
Tel: 0122 280496

Invoice no:	07891
Tax point:	1 May 20X1
VAT reg no:	431 7992 06
Your reference:	P2

	Amount excl of VAT £
Repair of window	66.00
Clearing of guttering	73.00
	139.00
VAT at 17.5%	23.83
Total amount payable	162.83

Deduct discount of 2% if paid within 14 days, net 30 days

INVOICE

Graham Haddow

Invoice to:
Stanton Associates
323 Main Road
Tonbridge TN1 6el

59 East Street
Medford
MF6 7TL
Tel: 0122 280496

Invoice no:	07892
Tax point:	3 May 20X1
VAT reg no:	431 7992 06
Your reference:	S3

	Amount excl of VAT £
Decoration of meeting room	1,100.00
VAT at 17.5%	188.65
Total amount payable	1,288.65

Deduct discount of 2% if paid within 14 days, net 30 days

INVOICE

Invoice to:
Boreham Bros
40/54 Hill Drive
Medford MF2 8AT

Graham Haddow
59 East Street
Medford
MF6 7TL
Tel: 0122 280496

Invoice no:	07893
Tax point:	5 May 20X1
VAT reg no:	431 7992 06
Your reference:	B7

	Amount excl of VAT £
Repair of door frames	106.00
Re-decorating of door frames	130.00
	236.00
VAT at 17.5%	41.30
Total amount payable	277.30

Sales day book

Date	Invoice no	Customer name	Code	Total £	VAT £	Maintenance £	Decorating £

Activity 25

Given below is an analysed sales day book.

Required

Total the sales day book and check that the totals cross-cast.

				Sales day book			
Date	Invoice no	Customer name	Code	Total £	VAT £	Group 01 £	Group 02 £
20X0							
1 Feb	61612	Worker Ltd	SL11	217.37	32.37	68.90	116.10
4 Feb	61613	P T Associates	SL04	122.38	18.22		104.16
5 Feb	61614	Paul Bros	SL13	289.27	43.08	106.19	140.00
8 Feb	61615	S D Partners	SL07	109.54	16.31	72.40	20.83
9 Feb	61616	Harper Ltd	SL08	399.97	59.57	160.18	180.22
11 Feb	C241	P T Associates	SL04	(23.68)	(3.52)		(20.16)

Show what the entries in the sales ledger will be:

Account name	Amount £	Dr ✓	Cr ✓

Show what the entries in the main ledger will be:

Account name	Amount £	Dr ✓	Cr ✓

Activity 26

Given below is an analysed sales returns day book for the month of April.

Sales returns day book								
Date	Credit note no	Customer name	Code	Total £	VAT £	01 £	02 £	03 £
7/4	2114	Gerard & Co	G01	34.36	5.11	16.80		12.45
15/4	2115	Filmer Ltd	F02	44.92	6.69	20.41	17.82	
20/4	2116	T Harrison	H04	24.44	3.64			20.80
28/4	2117	Rolls Ltd	R01	36.47	5.43	16.80	14.24	
				140.19	20.87	54.01	32.06	33.25

Show what the entries in the sales ledger will be:

Account name	Amount £	Dr ✓	Cr ✓

Show what the entries in the main ledger will be:

Account name	Amount £	Dr ✓	Cr ✓

7 Checking receipts

 Activity 27

Simon Harris is a self-employed accountant who has a number of clients who all pay by cheque. Today's date is 5 May 20X1 and in the last week he has received the following cheques.

Required

Inspect each one carefully to ensure that it is valid and make a note of any problems that you find.

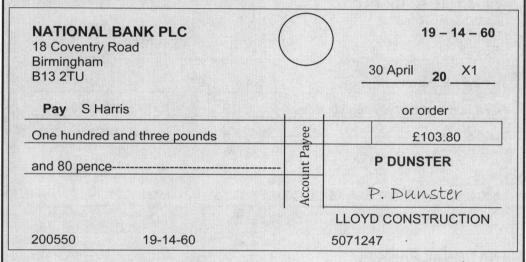

NATIONAL BANK PLC		19 – 14 – 60
18 Coventry Road Birmingham B13 2TU		30 April 20 X1

Pay   S Harris   or order

| One hundred and three pounds | | £103.80 |
| and 80 pence------------------------------------ | Account Payee | **P DUNSTER** P. Dunster LLOYD CONSTRUCTION |

200550   19-14-60   5071247

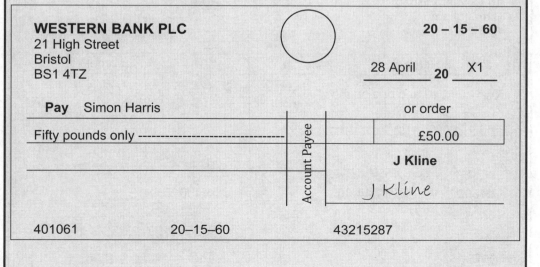

WESTERN BANK PLC		20 – 15 – 60
21 High Street Bristol BS1 4TZ		28 April 20 X1

Pay   Simon Harris   or order

| Fifty pounds only -------------------------------- | Account Payee | £50.00 |
| | | **J Kline** J Kline |

401061   20–15–60   43215287

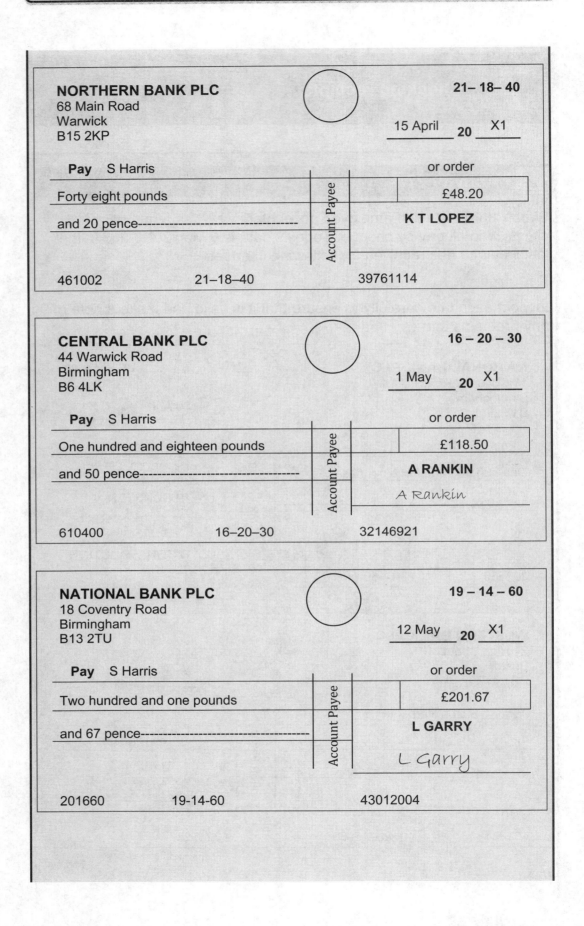

NORTHERN BANK PLC
68 Main Road
Warwick
B15 2KP

21– 18– 40

15 April   20   X1

Pay   S Harris   or order

Account Payee

Forty eight pounds   £48.20

and 20 pence------------------------------------   **K T LOPEZ**

461002   21–18–40   39761114

CENTRAL BANK PLC
44 Warwick Road
Birmingham
B6 4LK

16 – 20 – 30

1 May   20   X1

Pay   S Harris   or order

Account Payee

One hundred and eighteen pounds   £118.50

and 50 pence------------------------------------   **A RANKIN**

A Rankin

610400   16–20–30   32146921

NATIONAL BANK PLC
18 Coventry Road
Birmingham
B13 2TU

19 – 14 – 60

12 May   20   X1

Pay   S Harris   or order

Account Payee

Two hundred and one pounds   £201.67

and 67 pence------------------------------------   **L GARRY**

L Garry

201660   19-14-60   43012004

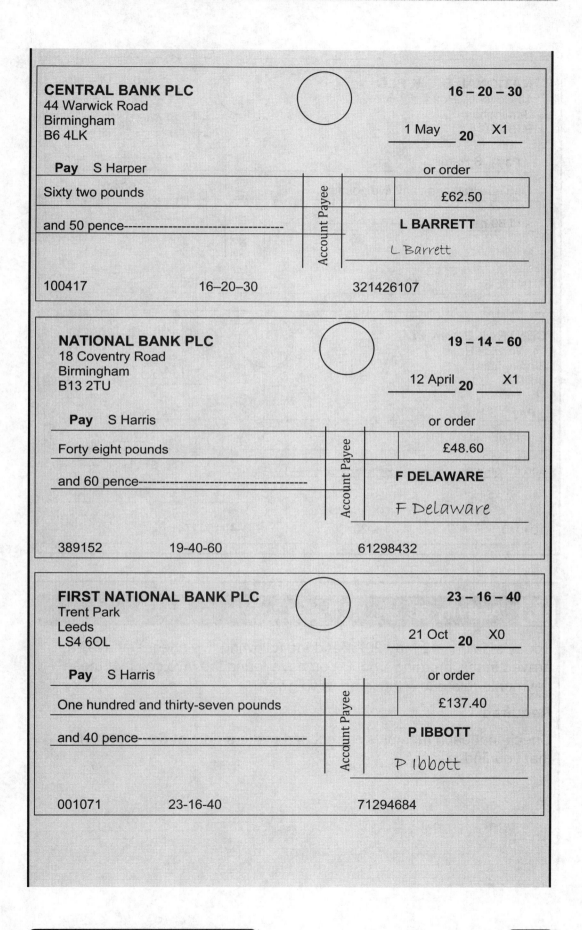

CENTRAL BANK PLC
44 Warwick Road
Birmingham
B6 4LK

16 – 20 – 30

1 May 20 X1

Pay   S Harper

or order

Sixty two pounds

Account Payee

£62.50

and 50 pence-----------------------------------

L BARRETT

L Barrett

100417   16–20–30   321426107

NATIONAL BANK PLC
18 Coventry Road
Birmingham
B13 2TU

19 – 14 – 60

12 April 20 X1

Pay   S Harris

or order

Forty eight pounds

Account Payee

£48.60

and 60 pence---------------------------------------

F DELAWARE

F Delaware

389152   19-40-60   61298432

FIRST NATIONAL BANK PLC
Trent Park
Leeds
LS4 6OL

23 – 16 – 40

21 Oct 20 X0

Pay   S Harris

or order

One hundred and thirty-seven pounds

Account Payee

£137.40

and 40 pence---------------------------------------

P IBBOTT

P Ibbott

001071   23-16-40   71294684

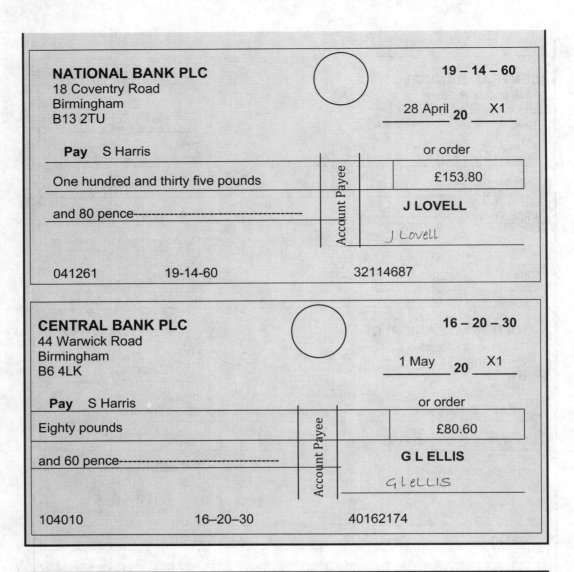

NATIONAL BANK PLC
18 Coventry Road
Birmingham
B13 2TU

19 – 14 – 60

28 April 20 X1

Pay   S Harris   or order

One hundred and thirty five pounds   £153.80

and 80 pence-------------------------------------   **J LOVELL**

Account Payee

J Lovell

041261   19-14-60   32114687

CENTRAL BANK PLC
44 Warwick Road
Birmingham
B6 4LK

16 – 20 – 30

1 May 20 X1

Pay   S Harris   or order

Eighty pounds   £80.60

and 60 pence-------------------------------------   **G L ELLIS**

Account Payee

G L ELLIS

104010   16–20–30   40162174

Activity 28

Today's date is 12 May 20X1 and the following five cheques have
arrived in this morning's post. You have found the invoices that these
payments relate to – these are also given.

Required

Check that each receipt is correct and make a note of any problems
that you find.

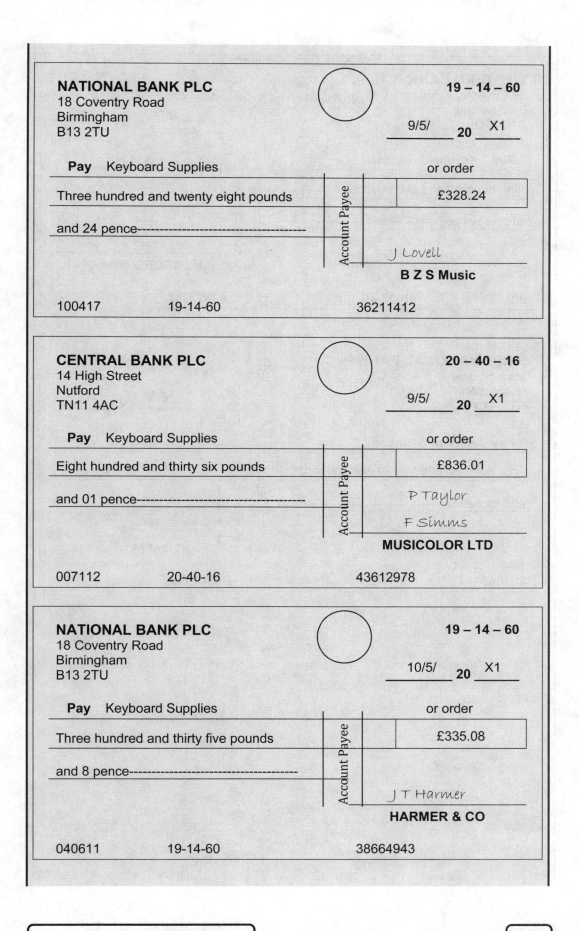

NATIONAL BANK PLC
18 Coventry Road
Birmingham
B13 2TU

19 – 14 – 60

9/5/ 20 X1

Pay   Keyboard Supplies

or order

Three hundred and twenty eight pounds

£328.24

and 24 pence--------------------------------------

Account Payee

J Lovell

B Z S Music

100417   19-14-60   36211412

CENTRAL BANK PLC
14 High Street
Nutford
TN11 4AC

20 – 40 – 16

9/5/ 20 X1

Pay   Keyboard Supplies

or order

Eight hundred and thirty six pounds

£836.01

and 01 pence-------------------------------------

Account Payee

P Taylor

F Simms

MUSICOLOR LTD

007112   20-40-16   43612978

NATIONAL BANK PLC
18 Coventry Road
Birmingham
B13 2TU

19 – 14 – 60

10/5/ 20 X1

Pay   Keyboard Supplies

or order

Three hundred and thirty five pounds

£335.08

and 8 pence--------------------------------------

Account Payee

J T Harmer

HARMER & CO

040611   19-14-60   38664943

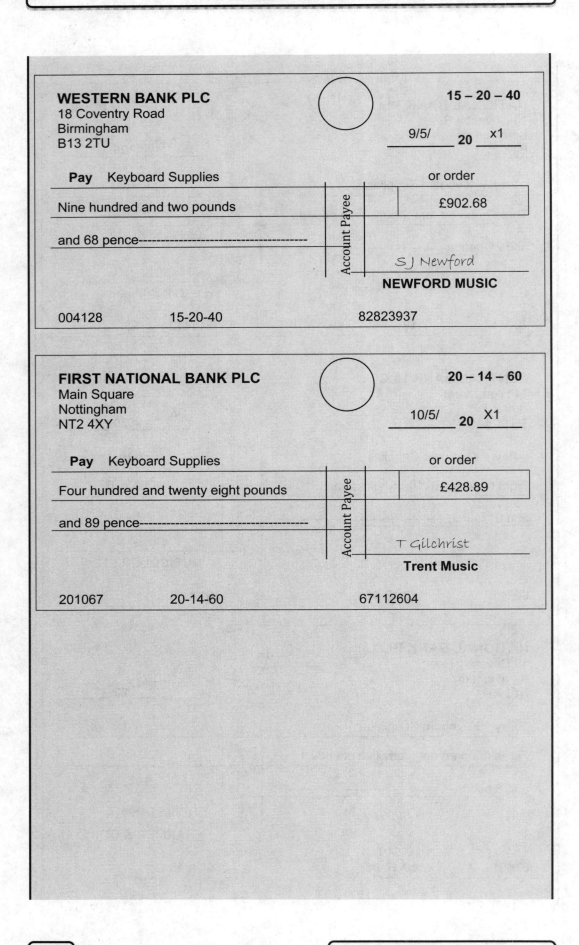

WESTERN BANK PLC
18 Coventry Road
Birmingham
B13 2TU

15 – 20 – 40

9/5/ 20 x1

Pay Keyboard Supplies   or order

Nine hundred and two pounds   £902.68

and 68 pence--------------------------------------

Account Payee

S J Newford
NEWFORD MUSIC

004128   15-20-40   82823937

FIRST NATIONAL BANK PLC
Main Square
Nottingham
NT2 4XY

20 – 14 – 60

10/5/ 20 X1

Pay Keyboard Supplies   or order

Four hundred and twenty eight pounds   £428.89

and 89 pence--------------------------------------

Account Payee

T Gilchrist
Trent Music

201067   20-14-60   67112604

INVOICE

Invoice to:
BZS Music
42 Westhill
Nutford TN11 3PQ

Keyboard Supplies
Trench Park Estate
Fieldham
Sussex TN21 4AF
Tel: 01829 654545
Fax: 01829 654646

Deliver to:

Invoice no:	06180
Tax point:	3 May 20X1
VAT reg no:	466 1128 30
Your reference:	SL01
Purchase order no:	77147

Code	Description	Quantity	VAT rate %	Unit price £	Amount excl of VAT £
B4012	Bento Keyboard	2	17.5	180.00	360.00
					360.00
Trade discount 20%					72.00
					288.00
VAT at 17.5%					48.88
Total amount payable					336.88

Deduct discount of 3% if paid within 10 days, net 30 days

INVOICE

Invoice to:
Musicolor Ltd
23 High Street
Nutford TN11 4 TZ

Keyboard Supplies
Trench Park Estate
Fieldham
Sussex TN21 4AF
Tel: 01829 654545
Fax: 01829 654646

Deliver to:

As above

Invoice no:	06176
Tax point:	1 May 20X1
VAT reg no:	466 1128 30
Your reference:	SL06
Purchase order no:	6362

Code	Description	Quantity	VAT rate %	Unit price £	Amount excl of VAT £
Z4600	Zanni Keyboard	3	17.5	185.00	555.00
A4802	Atol Keyboard	2	17.5	130.00	260.00
					815.00
Trade discount 10%					81.50
					733.50
VAT at 17.5%					124.51
Total amount payable					858.01

Deduct discount of 3% if paid within 10 days, net 30 days

INVOICE

Invoice to:
Harmer & Co
1 Acre Street
Nutford TN11 0HA

Keyboard Supplies
Trench Park Estate
Fieldham
Sussex TN21 4AF
Tel: 01829 654545
Fax: 01829 654646

Deliver to:

As above

Invoice no:	06183
Tax point:	3 May 20X1
VAT reg no:	466 1128 30
Your reference:	SL17
Purchase order no:	047786

Code	Description	Quantity	VAT rate %	Unit price £	Amount excl of VAT £
G4326	Garland Keyboard	3	17.5	98.00	294.00
					294.00

VAT at 17.5%	49.90
Total amount payable	343.90

Deduct discount of 3% if paid within 10 days, net 30 days

INVOICE

Keyboard Supplies

Invoice to:
Newford Music
32/34 Main Street
Welland
Sussex TN4 6BD

Trench Park Estate
Fieldham
Sussex TN21 4AF
Tel: 01829 654545
Fax: 01829 654646

Deliver to:

As above

Invoice no:	06171
Tax point:	30 April 20X1
VAT reg no:	466 1128 30
Your reference:	SL18
Purchase order no:	47202

Code	Description	Quantity	VAT rate %	Unit price £	Amount excl of VAT £
Z4406	Zanni Keyboard	6	17.5	165.00	990.00
					990.00
Trade discount 20%					198.00
					792.00
VAT at 17.5%					134.44
Total amount payable					926.44

Deduct discount of 3% if paid within 10 days, net 30 days

INVOICE

Keyboard Supplies

Invoice to:
Trent Music
Trent House
Main Street
Fieldham TN21 6ZF

Trench Park Estate
Fieldham
Sussex TN21 4AF
Tel: 01829 654545
Fax: 01829 654646

Deliver to:

Invoice no:	06184
Tax point:	3 May 20X1
VAT reg no:	466 1128 30
Your reference:	SL41
Purchase order no:	93754

Code	Description	Quantity	VAT rate %	Unit price £	Amount excl of VAT £
G4030	Garland Keyboard	4	17.5	105.00	420.00
					420.00
Trade discount 10%					42.00
					378.00
VAT at 17.5%					64.16
Total amount payable					442.16

Deduct discount of 3% if paid within 10 days, net 30 days

8 The analysed cash receipts book

 Activity 29

Your organisation receives a number of cheques from debtors through the post each day and these are listed on the cheque listing. It also makes some sales to non-credit customers each day which include VAT at the standard rate and are paid for by cheque.

Today's date is 28 April 20X1 and the cash receipts book is given below:

			Cash receipts book				
Date	Narrative	SL Code	Discount £	Bank £	SLCA £	Sales £	VAT £
20X1							
28/4	G Heilbron	SL04		108.45	108.45		
	L Tessa	SL15	3.31	110.57	110.57		
	J Dent	SL17	6.32	210.98	210.98		
	F Trainer	SL21		97.60	97.60		
	A Winter	SL09	3.16	105.60	105.60		
	Non-credit sales			265.08		225.60	39.48
			12.79	898.28	633.20	225.60	39.48

Required

Show what the entries in the sales ledger will be:

Account name	Amount £	Dr ✓	Cr ✓

Show what the entries in the main ledger will be:

Account name	Amount £	Dr ✓	Cr ✓

Activity 30

Given below is the debit side of the cash book completed for transactions that took place on 15th May:

Cash Book – Debit side				
Date	Narrative	SL Code	Discount £	Bank £
20X1				
15/5	McCaul & Partners	M04	2.95	147.56
	P Martin	M02		264.08
	F Little	L03		167.45
	D Raine	R01	7.97	265.89
			10.92	844.98

Required

Show what the entries in the sales ledger will be:

Account name	Amount £	Dr ✓	Cr ✓

Show what the entries in the main ledger will be:

Account name	Amount £	Dr ✓	Cr ✓

9 Debtors Statements

 Activity 31

You work in the accounts department of Farmhouse Pickles Ltd and given below are two debtors' accounts from the sales ledger.

Grant & Co					SL07
		£			£
1 April	Balance b/d	337.69	12 April	SRDB – 0335	38.70
4 April	SDB 32656	150.58	20 April	CRB	330.94
18 April	SDB 32671	179.52	20 April	CRB – discount	6.75
25 April	SDB 32689	94.36	24 April	SRDB – 0346	17.65

Mitchell Partners					SL10
		£			£
1 April	Balance b/d	180.46	12 April	SRDB – 0344	66.89
7 April	SDB 32662	441.57	21 April	CRB	613.58
20 April	SDB 32669	274.57	21 April	CRB – discount	8.45

Required

Prepare statements to be sent to each of these customers at the end of April 20X1 on the blank statements provided.

F A R M H O U S E
PICKLES
LTD

225 School Lane
Weymouth
Dorset
WE36 5NR
Tel: 0261 480444
Fax: 0261 480555
Date:

To:

STATEMENT

Date	Transaction	Debit £	Credit £	Balance £

May we remind you that our credit terms are 30 days

To:

FARMHOUSE PICKLES LTD

225 School Lane
Weymouth
Dorset
WE36 5NR
Tel: 0261 480444
Fax: 0261 480555
Date:

STATEMENT

Date	Transaction	Debit £	Credit £	Balance £

May we remind you that our credit terms are 30 days

Activity 32

Shown below is a customer's account from the sales ledger of Ryan's Toy Shop Ltd, along with a statement of account to be sent to that customer.

Arnold's Toys Ltd							
Dr							Cr
Date	Transaction	£		Date	Transaction	£	
19/11	Invoice 2195	118	08	20/11	Credit note 2198	323	60
20/11	Invoice 2198	2,201	95	22/11	Cheque c/f	118	08
		2,320	03			2,320	03
23/11	b/f	1,996	43				

Required

Complete the statement of account below.

Ryan's Toy Shop LTD
125 Finchley Way Bristol BS1 4PL Tel: 01272 200299

STATEMENT OF ACCOUNT

Customer name: Arnold's Toys Ltd
Customer address: 14 High Street, Bristol, BS2 5FL

Statement date 1st December		Amount		Balance	
Date	Transaction	£	p	£	P

10 Consolidation – sales

 Activity 33

Diana Moore is the owner of a business called The Last Bite.

You are employed by the business as a bookkeeper.

The business uses a manual accounting system.

Double entry takes place in the main ledger. Individual accounts of debtors and creditors are kept in the sales ledger and purchases ledger as memorandum accounts.

Assume today's date is 30 November 20X9, unless you are told otherwise.

Balances at the start of the date on 30 November 20X9

Credit customers

	Tony's	5,600
	Bella's	1,860
	Jasper's	14,228
	Jack's	25,000
Cash		1,495
Sales		74,472
Sales returns		1,110
Sales ledger control		71,047
Discount allowed		1,210
VAT (credit balance)		11,047

Task 1

Enter the opening balances above into the 'T' accounts given.

Transactions

The following transactions took place on 30 November 20X9 and have been entered into the daybooks below:

Sales day book					
Date	Details	Inv. No.	Total £	VAT £	Net £
30/11/X9	Tony's	879	18,330	2,730	15,600
30/11/X9	Bella's	880	1,175	175	1,000
30/11/X9	Jasper's	881	3,525	525	3,000
30/11/X9	Jack's	882	4,230	630	3,600
			27,260	4,060	23,200

Sales returns day book					
Date	Details	Credit No.	Total £	VAT £	Net £
30/11/X9	Bella's	16	1,410	210	1,200
30/11/X9	Jack's	17	423	63	360
			1,833	273	1,560

Cash receipts book					
Date	Details	Total £	SLCA £	VAT £	Cash sales £	Discount allowed £
30/11/X9	Jack's	6,600	6,600			132
30/11/X9	Cash sale	470		70	400	
		7,070	6,600	70	400	132

Task 2

From the daybooks and cash book shown, make the relevant entries into the accounts in the main ledger and the sales ledger.

Task 3

Balance the accounts showing clearly the balances carried down at 30 November and brought down at 1 December.

Task 4

List the balances you have calculated in Task 3 in the trial balance.

Sales ledger

Tony's					
Date	**Details**	**£**	**Date**	**Detail**	**£**

Bella's					
Date	**Details**	**£**	**Date**	**Detail**	**£**

KAPLAN PUBLISHING

Jasper's

Date	Details	£	Date	Detail	£

Jack's

Date	Details	£	Date	Detail	£

Main ledger

Cashbook

Date	Details	£	Date	Detail	£

Sales					
Date	**Details**	**£**	**Date**	**Detail**	**£**

Sales returns					
Date	**Details**	**£**	**Date**	**Detail**	**£**

Sales ledger control					
Date	**Details**	**£**	**Date**	**Detail**	**£**

KAPLAN PUBLISHING

Discounts allowed					
Date	Details	£	Date	Detail	£

VAT					
Date	Details	£	Date	Detail	£

Other balances

Fixtures & Fittings	11,400
Motor vehicles	21,485
Stock	5,400
Petty cash control	150
Capital	25,000
Loan from bank	20,000
Discounts received	144
Purchases	11,756
Purchases returns	487
Purchases ledger control	19,432
Motor expenses	1,940
Wages	19,450
Rent	1,100
Heat & light	876
Stationery	331
Telephone	794
Insurance	411
Miscellaneous expenses	627

Task 5

List the remaining balances shown above in the trial balance and total each column.

Trial balance

	Dr £	Cr £
Cashbook		
Sales		
Sales returns		
Sales ledger control		
Discounts allowed		
VAT		
Fixtures & Fittings		
Motor vehicles		
Stock		
Petty cash control		
Capital		
Loan from bank		
Discounts received		
Purchases		
Purchases returns		
Purchases ledger control		
Motor expenses		
Wages		
Rent		
Heat & light		
Stationery		
Telephone		
Insurance		
Miscellaneous expenses		
Totals		

KAPLAN PUBLISHING

11 Credit purchases – documents

Activity 34

Nethan Builders have just received the following credit note. You are required to check that the credit note is clerically accurate and note the details of any problems. Trade discount is 15%.

CREDIT NOTE

Credit note to:
Nethan Builders
Brecon House
Stamford Road
Manchester
M16 4PL

J M Bond & Co
North Park Industrial Estate
Manchester
M12 4TU
Tel: 0161 561 3214
Fax: 0161 561 3060

Credit note no: 06192
Tax point: 22 April 20X1
VAT reg no: 461 4367 91
Invoice no: 331624

Code	Description	Quantity	VAT rate %	Unit price £	Amount excl of VAT £
DGSS4163	Structural softwood untreated	6 m	17.5	6.85	41.10

	41.10
Trade discount 15%	8.22
	32.88
VAT at 17.5%	5.75
Total amount of credit	38.63

Activity 35

You work in the accounts department of Nethan Builders and given below are three purchase invoices together with the related purchase orders and delivery note. You are to check each invoice carefully and note any problems or discrepancies that you find. You may assume that the rates of trade and settlement discounts are correct.

INVOICE

Invoice to:
Nethan Builders
Brecon House
Stamford Road
Manchester
M16 4PL

A J Broom & Company Limited
59 Parkway
Manchester
M2 6EG
Tel: 0161 560 3392
Fax: 0161 560 5322

Deliver to:
As above

Invoice no:	046123
Tax point:	22 April 20X1
VAT reg no:	661 2359 07
Purchase order no::	7164

Code	Description	Quantity	VAT rate %	Unit price £	Amount excl of VAT £
DGS472	SDG Softwood	9.6 m	17.5	8.44	81.02
CIBF653	Joist hanger	7	17.5	12.30	86.10
					167.12
Trade discount 10%					16.71
					150.41
VAT at 17.5%					26.32
Total amount payable					176.73

INVOICE

Invoice to:
Nethan Builders
Brecon House
Stamford Road
Manchester
M16 4PL

Jenson Ltd
30 Longfield Park
Kingsway
M45 2TP

Invoice no: 47792
Tax point: 22 April 20X1
VAT reg no: 641 3229 45
Purchase order no:: 7162

Deliver to:
As above

Code	Description	Quantity	VAT rate %	Unit price £	Amount excl of VAT £
PL432115	Door lining set 32 × 115 mm	14	17.5	30.25	423.50
PL432140	Door lining set 32 × 138 mm	8	17.5	33.15	265.20

	688.70
Trade discount 15%	103.30
	585.40
VAT at 17.5%	102.44
Total amount payable	687.84

Deduct discount of 3% if paid within 14 days

INVOICE

Haddow Bros

Invoice to:
Nethan Builders
Brecon House
Stamford Road
Manchester
M16 4PL

The White House
Standing Way
Manchester
M13 6FH
Tel: 0161 560 3140
Fax: 0161 560 5140

Deliver to:
As above

Invoice no: 033912
Tax point: 22 April 20X1
VAT reg no: 460 3559 71
Purchase order no:: 7166

Code	Description	Quantity	VAT rate %	Unit price £	Amount excl of VAT £
PLY8FE1	Plywood Hardwood 2440 × 1220 mm	12 sheets	17.5	17.80	213.60

	213.60
VAT at 17.5%	36.63
Total amount payable	250.23

Deduct discount of 2% if paid within 10 days

PURCHASE ORDER

Nethan Builders
Brecon House
Stamford Road
Manchester
M16 4PL

To: Jenson Ltd
       30 Longfield Park
       Kingsway
       M45 2TP

Tel: 0161 521 6411
Fax: 0161 521 6
Date: 14 April 20X1
Purchase order no: 7162

Delivery address
(If different fs from above)

Invoice address
(If different from above)

Code	Quantity	Description	Unit price (exclusive of VAT)
			£
PL432140	8	Door lining set 32 × 138 mm	33.15
PL432115	14	Door lining set 32 × 115 mm	30.25

PURCHASE ORDER

Nethan Builders
Brecon House
Stamford Road
Manchester
M16 4PL

To: A J Broom & Co Ltd
       59 Parkway
       Manchester
       M2 6EG

Tel: 0161 521 6411
Fax: 0161 521 6
Date: 14 April 20X1
Purchase order no: 7164

Delivery address
(If different from above)

Invoice address
(If different from above)

Code	Quantity	Description	Unit price (exclusive of VAT)
			£
DGS472	9.6 m	SDG Softwood	8.44
CIBF653	5	Joist hanger	12.30

PURCHASE ORDER

Nethan Builders
Brecon House
Stamford Road
Manchester
M16 4PL

To: Haddow Bros
The White House
Standing Way
Manchester
M13 6FH

Tel: 0161 521 6411
Fax: 0161 521 6
Date: 14 April 20X1
Purchase order no: 7165

Delivery address (If different from above)	Invoice address (If different from above)

Code	Quantity	Description	Unit price (exclusive of VAT)
			£
PLY8FE1	12 sheets	Plywood Hardwood 2440 × 1220 mm	17.80

DELIVERY NOTE

Jenson Ltd
30 Longfield Park
Kingsway
M45 2TP
Tel: 0161 511 4666
Fax: 0161 511 4777

Deliver to:
Nethan Builders
Brecon House
Stamford Road
Manchester
M16 4PL

Delivery note no: 47823
Tax point: 19 April 20X1
VAT reg no: 641 3229 45

Code	Description	Quantity	VAT rate %	Unit price £	Amount excl of VAT £
PL432115	Door lining set 32 × 115 mm	14			
PL432140	Door lining set 32 × 138 mm	8			

Goods received in good condition

Print name	C JULIAN
Signature	C JULIAN
Date	19/4/X1

DELIVERY NOTE

A.J. Broom & Company Limited

Deliver to:
Nethan Builders
Brecon House
Stamford Road
Manchester
M16 4PL

59 Parkway
Manchester
M2 6EG
Tel: 0161 560 3392
Fax: 0161 560 5322

Delivery note no:	076429
Tax point:	20 April 20X1
VAT reg no:	661 2359 07
Purchase order no:	7164

Code	Description	Quantity	VAT rate %	Unit price £	Amount excl of VAT £
CIBF653	Joist hanger	7			
DGS472	SDG Softwood	9.6 m			

Goods received in good condition

Print name	C JULIAN
Signature	C JULIAN
Date	19/4/X1

DELIVERY NOTE

Haddow Bros

Deliver to:
Nethan Builders
Brecon House
Stamford Road
Manchester
M16 4PL

The White House
Standing Way
Manchester
M13 6FH
Tel: 0161 560 3140
Fax: 0161 560 6140

Delivery note no:	667713
Tax point:	17 April 20X1
VAT reg no:	460 3559 71

Code	Description	Quantity	VAT rate %	Unit price £	Amount excl of VAT £
PLY8FE1	Plywood Hardwood 2440 × 1220 mm	10			

Goods received in good condition

Print name	C JULIAN
Signature	C JULIAN
Date	17/4/X1

Activity 36

Nethan Builders codes all purchase invoices and credit notes with a supplier code and a general ledger code. Codes from their accounting system are given below:

Supplier	Supplier Account Code
Haddow Bros	HAD29
AJ Broom & Company Ltd	AJB14
Jenson Ltd	JEN32
JM Bond & Co	JMB33

Item	General Ledger Code
Softwood	GL110
Hardwood	GL112
Sand	GL130
Steel	GL140
Brick	GL145

Required

For each of the invoices and credit notes shown below select the appropriate supplier account code and general ledger code to be used to code them.

INVOICE

Haddow Bros

Invoice to:
Nethan Builders
Brecon House
Stamford Road
Manchester
M16 4PL

Deliver to:
As above

The White House, Standing Way, Manchester
M13 6FH
Tel: 0161 560 3140
Fax: 0161 560 5140

Invoice no: 033912
Tax point: 22 April 20X1
VAT reg no: 460 3559 71
Purchase order no:: 7166

Code	Description	Quantity	VAT rate %	Unit price £	Amount excl of VAT £
PLY8FE1	Plywood Hardwood 2440 × 1220 mm	12 sheets	17.5	17.80	213.60
					213.60
VAT at 17.5%					36.63
Total amount payable					250.23
Deduct discount of 2% if paid within 10 days					

INVOICE

Invoice to:
Nethan Builders
Brecon House
Stamford Road
Manchester
M16 4PL

Deliver to:
As above

Jenson Ltd
30 Longfield Park, Kingsway, M45 2TP

Invoice no:	47792
Tax point:	22 April 20X1
VAT reg no:	641 3229 45
Purchase order no:: 7162	

Code	Description	Quantity	VAT rate %	Unit price £	Amount excl of VAT £
PL432115	Steel rods 32 × 115 mm	14	17.5	30.25	423.50
PL432140	Steel rods 32 × 138 mm	8	17.5	33.15	265.20
					688.70
Trade discount 15%					103.30
					585.40
VAT at 17.5%					99.37
Total amount payable					684.77

Deduct discount of 3% if paid within 14 days

INVOICE

Invoice to:
Nethan Builders
Brecon House
Stamford Road
Manchester
M16 4PL

Deliver to:
As above

A J Broom & Company Limited
59 Parkway, Manchester, M2 6EG
Tel: 0161 560 3392
Fax: 0161 560 5322

Invoice no:	046123
Tax point:	22 April 20X1
VAT reg no:	661 2359 07
Purchase order no:: 7164	

Code	Description	Quantity	VAT rate %	Unit price £	Amount excl of VAT £
DGS472	SDG Softwood	9.6 m	17.5	8.44	81.02
CIBF653	BIC Softwood	7	17.5	12.30	86.10
					167.12
Trade discount 10%					16.71
					150.41
VAT at 17.5%					26.32
Total amount payable					176.73

CREDIT NOTE

J M Bond & Co

Credit note to:
Nethan Builders
Brecon House
Stamford Road
Manchester
M16 4PL

North Park Industrial Estate, Manchester, M12 4TU
Tel: 0161 561 3214
Fax: 0161 561 3060

Credit note no: 06192
Tax point: 22 April 20X1
VAT reg no: 461 4367 91
Invoice no: 331624

Code	Description	Quantity	VAT rate %	Unit price £	Amount excl of VAT £
DGSS4163	Sand	2000 kg	17.5	6.85	41.10
					41.10
Trade discount 15%					8.22
					32.88
VAT at 17.5%					5.75
Total amount of credit					38.63

12   Credit purchases – discounts and VAT

 Activity 37

Calculate the VAT for the following:

(a)   X purchases £400 goods from Y net of VAT.

(b)   X purchases £650 goods from Y net of VAT.

(c)   X purchases £425 goods from Y including VAT.

(d)   X purchases £77 goods from Y including VAT.

Activity 38

Calculate the VAT on the following:

(a) X purchases £850 goods from Y and takes the 3% settlement discount offered.

(b) X purchases £600 goods from Y and takes the 5% settlement discount offered.

(c) X purchases £325 goods from Y and does not take the 2% settlement discount offered.

(d) X purchases £57 goods from Y and does not take the 4% settlement discount offered.

 Activity 39

Z buys £600 of goods net of VAT from A and takes the 3% settlement discount offered.

Post these transactions in the ledger accounts of Z.

13 The purchases day book – main and purchases ledgers

 Activity 40

Curtain Decor is a business that makes curtains and blinds to order. Its purchases are analysed between fabric purchases, header tape purchases and others. A separate purchases returns day book is not kept so any credit notes received are recorded as negative amounts in the purchases day book. The business only has five credit suppliers and they are as follows:

Mainstream Fabrics	PL01
C R Thorne	PL02
Fabric Supplies Ltd	PL03
Lillian Fisher	PL04
Headstream & Co	PL05

Today's date is 12 April 20X1 and given below are three invoices and a credit note. These are to be entered into the analysed purchases day book and each column is to be totalled.

INVOICE

Fabric Supplies Ltd

Invoice to:
Curtain Décor
Field House
Warren Lane
Hawkhurst TN23 1AT

12/14 Tike Road
Wadfield
TN11 4ZP
Tel: 01882 467111
Fax: 01882 467112

Deliver to:

As above

Invoice no:	06783
Tax point:	7 April 20X1
VAT reg no:	532 6741 09

Code	Description	Quantity	VAT rate %	Unit price £	Amount excl of VAT £
B116-14	Header Tape 14cm	30 m	17.5	4.62	138.60
P480-G	Fabric – Green	56 m	17.5	14.25	798.00
					936.60

VAT at 17.5%	160.62
Total amount payable	1,097.22

Deduct discount of 2% if paid within 10 days

INVOICE

Invoice to:
Curtain Décor
Field House
Warren Lane
Hawkhurst TN23 1AT

Lillian Fisher
61 Park Crescent
Hawkhurst
TN23 8GF
Tel: 01868 463501
Fax: 01868 463502

Deliver to:

As above

Invoice no: 0328
Tax point: 6 April 20X1
VAT reg no: 469 7153 20

Code	Description	Quantity	VAT rate %	Unit price £	Amount excl of VAT £
TB06	Tie Back Cord – Yellow	10 m	17.5	6.55	65.50
TB09	Tie Back Cord – Green	4 m	17.5	6.55	26.20
					91.70
VAT at 17.5%					16.04
Total amount payable					107.74

CREDIT NOTE

Credit note to:
Curtain Décor
Field House
Warren Lane
Hawkhurst TN23 1AT

Headstream & Co
140 Myrtle Place
Fenham
TN16 4SJ
Tel: 01842 303136
Fax: 01842 303137

Credit note no: CN0477
Tax point: 7 April 20X1
VAT reg no: 663 4892 77

Code	Description	Quantity	VAT rate %	Unit price £	Amount excl of VAT £
HT479	Header Tape 22 cm	2 m	17.5	8.30	16.60
CCF614Y	CC Fabric – Yellow	4 m	17.5	12.85	51.40
					68.00
VAT at 17.5%					11.90
Total credit					79.90

INVOICE

Mainstream Fabrics

Invoice to:
Curtain Décor
Field House
Warren Lane
Hawkhurst TN23 1AT

Tree Tops House
Farm Road
Tonbridge
TN2 4XT
Tel: 01883 214121
Fax: 01883 214122

Deliver to:

As above

Invoice no: 07359
Tax point: 8 April 20X1
VAT reg no: 379 4612 04

Code	Description	Quantity	VAT rate %	Unit price £	Amount excl of VAT £
DG4167F	Design Guild Fabric – Fuchsia	23 m	17.5	13.60	312.80
					312.80
Trade discount 10%					31.28
					281.52
VAT at 17.5%					48.52
Total amount payable					330.04

Deduct discount of 1½% if paid within 14 days

Purchases day book								
Date	Invoice no	Code	Supplier	Total	VAT	Fabric	Header tape	Other

Activity 41

Kingdon Builders analyse their purchases into wood, bricks and cement, and small consumables such as nails and screws. You are given three purchase invoices, recently received, to enter into the purchases day book given.

An extract from the purchase ledger coding manual is given:

Supplier	Purchase ledger code
JR Ryan & Co	PL08
HT Todd Plc	PL13
Magnum Supplies	PL16

Today's date is 3 May 20X1.

Enter the invoices into the analysed purchases day book and total each of the columns.

INVOICE

Invoice to:
Kingdon Builders
Brecon House
Stamford Road
Manchester
M16 4PL

Magnum Supplies
140/150 Park Estate
Manchester
M20 6EG
Tel: 0161 561 3202
Fax: 0161 561 3200

Deliver to:

As above

Invoice no:	077401
Tax point:	1 May 20X1
VAT reg no:	611 4337 90

Code	Description	Quantity	VAT rate %	Unit price £	Amount excl of VAT £
BH47732	House Bricks – Red	400	17.5	1.24	496.00
					496.00
Trade discount 15%					74.40
					421.60
VAT at 17.5%					72.30
Total amount payable					493.90

Deduct discount of 2% if paid within 10 days

KAPLAN PUBLISHING

INVOICE

Invoice to:
Kingdon Builders
Brecon House
Stamford Road
Manchester
M16 4PL

J.R. Ryan & Co
59 Parkway
Manchester
M2 6EG
Tel: 0161 560 3392
Fax: 0161 560 5322

Deliver to:

As above

Invoice no: 046193
Tax point: 1 May 20X1
VAT reg no: 661 2359 07

Code	Description	Quantity	VAT rate %	Unit price £	Amount excl of VAT £
DGT 472	SDGS Softwood 47 × 225 mm	11.2 m	17.5	8.44	94.53
NBD021	Oval Wire Nails	7 boxes	17.5	2.50	17.50
					112.03
Trade discount 10%					11.20
					100.83
VAT at 17.5%					17.64
Total amount payable					118.47

INVOICE

Invoice to:
Kingdon Builders
Brecon House
Stamford Road
Manchester
M16 4PL

HT Todd Plc
30 Longfield Park
Kingsway
M45 2TP
Tel: 0161 511 4666
Fax: 0161 511 4777

Deliver to:

As above

Invoice no:	47823
Tax point:	1 May 20X1
VAT reg no:	641 3229 45
Purchase order no:	7211

Code	Description	Quantity	VAT rate %	Unit price £	Amount excl of VAT £
PLY8FU	Plywood Hardboard	16 sheets	17.5	17.80	284.80
BU611	Ventilator Block	10	17.5	8.60	86.00
					370.80

VAT at 17.5%	62.94
Total amount payable	433.74

Deduct discount of 3% if paid within 14 days

Purchases day book

Date	Invoice no	Code	Supplier	Total	VAT	Wood	Bricks/ Cement	Consum- ables

Activity 42

Kingdon Builders have recently received the three credit notes given. They are to be recorded in the analysed purchases returns day book given.

An extract from the purchase ledger coding manual shows:

Supplier	Purchase ledger code	Settlement discount on original purchase
HT Todd Plc	PL13	3%
BL Lukey Ltd	PL03	2%
Magnum Supplies	PL16	2%

Today's date is 3 May 20X1.

You are required to enter the credit notes into the analysed purchases returns day book and to total each of the columns.

CREDIT NOTE

HT Todd Plc
30 Longfield Park
Kingsway
M45 2TP
Tel: 0161 511 4666
Fax: 0161 511 4777

Credit note to:
Kingdon Builders
Brecon House
Stamford Road
Manchester
M16 4PL

Deliver to:

As above

Credit note no:	CN06113
Tax point:	28 April 20X1
VAT reg no:	641 3229 45
Purchase order no:	47792

Code	Description	Quantity	VAT rate %	Unit price £	Amount excl of VAT £
PL432115	Door Lining Set – wood 32 × 115 mm	1	17.5	30.25	30.25
					30.25
Trade discount 15%					4.54
					25.71
VAT at 17.5%					4.36
Total amount of credit					30.07

CREDIT NOTE

BL Lukey Ltd

The White House
Standing Way
Manchester
M13 6FH
Tel: 0161 560 3140
Fax: 0161 560 6140

Credit note to:
Kingdon Builders
Brecon House
Stamford Road
Manchester
M16 4PL

Deliver to:

As above

Credit note no:				06132	
Tax point:				27 April 20X1	
VAT reg no:				460 3559 71	

Code	Description	Quantity	VAT rate %	Unit price £	Amount excl of VAT £
PLY8FE1	Plywood Hardwood 2440 × 1220 mm	2	17.5	17.80	35.60
					35.60
VAT at 17.5%					6.10
Total amount of credit					41.70

CREDIT NOTE

Magnum Supplies

140/150 Park Estate
Manchester
M20 6EG
Tel: 0161 561 3202
Fax: 0161 561 3200

Credit note to:
Kingdon Builders
Brecon House
Stamford Road
Manchester
M16 4PL

Deliver to:

As above

Credit note no:				C4163	
Tax point:				30 April 20X1	
VAT reg no:				611 4337 90	

Code	Description	Quantity	VAT rate %	Unit price £	Amount excl of VAT £
BU1628	Ventilator Brick	5	17.5	9.20	46.00
					46.00
Trade discount 15%					6.90
					39.10
VAT at 17.5%					6.70
Total amount of credit					45.80

Purchases returns day book								
Date	Credit note no	Code	Supplier	Total	VAT	Wood	Bricks/ Cement	Consum- ables

 Activity 43

Given below is a purchases returns day book.

Purchases returns day book									
Date	Credit note	Code	Supplier	Total £	VAT £	01 £	02 £	03 £	04 £
15/4/X1	C0179	PL16	J D Withers	27.49	4.09		23.40		
18/4/X1	C4772	PL06	F Williams	164.50	24.50	32.00		108.00	
19/4/X1	06638	PL13	K Bartlett	53.11	7.91	28.40			16.80
				245.10	36.50	60.40	23.40	108.00	16.80

Required

Show what the entries in the purchases ledger will be:

Account name	Amount £	Dr ✓	Cr ✓

Show what the entries in the main ledger will be:

Account name	Amount £	Dr ✓	Cr ✓

Activity 44

Given below is the purchases day book for a business.

				Total £	VAT £	Net £
PURCHASES DAY BOOK						
Date	Invoice no	Code	Supplier	Total £	VAT £	Net £
20X1						
1 May	36558	PL03	L Jameson	393.91	58.66	335.25
1 May	102785	PL07	K Davison	124.96	18.61	106. 35
3 May	92544	PL02	H Samuels	109.79	16.35	93.44
4 May	03542	PL04	G Rails	180.93	26.94	153.99
5 May	002633	PL01	T Ives	192.98	28.74	164.24
				1,002.57	149.30	853.27

Show what the entries in the purchases ledger will be:

Account name	Amount £	Dr ✓	Cr ✓

Show what the entries in the main ledger will be:

Account name	Amount £	Dr ✓	Cr ✓

14 Making Payments

 Activity 45

Given below are four invoices received by Nethan Builders that are to be paid today, 18 May 20X1. It is the business policy to take advantage of any settlement discounts possible.

You are required to complete a remittance advice for each payment.

INVOICE

Building Contract Supplies

Invoice to:
Nethan Builders
Brecon House
Stamford Road
Manchester
M16 4PL

Unit 15
Royal Estate
Manchester
M13 2EF
Tel: 0161 562 3041
Fax: 0161 562 3042

Deliver to:
As above

Invoice no: 07742
Tax point: 8 May 20X1
VAT reg no: 776 4983 06

Code	Description	Quantity	VAT rate %	Unit price £	Amount excl of VAT £
SDGSL6	SDGS Softwood 47 × 225 mm	20.5 m	17.5	8.30	170.15
					170.15

VAT at 17.5%   29.32

Total amount payable   199.47

Deduct discount of 1½% if paid within 14 days

INVOICE

Jenson Ltd
30 Longfield Park, Kingsway
M45 2TP
Tel: 0161 511 4666
Fax: 0161 511 4777

Invoice to:
Nethan Builders
Brecon House
Stamford Road
Manchester
M16 4PL

Deliver to:
As above

Invoice no:	47811
Tax point:	5 May 20X1
VAT reg no:	641 3229 45
Purchase order no:	7174

Code	Description	Quantity	VAT rate %	Unit price £	Amount excl of VAT £
PL432115	Door Lining set 32 × 115 mm	6	17.5	30.25	181.50
					181.50
Trade discount 15%					27.22
					154.28
VAT at 17.5%					26.18
Total amount payable					180.46

Deduct discount of 3% if paid within 14 days

INVOICE

Invoice to:
Nethan Builders
Brecon House
Stamford Road
Manchester
M16 4PL

Deliver to:
As above

Magnum Supplies
140/150 Park Estate
Manchester
M20 6EG
Tel: 0161 561 3202
Fax: 0161 561 3200

Invoice no:	077422
Tax point:	11 May 20X1
VAT reg no:	611 4337 90

Code	Description	Quantity	VAT rate %	Unit price £	Amount excl of VAT £
BH47732	House Bricks – Red	600	17.5	1.24	744.00
					744.00
Trade discount 15%					111.60
					632.40
VAT at 17.5%					108.45
Total amount payable					740.85

Deduct discount of 2% if paid within 10 days

INVOICE

Invoice to:
Nethan Builders
Brecon House
Stamford Road
Manchester
M16 4PL

Deliver to:
As above

Haddow Bros
The White House
Standing Way
Manchester
M13 6FH
Tel: 0161 560 3140
Fax: 0161 560 6140

Invoice no: G33940
Tax point: 9 May 20X1
VAT reg no: 460 3559 71

Code	Description	Quantity	VAT rate %	Unit price £	Amount excl of VAT £
PLY8FE1	Plywood Hardwood 2440 × 1220 mm	24	17.5	17.80	427.20
					427.20
VAT at 17.5%					73.26
Total amount payable					500.46
Deduct discount of 2% if paid within 10 days					

REMITTANCE ADVICE

To:

Nethan Builders
Brecon House
Stamford House
Manchester
M16 4PL

Tel: 0161 521 6411
Fax: 0161 530 6412
VAT Reg no: 471 3860 42
Date:

Date	Invoice no	Amount £	Discount taken £	Paid £

Total paid £

Cheque no

REMITTANCE ADVICE

To:

Nethan Builders
Brecon House
Stamford House
Manchester
M16 4PL

Tel: 0161 521 6411
Fax: 0161 530 6412
VAT Reg no: 471 3860 42
Date:

Date	Invoice no	Amount £	Discount taken £	Paid £

Total paid £

Cheque no

REMITTANCE ADVICE

To:

Nethan Builders
Brecon House
Stamford House
Manchester
M16 4PL

Tel: 0161 521 6411
Fax: 0161 530 6412
VAT Reg no: 471 3860 42
Date:

Date	Invoice no	Amount £	Discount taken £	Paid £

Total paid £

Cheque no

REMITTANCE ADVICE				

To:

Nethan Builders
Brecon House
Stamford House
Manchester
M16 4PL

Tel: 0161 521 6411
Fax: 0161 530 6412
VAT Reg no: 471 3860 42
Date:

Date	Invoice no	Amount £	Discount taken £	Paid £

Total paid   £

Cheque no

15 The analysed cash payments book

 Activity 46

Given below is the cash payments book for a business.

							CASH PAYMENTS BOOK		
Date	Details	Cheque no	Code	Discount £	Bank £	PLCA £	Cash purchases £	VAT £
12/3	Homer Ltd	03648	PL12	5.06	168.70	168.70		
	Forker & Co	03649	PL07	5.38	179.45	179.45		
	Purchases	03650			334.87		285.00	49.87
	Print Ass.	03651	PL08		190.45	190.45		
	ABG Ltd	03652	PL02	6.62	220.67	220.67		
	Purchases	03653			193.87		165.00	28.87
	G Greg	03654	PL19		67.89	67.89		
				17.06	1,355.90	827.16	450.00	78.74

Required

Show what the entries in the purchases ledger will be:

Account name	Amount £	Dr ✓	Cr ✓

Show what the entries in the main ledger will be:

Account name	Amount £	Dr ✓	Cr ✓

Activity 47

Given below is the credit side of Nethan Builders cashbook.

							CASH BOOK – CREDIT SIDE		
Date	Details	Cheque no	Code	Discount £	Bank £	PLCA £	Cash purchases £	VAT £
20X1								
30/5	J M Bond	200572	PL01		247.56	247.56		
	Magnum Supplies	200573	PL16	13.25	662.36	662.36		
	A J Broom	200574	PL08		153.57	153.57		
	Jenson Ltd	200575	PL13	6.73	336.57	336.57		
	KKL Traders	200576	PL20	8.85	442.78	442.78		
	Purchases	200577			108.66		92.48	16.18
				28.83	1,951.50	1,842.84	92.48	16.18

Required

Show what the entries in the purchases ledger will be:

Account name	Amount £	Dr ✓	Cr ✓

Show what the entries in the main ledger will be:

Account name	Amount £	Dr ✓	Cr ✓

16 The Cashbook

Activity 48

Below is Jenny's cash book for the month of March 20X9:

Date	Detail	Disc Allowed £	Bank £	Date	Detail	Bank £
01/03	Bal b/f		12534	08/03	Stationery	200
20/03	H Ltd	234	5230	11/03	Rent	1000
				21/03	Q Ltd	3561
				30/03	Insurance	450
		234	17764			5211

Show what the entries in the main ledger will be:

Account name	Amount £	Dr ✓	Cr ✓

Show what the entries in the sales and purchases ledgers will be:

Account name	Amount £	Dr ✓	Cr ✓

KAPLAN PUBLISHING

Activity 49

Below is Lynn's cash book for the month of June 20X9:

Date	Detail	Bank £	Date	Detail	VAT £	Bank £
01/06	Bal b/f	12500	06/06	Telephone	70	470
05/06	ABC Ltd	2455	15/06	Motor vehicles	875	5875
20/06	VAT refund	5222	21/06	Insurance		4000
			29/06	Rent&Rates		2000
			30/06	Bal c/d		7832
		20177			945	20177

Show what the entries in the main ledger will be:

Account name	Amount £	Dr ✓	Cr ✓

Show what the entries in the sales and purchases ledgers will be:

Account name	Amount £	Dr ✓	Cr ✓

Activity 50

Below is Brendon's cash book for the month of August 20X9:

Date	Detail	Bank £	Date	Detail	Disc. Received £	Bank £
01/08	Bal b/f	5482	03/08	TV Ltd	21	189
06/08	VAT refund	214	08/08	General expenses		687
			10/08	Electricity		200
			27/08	Gas		540
			31/08	Bal c/d		4080
		5696			21	5696

Show what the entries in the main ledger will be:

Account name	Amount £	Dr ✓	Cr ✓

Show what the entries in the sales and purchases ledgers will be:

Account name	Amount £	Dr ✓	Cr ✓

17 Consolidation – Purchases

 Activity 51

James Dean is the owner of a retail business called Bodgit & Scarper.

You are employed by the business as a bookkeeper.

The business uses a manual accounting system.

Double entry takes place in the main ledger. Individual accounts of debtors and creditors are kept in the sales and purchases ledgers.

Assume today's date is 30 June 20X9, unless you are told otherwise.

Balances at the start of the date on 30 June 20X9

Credit suppliers

Company A	11,200
Company B	3,720
Company C	28,456
Company D	50,400
Motor vehicles	38,700
Purchases	343,600
Purchases returns	1,200
Purchases ledger control	162,094
Discount received	1,800
Miscellaneous (debit balance)	4,000
Loan from bank	31,500
VAT (debit balance)	12,840

Task 1

Enter the opening balances above into the 'T' accounts given.

Transactions

The following transactions took place on 30 June 20X9 and have been entered into the daybooks below:

Purchases day book					
Date	Details	Inv. No.	Total £	VAT £	Net £
30/06/X9	Company A	131	27,495	4,095	23,400
30/06/X9	Company B	132	1,586	236	1,350
30/06/X9	Company C	133	7,931	1,181	6,750
30/06/X9	Company D	134	3,172	472	2,700
			40,184	5,984	34,200

Purchases returns day book					
Date	Details	Credit No.	Total £	VAT £	Net £
30/06/X9	Company A	62	528	78	450
30/06/X9	Company D	G7	105	15	90
			633	93	540

Cash book						
Date	Detail	Bank £	Date	Details	VAT £	Bank £
30/6/X9	HMRC	12,840	30/6/X9	Bal b/d		22,681
			30/6/X9	Motor Vehicles		19,125
			30/6/X9	Loan repayment		1,125
30/6/X9	Bal c/d	31,171	30/6/X9	Miscellaneous	160	1,080
		44,011				44,011
			1/07/X9	Bal b/d		31,171

Task 2

From the daybooks and cash book shown, make the relevant entries into the accounts in the main ledger and the purchases ledger.

Task 3

Balance the accounts showing clearly the balances carried down at 30 June and brought down at 1 July.

Task 4

List the balances you have calculated in Task 3 in the trial balance

Purchases ledger

Company A					
Date	**Details**	**£**	**Date**	**Detail**	**£**

Company B					
Date	**Details**	**£**	**Date**	**Detail**	**£**

Company C					
Date	**Details**	**£**	**Date**	**Detail**	**£**

Company D					
Date	**Details**	**£**	**Date**	**Detail**	**£**

Main ledger

Motor vehicles					
Date	**Details**	**£**	**Date**	**Detail**	**£**

KAPLAN PUBLISHING

Purchases

Date	Details	£	Date	Detail	£

Purchases returns

Date	Details	£	Date	Detail	£

Purchases ledger control

Date	Details	£	Date	Detail	£

Discounts received					
Date	Details	£	Date	Detail	£

Miscellaneous					
Date	Details	£	Date	Detail	£

Loan from bank					
Date	Details	£	Date	Detail	£

KAPLAN PUBLISHING

VAT					
Date	Details	£	Date	Detail	£

Other balance

Plant & machinery	25,530
Stock	15,225
Petty cash control	456
Sales ledger control	237,243
Capital	6,669
Sales	491,325
Sales returns	2,100
Discounts allowed	360
Wages	19,400
Rent	4,575
Heat & light	3,900
Rates	472
Telephone	933
Insurance	4,875
Stationery	3,060

Task 5

List the remaining balances shown above in the trial balance and total each column.

Trial balance

	Dr £	Cr £
Plant & machinery		
Motor vehicles		
Bank		
Stock		
Petty cash control		
Sales ledger control		
Purchases ledger control		
Capital		
VAT		
Loan from bank		
Sales		
Sales returns		
Discounts received		
Purchases		
Purchases returns		
Discounts allowed		
Wages		
Rent		
Heat & light		
Rates		
Stationery		
Telephone		
Insurance		
Miscellaneous expenses		
Totals		

KAPLAN PUBLISHING

18 Petty cash

 Activity 52

Given below is a business' petty cash book for the week.

Petty cash book

Receipts			Payments								
Date	Narrative	Total	Date	Details	Voucher no	Amount £	Postage £	Staff welfare £	Station-ery £	Travel expenses £	VAT £
5/1/X1	Bal b/d	150.00	12/1/X1	Postage	03526	13.68	13.68				
				Staff welfare	03527	25.00		25.00			
				Stationery	03528	14.80			12.60		2.20
				Taxi fare	03529	12.00				10.21	1.79
				Staff welfare	03530	6.40		6.40			
				Postage	03531	12.57	12.57				
				Rail fare	03532	6.80				6.80	
				Stationery	03533	7.99			6.80		1.19
				Taxi fare	03534	18.80				16.00	2.80
						118.04	26.25	31.40	19.40	33.01	7.98

Required

Show what the entries in the main ledger will be:

Account name	Amount £	Dr ✓	Cr ✓

Activity 53

Given below is a completed petty cash book for transactions that took place on 12th April 20X1:

Petty cash book

Receipts			Payments								
Date	Narrative	Total	Date	Narrative	Voucher no	Total	Postage	Staff welfare	Tea and coffee	Travel expenses	VAT
						£	£	£	£	£	£
12/04	Bal b/d	50.00	12/04	Coffee/milk	2534	4.68		4.68			
12/04	Bank	11.22		Postage	2535	13.26	13.26				
				Stationery	2536	10.27			8.74		1.53
				Taxi fare	2537	15.00				12.77	2.23
				Postage	2538	6.75	6.75				
				Train fare	2539	7.40				7.40	
				Stationery	2540	3.86			3.29		0.57
						61.22	20.01	4.68	12.03	20.17	4.33

Required

Show what the entries in the main ledger will be:

Account name	Amount £	Dr ✓	Cr ✓

Activity 54

Given below is the completed petty cash book for the week.

Petty cash book

Receipts			Payments								
Date	Narrative	Total	Date	Narrative	Voucher no	Total	Postage	Staff welfare	Tea and coffee	Travel expenses	VAT
						£	£	£	£	£	£
	Bal b/d	100.00	30/4/X1	Coffee/milk	2534	4.68		4.68			
				Postage	2535	13.26	13.26				
				Stationery	2536	10.27			8.74		1.53
				Taxi fare	2537	15.00				12.77	2.23
				Postage	2538	6.75	6.75				
				Train fare	2539	7.40				7.40	
				Stationery	2540	3.86			3.29		0.57
						61.22	20.01	4.68	12.03	20.17	4.33

Required

Post the totals from the petty bash book to the main ledger accounts given below.

Main ledger accounts

Postage account

		£		£
23 Apr	Balance b/d	231.67		

Staff welfare account

		£		£
23 Apr	Balance b/d	334.78		

Stationery account

		£			£
23 Apr	Balance b/d	53.36			

Travel expenses account

		£			£
23 Apr	Balance b/d	579.03			

VAT account

		£			£
			23 Apr	Balance b/d	967.44

ANSWERS

Practice activities answers

Double entry bookkeeping for Basic Accounting I

1 Double entry bookkeeping – introduction

Activity 1

(a) Opening capital

	£		£
Assets Cash	5,000	Capital	5,000

(b) Cash purchase

	£		£
Assets Stock	500	Capital	5,000
Cash (5,000 – 500)	4,500		
	5,000		5,000

(c) Credit purchase

	£		£
Assets Stock (500 + (5 × 200))	1,500	Capital	5,000
Cash	4,500		
	6,000		
Liabilities Creditors	(1,000)		
	5,000		5,000

(d) Cash sale

	£		£
Assets Stock (1,500 – 500)	1,000	Capital	5,000
Cash (4,500 + 750)	5,250	Profit (750 – 500)	250
	6,250		
Liabilities Creditors	(1,000)		
	5,250		5,250

(e) Cash sale

Assets		£		£
	Stock (1,000 – 800)	200	Capital	5,000
	Debtors	1,200	Profit (250 + 1,200 – 800)	650
	Cash	5,250		
		6,650		
Liabilities	Creditors	(1,000)		
		5,650		5,650

(f) Paid rent

Assets		£		£
	Stock	200	Capital	5,000
	Debtors	1,200	Profit (650 – 250)	400
	Cash (5,250 – 250)	5,000		
		6,400		
Liabilities	Creditors	(1,000)		
		5,400		5,400

(g) Drawings

Assets		£		£
	Stock	200	Capital	5,000
	Debtors	1,200	Profit	400
	Cash (5,000 – 100)	4,900		
		6,300	Drawings	(100)
Liabilities	Creditors	(1,000)		
		5,300		5,300

(h) Sundry income

Assets		£		£
	Stock	200	Capital	5,000
	Debtors (1,200 + 50)	1,250	Profit (400 + 50)	450
	Cash	4,900		
		6,350	Drawings	(100)
Liabilities	Creditors	(1,000)		
		5,350		5,350

(i)   Payment to creditor

		£		£
Assets	Stock	200	Capital	5,000
	Debtors	1,250	Profit	450
	Cash (4,900 – 500)	4,400		
		———		
		5,850	Drawings	(100)
Liabilities	Creditors (1,000 – 500)	(500)		
		———		———
		5,350		5,350
		———		———

(j)   Receipt from debtor

		£		£
Assets	Stock	200	Capital	5,000
	Debtors (1,250 – 1,200)	50	Profit	450
	Cash (4,400 + 1,200)	5,600		
		———		
		5,850	Drawings	(100)
Liabilities	Creditors	(500)		
		———		———
		5,350		5,350
		———		———

(k)   Purchase of van

		£		£
Assets	Van	4,000	Capital	5,000
	Stock	200	Profit	450
	Debtors	50		———
	Cash (5,600 – 4,000)	1,600		5,450
		———	Drawings	(100)
		5,850		
Liabilities	Creditors	(500)		
		———		———
		5,350		5,350
		———		———

(l)   Telephone bill

		£		£
Assets	Van	4,000	Capital	5,000
	Stock	200	Profit (450 – 150)	300
	Debtors	50		———
	Cash	1,600		5,300
		———	Drawings	(100)
		5,850		
Liabilities	Creditors (500 + 150)	(650)		
		———		———
		5,200		5,200
		———		———

Activity 2

Accounting equation at 31 January 20X9

		£		£
Assets	Display equipment	50	Capital	3,000
	Stocks of sports equipment (W1)	2,000	Profit (balancing figure)	230
	Debtors	30		
	Cash (W2)	2,500		3,230
		4,580		
Liabilities	Creditors	1,500	Drawings	(150)
		3,080		3,080

Workings

(1) Stock

	£	£
Purchased 10 January		1,000
Purchased 31 January		1,500
Sold during January (½× £1,000)		(500)
		2,000

(2) Cash

		£
Receipts	Capital paid in	3,000
	From customers	800
		3,800
Payments	Rent	100
	Suppliers of stock	1,000
	Suppliers of display equipment	50
	Drawings	150
		(1,300)
Balance at 31 January		2,500

2 Ledger accounting

Activity 3

Bank

		£			£
(a)	Capital	4,000	(b)	Computer	1,000
(d)	Sales	800	(c)	Rent	400

Capital

		£			£
			(a)	Bank	4,000

Rent

		£			£
(c)	Bank	400			

Sales

		£			£
			(d)	Bank	800

Computers

		£			£
(b)	Bank	1,000			

Activity 4

Bank

		£			£
(a)	Capital	5,000	(b)	Purchases	800
(e)	Sales	600	(c)	Rent	500
(f)	Sales	700	(d)	Van	2,000
			(g)	Purchases	1,000
			(h)	Stationery	200
			(i)	Drawings	500

Purchases

		£		£
(b)	Bank	800		
(g)	Bank	1,000		

Capital

	£			£
		(a)	Bank	5,000

Rent

		£		£
(c)	Bank	500		

Van

		£		£
(d)	Bank	2,000		

Sales

	£			£
		(e)	Bank	600
		(f)	Bank	700

Stationery

		£		£
(h)	Bank	200		

Drawings

		£		£
(i)	Bank	500		

KAPLAN PUBLISHING

Activity 5

Capital

		£			£
			(a)	Bank	4,000

Purchases

		£		£
(b)	Bank	700		
(g)	Bank	1,200		

Entertainment

		£		£
(c)	Bank	300		

Computers

		£		£
(d)	Bank	3,000		

Sales

		£			£
			(e)	Bank	1,500

Drawings

		£		£
(f)	Bank	500		

Telephone

		£			£
(h)	Bank	600	(i)	Bank	200

Stationery

		£		£
(j)	Bank	157		

Bank

		£			£
(a)	Capital	4,000	(b)	Purchases	700
(e)	Sales	1,500	(c)	Entertainment	300
(i)	Telephone	200	(d)	Computers	3,000
			(f)	Drawings	500
			(g)	Purchases	1,200
			(h)	Telephone	600
			(j)	Stationery	157

Activity 6

Capital

		£			£
			(a)	Bank	2,000

Purchases

		£		£
(b)	Creditors	1,000		
(f)	Bank	1,000		
(i)	Bank	200		

Van

		£		£
(c)	Bank	900		

Sales

	£			£
		(d)	Debtors	2,500
		(h)	Bank	800

Consultancy services

	£			£
		(e)	Bank	3,000

Stationery

		£			£
(g)	Bank	260	(j)	Bank	100

Debtors

		£			£
(d)	Sales	2,500			

Creditors

	£			£
		(b)	Purchases	1,000

Bank

		£			£
(a)	Capital	2,000	(c)	Van	900
(e)	Consultancy	3,000	(f)	Purchases	1,000
(h)	Sales	800	(g)	Stationery	260
(j)	Stationery	100	(i)	Purchases	200

Activity 7

Sales

	£		£
		B	1,000
		C	90

B Debtor

	£		£
Sales	1,000	Bank	500

C Debtor

	£		£
Sales	90	Bank	90

Bank

	£		£
B	500		
C	90		

Activity 8

Purchases

	£		£
Y	600		
Z	750		

Y Creditor

	£		£
Bank	300	Purchases	600

Z Creditor

	£		£
Bank	500	Purchases	750

Bank

	£		£
		Y	300
		Z	500

3 Drafting an initial Trial Balance

Activity 9

Bank

	£		£
Capital	10,000	Computer	1,000
Sales	2,000	Telephone	567
Sales	3,000	Rent	1,500
Sales	2,000	Rates	125
		Stationery	247
		Petrol	49
		Purchases	2,500
		Drawings	500
		Petrol	42
Sub-total	17,000	Sub-total	6,530
		Balance c/d	10,470
	17,000		17,000
Balance b/d	10,470		

Activity 10

Bank

	£		£
Capital	5,000	Purchases	850
Sales	1,000	Fixtures	560
Sales	876	Van	1,500
Rent rebate	560	Rent	1,300
Sales	1,370	Rates	360
		Telephone	220
		Stationery	120
		Petrol	48
		Car repairs	167
Sub-total	8,806	Sub-total	5,125
		Balance c/d	3,681
	8,806		8,806
Balance b/d	3,681		

Activity 11

Bank

	£		£
Balance b/f	23,700	Drawings	4,000
Sales	2,300	Rent	570
Sales	1,700	Purchases	6,000
Debtors	4,700	Rates	500
		Salaries	3,600
		Car expenses	460
		Petrol	49
		Petrol	38
		Electricity	210
		Stationery	89
Sub-total	32,400	Sub-total	15,516
		Balance c/d	16,884
	32,400		32,400
Balance b/d	16,884		

Activity 12

TRIAL BALANCE AT 31 AUGUST 20X9

	DR £	CR £
Sales		41,770
Purchases	34,680	
Debtors	6,790	
Creditors		5,650
General expenses	12,760	
Loan		10,000
Plant and machinery at cost	5,000	
Motor van at cost	6,000	
Drawings	2,000	
Rent and rates	6,700	
Insurance	4,000	
Bank overdraft		510
Capital		20,000
	77,930	77,930

Activity 13

Purchases

		£			£
(a)	Creditors	1,000			
(j)	Bank	400	Balance c/d		1,400
		1,400			1,400
	Balance b/d	1,400			

Creditors

		£			£
(g)	Bank	300	(a)	Purchases	1,000
	Balance c/d	700			
		1,000			1,000
				Balance b/d	700

Rent

		£		£
(b)	Bank	500	Balance c/d	500
		500		500
	Balance b/d	500		

Sales

	£			£
		(c)	Debtors	1,500
Balance c/d	3,500	(k)	Bank	2,000
	3,500			3,500
			Balance b/d	3,500

Debtors

	£		£
(c) Sales	1,500	(f) Bank	400
		Balance c/d	1,100
	1,500		1,500
Balance b/d	1,100		

Computers

	£		£
(d) Bank	900	Balance c/d	900
	900		900
Balance b/d	900		

Wages

	£		£
(e) Bank	1,000	Balance c/d	1,000
	1,000		1,000
Balance b/d	1,000		

Telephone

	£		£
(h) Bank	200	(i) Bank	50
		Balance c/d	150
	200		200
Balance b/d	150		

Bank

		£			£
(f)	Debtors	400	(b)	Rent	500
(i)	Telephone	50	(d)	Computer	900
(k)	Sales	2,000	(e)	Wages	1,000
			(g)	Creditors	300
			(h)	Telephone	200
			(j)	Purchases	400
	Balance c/d	850			
		3,300			3,300
				Balance b/d	850

Trial Balance as at 31 July 20X9:

	DR £	CR £
Purchases	1,400	
Creditors		700
Rent	500	
Sales		3,500
Debtors	1,100	
Computers	900	
Wages	1,000	
Telephone	150	
Bank overdraft		850
	5,050	5,050

4 Credit sales: documents

 Activity 14

CREDIT NOTE

Keyboard Supplies

Credit note to:
H M Music
Tenant House
Perley
TN7 8ER

Trench Park Estate
Fieldham
Sussex TN21 4AF
Tel: 01829 654545
Fax: 01829 654646

Credit note no:	CN0337
Tax point:	17 April 20X1
VAT reg no:	466 1128 30
Purchase order no:	SL09

Code	Description	Quantity	VAT rate %	Unit price £	Amount excl of VAT £
B3060	Bento Keyboard	1	17.5	126.00	126.00
					126.00
Trade discount 15%					18.90
					107.10
VAT at 17.5%					18.74
Total amount					125.84

Activity 15

INVOICE

Invoice to:
Musicolor Ltd
23 High Street
Nutford
Sussex
TN11 4TZ

Keyboard Supplies
Trench Park Estate
Fieldham
Sussex TN21 4AF
Tel: 01829 654545
Fax: 01829 654646

Deliver to:
As above

Invoice no:	06113
Tax point:	17 April 20X1
VAT reg no:	466 1128 30
Your reference:	SL06
Purchase order no:	04318

Code	Description	Quantity	VAT rate %	Unit price £	Amount excl of VAT £
Z4600	Zanni Keyboard	2	17.5	185.00	370.00
A4802	Atol Keyboard	3	17.5	130.00	390.00
					760.00
Trade discount 10%					76.00
					684.00
VAT at 17.5%					116.10
Total amount payable					800.10

Deduct discount of 3% if paid within 10 days, 30 days net

INVOICE

Keyboard Supplies

Invoice to:
Newford Music
32/34 Main Street
Welland
Sussex
TN4 6BD

Trench Park Estate
Fieldham
Sussex TN21 4AF
Tel: 01829 654545
Fax: 01829 654646

Deliver to:
As above

Invoice no:	06114
Tax point:	17 April 20X1
VAT reg no:	466 1128 30
Your reference:	SL18
Purchase order no:	47115

Code	Description	Quantity	VAT rate %	Unit price £	Amount excl of VAT £
Z4406	Zanni Keyboard	4	17.5	165.00	660.00
					660.00
Trade discount 20%					132.00
					528.00
VAT at 17.5%					89.62
Total amount payable					617.62

Deduct discount of 3% if paid within 10 days, 30 days net

INVOICE

Invoice to:
FT Music Supplies
The Barn
Nutford
Sussex TN11 7AJ

Deliver to:
As above

Keyboard Supplies

Trench Park Estate
Fieldham
Sussex TN21 4AF
Tel: 01829 654545
Fax: 01829 654646

Invoice no:	06115
Tax point:	17 April 20X1
VAT reg no:	466 1128 30
Your reference:	SL23
Purchase order no:	71143

Code	Description	Quantity	VAT rate %	Unit price £	Amount excl of VAT £
B2010	Bento Keyboard	2	17.5	148.00	296.00
G4706	Garland Keyboard	3	17.5	96.00	288.00
					584.00
Trade discount 15%					87.60
					496.40
VAT at 17.5%					86.87
Total amount payable					583.27

📝 Activity 16

(i) Has the correct pricing been used on the invoice?

Yes – the price quoted on the purchase order was £40 per 100 which is equal to £0.40 for each item.

(ii) Has the correct discount been applied?

No – the trade discount agreed on the purchase order was 10%, not the 20% charged on the invoice.

(iii) What should the correct amount of VAT charged be?

The VAT should have been charged on the correct discounted amount of £160 less 10% discount, therefore a net amount of £144.

VAT should have been £144 × 17.5% = £25.20

(iv) **What should the correct total amount payable be?**

The correct amount payable be the correct discounted amount of £144 plus the correct VAT of £25.20, so the total amount payable should be £169.20

Activity 17

(a) To allow for expansion of the number of accounts in the general ledger

(b) Any three from:

- Customer account codes
- Supplier account codes
- Product codes
- Stock codes
- VAT codes
- Department codes

(c)

	TRUE/FALSE
General ledger codes help when barcoding an item of stock	FALSE
General ledger codes help when filing a financial document	FALSE
General ledger codes help trace relevant accounts quickly and easily	TRUE
General ledger codes help find the total amount owing to a supplier	FALSE

5 Credit sales – discounts and VAT

Activity 18

(a) VAT = £140.00 × 17.5% = £24.50

(b) VAT = £560.00 × 17.5% = £98.00

(c) VAT = £780.00 × $\frac{17.5}{117.5}$ = £116.17

(d) VAT = £970.00 × $\frac{17.5}{117.5}$ = £144.46

Activity 19

(a) VAT = £(280 − (2% × 280)) × 17.5% = £48.02

(b) VAT = £(480 − (3% × 480)) × 17.5% = £81.48

(c) VAT = £(800 − (5% × 800)) × 17.5% = £133.00

(d) VAT = £(650 − (4% × 650)) × 17.5% = £109.20

Activity 20

(a) B takes the settlement discount:

	£
Net price	600.00
VAT £(600 − (3% × 600)) × 17.5%	101.85
Invoice value	701.85

Amount paid by B:

	£
Invoice value	701.85
Less: 3% × 600	(18.00)
Amount paid	683.85

KAPLAN PUBLISHING

(b) B does not take the settlement discount:

	£
Net price	600.00
VAT £(600 – (3% × 600)) × 17.5%	101.85
Invoice value	701.85

If B does not take the settlement discount, B will pay the full £701.85.

Activity 21

(a) C takes the settlement discount:

	£
Net price	700.00
VAT £(700 – (5% × 700)) × 17.5%	116.37
Invoice value	816.37
Less: 5% discount = 700 × 5%	(35.00)
Amount paid by C	781.37

Sales

	£		£
		SLCA	700.00

SLCA

	£		£
Sales + VAT	816.37	Bank	781.37
		Discount allowed	35.00
	816.37		816.37

Bank

	£		£
SLCA	781.37		

VAT

	£		£
		SLCA	116.37

Discount allowed

	£		£
SLCA	35.00		

(b)   C does not take the settlement discount:

	£
Invoice value (per (a))	816.37

As C does not take the settlement discount, he pays the full amount (£816.37).

Sales

	£		£
		SLCA	700.00

SLCA

	£		£
Sales + VAT	816.37	Bank	816.37

Bank

	£		£
SLCA	816.37		

VAT

	£		£
		SLCA	116.37

6 The sales day book – main and subsidiary ledgers

Activity 22

Sales day book

Date	Invoice no	Customer name	Code	Total £	VAT £	Net £
20X1						
1/5	03466	Fraser & Co	SL14	151.19	22.51	128.68
	03467	Letterhead Ltd	SL03	303.03	45.13	257.90
2/5	03468	Jeliteen Traders	SL15	113.48	16.90	96.58
	CN0746	Garner & Co	SL12	(80.72)	(12.02)	(68.70)
3/5	03469	Harper Bros	SL22	315.07	46.92	268.15
	03470	Juniper Ltd	SL17	123.82	18.44	105.38
4/5	03471	H G Frank	SL30	346.23	51.56	294.67
	CN0747	Hill Traders	SL26	(138.27)	(20.59)	(117.68)
5/5	03472	Keller Assocs	SL07	129.93	19.35	110.58
				1,263.76	188.20	1,075.56

Activity 23

Sales day book

Date	Invoice no	Customer name	Code	Total £	VAT £	01 £	02 £	03 £	04 £
18/4/X1	06116	B Z S Music		1,426.15	206.95		432.00		787.20
18/4/X1	06117	M T Retail		628.62	93.62	210.00			325.00
18/4/X1	06118	Harmer & Co		1,016.51	147.51		575.00	294.00	
				3,071.28	448.08	210.00	1,007.00	294.00	1,112.20

Note that when a trade discount has been deducted on the invoice in total it must be deducted from each type of sale when entering the figures in the analysed sales day book.

Activity 24

Sales day book							
Date	Invoice no	Customer name	Code	Total £	VAT £	Maintenance £	Decorating £
01/5/X1	07891	Portman & Co	P2	162.83	23.83	139.00	
03/5/X1	07892	Stanton Assocs	S3	1,288.65	188.65		1,100.00
05/5/X1	07893	Boreham Bros	B7	277.30	41.30	106.00	130.00
				1,728.78	253.78	245.00	1,230.00

Activity 25

Sales day book							
Date	Invoice no	Customer name	Code	Total £	VAT £	Group 01 £	Group 02 £
20X0							
1 Feb	61612	Worker Ltd	SL11	217.37	32.37	68.90	116.10
4 Feb	61613	P T Associates	SL04	122.38	18.22		104.16
5 Feb	61614	Paul Bros	SL13	289.27	43.08	106.19	140.00
8 Feb	61615	S D Partners	SL07	109.54	16.31	72.40	20.83
9 Feb	61616	Harper Ltd	SL08	399.97	59.57	160.18	180.22
11 Feb	C241	P T Associates	SL04	(23.68)	(3.52)		(20.16)
				1,114.85	166.03	407.67	541.15

The entries in the sales ledger will be:

Account name	Amount £	Dr ✓	Cr ✓
Worker Ltd	217.37	✓	
P T Associates	122.38	✓	
Paul Bros	289.27	✓	
S D Partners	109.54	✓	
Harper Ltd	399.97	✓	
P T Associates	23.68		✓

The entries in the main ledger will be:

Account name	Amount £	Dr ✓	Cr ✓
Sales Ledger Control Account	1,114.85	✓	
VAT	166.03		✓
Sales account – 01	407.67		✓
Sales account – 02	541.15		✓

Activity 26

The entries in the sales ledger will be:

Account name	Amount £	Dr ✓	Cr ✓
Gerard & Co	34.36		✓
Filmer Ltd	44.92		✓
T Harrison	24.44		✓
Rolls Ltd	36.47		✓

The entries in the main ledger will be:

Account name	Amount £	Dr ✓	Cr ✓
Sales Ledger Control Account	140.19		✓
VAT	20.87	✓	
Sales returns account – 01	54.01	✓	
Sales returns account – 02	32.06	✓	
Sales returns account – 03	33.25	✓	

7 Checking receipts

 Activity 27

The following problems exist on the cheques received:

Cheque from K T Lopez – not signed;

Cheque from L Garry – post dated;

Cheque from L Barrett – made out to wrong name;

Cheque from P Ibbott – more than six months old;

Cheque from J Lovell – discrepancy between words and figures.

 Activity 28

Cheque from BZS Music – settlement discount of £8.64 has been taken – this is valid.

Cheque from Musicolor Ltd – settlement discount of £22.00 has been taken – but is not valid as the cheque has been received after 10 days from the invoice date. However, in the interest of good customer relations, perhaps the discount should be granted but the customer should be informed and reminded of the settlement discount terms.

Cheque from Harmer & Co – settlement discount of £8.82 has been taken – this is valid.

Cheque from Newford Music – settlement discount of £23.76 has been taken – this is not valid as the receipt is too late to claim the discount. Again the discount might be granted in the interest of good customer relations but the customer should be informed and reminded of the settlement discount terms.

Cheque from Trent Music – settlement discount of £13.27 has been taken – however it should have been £11.34 (3% × £378.00). Customer should be informed of the error.

8 The analysed cash receipts book

 Activity 29

The entries in the sales ledger will be:

Account name	Amount £	Dr ✓	Cr ✓
G Heilbron	108.45		✓
L Tessa	110.57		✓
L Tessa	3.31		✓
J Dent	210.98		✓
J Dent	6.32		✓
F Trainer	97.60		✓
A Winter	105.60		✓
A Winter	3.16		✓

The entries in the main ledger will be:

Account name	Amount £	Dr ✓	Cr ✓
Discounts Allowed	12.79	✓	
Sales Ledger Control Account	12.79		✓
Sales Ledger Control Account	633.20		✓
Sales	225.60		✓
VAT	39.48		✓

Activity 30

The entries in the sales ledger will be:

Account name	Amount £	Dr ✓	Cr ✓
McCaul & Partners	147.56		✓
McCaul & Partners	2.95		✓
P Martin	264.08		✓
F Little	167.45		✓
D Raine	265.89		✓
D Raine	7.97		✓

Show what the entries in the main ledger will be:

Account name	Amount £	Dr ✓	Cr ✓
Discounts allowed	10.92	✓	
Sales Ledger Control Account	10.92		✓
Sales Ledger Control Account	844.98		✓

9 Debtors' statements

Activity 31

To: Grant & Co

FARMHOUSE PICKLES LTD

225 School Lane
Weymouth
Dorset
WE36 5NR
Tel: 0261 480444
Fax: 0261 480555
Date: 30 April 20X1

STATEMENT

Date	Transaction	Debit £	Credit £	Balance £
1 April	Opening balance			337.69
4 April	Inv 32656	150.58		488.27
12 April	Credit 0335		38.70	449.57
18 April	Inv 32671	179.52		629.09
20 April	Payment		330.94	298.15
20 April	Discount		6.75	291.40
24 April	Credit 0346		17.65	273.75
25 April	Inv 32689	94.36		368.11

May we remind you that our credit terms are 30 days

FARMHOUSE PICKLES LTD

225 School Lane
Weymouth
Dorset
WE36 5NR
Tel: 0261 480444
Fax: 0261 480555
Date: 30 April 20X1

To: Mitchell Partners

STATEMENT

Date	Transaction	Debit £	Credit £	Balance £
1 April	Opening balance			180.46
7 April	Inv 32662	441.57		622.03
12 April	Credit 0344		66.89	555.14
20 Aprill	Inv 32669	274.57		829.71
21 April	Payment		613.58	216.13
21 April	Discount		8.45	207.68

May we remind you that our credit terms are 30 days

Activity 32

		TOYBOX GAMES LTD				
		125 Finchley Way Bristol BS1 4PL Tel: 01272 200299				

STATEMENT OF ACCOUNT

Customer name Arnold's Toys Ltd
Customer address 14 High Street, Bristol, BS2 5FL

Statement date 1st December		Amount		Balance	
Date	Transaction	£	p	£	. p
19/11	Invoice 2095	118	08	118	08
20/11	Invoice 2098	2201	95	2320	03
20/11	Credit note 2098	323	60	1996	43
22/11	Cheque	118	08	1878	35
				1878	35

10 Consolidation – sales

Activity 33

Sales ledger

Tony's

Date	Details	£	Date	Detail	£
30/11	Bal b/f	5600			
30/11	SDB	18330	30/11	Bal c/d	23930
		23930			**23930**
01/12	Bal b/d	23930			

Bella's

Date	Details	£	Date	Detail	£
30/11	Bal b/f	1860	30/11	SRDB	1410
30/11	SDB	1175	30/11	Bal c/d	1625
		3035			**3035**
01/12	Bal b/d	1625			

Jasper's

Date	Details	£	Date	Detail	£
30/11	Bal b/f	14228			
30/11	SDB	3525	30/11	Bal c/d	17753
		17753			**17753**
01/12	Bal b/d	17753			

Jack's

Date	Details	£	Date	Detail	£
30/11	Bal b/f	25000	30/11	SRDB	423
30/11	SDB	4230	30/11	CRB	6600
			30/11	Discounts	132
			30/11	Bal c/d	22075
		29230			**29230**
01/12	Bal b/d	22075			

Main (general) ledger

Cashbook

Date	Details	£	Date	Detail	£
30/11	Bal b/f	1495			
30/11	CRB	7070	30/11	Bal c/d	8565
		8565			**8565**
01/12	Bal b/d	8565			

Sales

Date	Details	£	Date	Detail	£
			30/11	Bal b/f	74472
			30/11	SDB	23200
30/11	Bal c/d	98072	30/11	CRB	400
		98072			**98072**
			01/12	Bal b/d	98072

Sales returns

Date	Details	£	Date	Detail	£
30/11	Bal b/f	1110			
30/11	SRDB	1560	30/11	Bal c/d	2670
		2670			**2670**
01/12	Bal b/d	2670			

Sales ledger control

Date	Details	£	Date	Detail	£
30/11	Bal b/f	71047	30/11	SRDB	1833
30/11	SDB	27260	30/11	CRB	6600
			30/11	Discounts	132
			30/11	Bal c/d	89742
		98307			**98307**
01/12	Bal b/d	89742			

Discounts allowed

Date	Details	£	Date	Detail	£
30/11	Bal b/f	1210			
30/11	CRB	132	30/11	Bal c/d	1342
		1342			**1342**
01/12	Bal b/d	1342			

VAT

Date	Details	£	Date	Detail	£
30/11	SRDB	273	30/11	Bal b/f	11047
			30/11	SDB	4060
30/11	Bal c/d	14904	30/11	CRB	70
		15177			**15177**
			01/12	Bal b/d	14904

Trial balance

	Dr £	Cr £
Cashbook	8565	
Sales		98072
Sales returns	2670	
Sales ledger control	89742	
Discounts allowed	1342	
VAT		14904
Fixtures & Fittings	11400	
Motor vehicles	21485	
Stock	5400	
Petty cash control	150	
Capital		25000
Loan from bank		20000
Discounts received		144
Purchases	11756	
Purchases returns		487
Purchases ledger control		19432
Motor expenses	1940	
Wages	19450	
Rent	1100	
Heat & light	876	
Stationery	331	
Telephone	794	
Insurance	411	
Miscellaneous expenses	627	
Totals	**178039**	**178039**

11 Credit purchases: documents

 ### Activity 34

Credit note from J M Bond & Co

The trade discount deducted should have been £6.16. Therefore, the total amount of credit is wrong.

 ### Activity 35

Invoice from A J Broom & Company Ltd

Seven joist hangers were invoiced and delivered but only five were ordered.

Invoice from Jenson Ltd

The VAT calculation is incorrect – the amount should be £99.37.

Invoice from Haddow Bros

12 sheets were invoiced and ordered but only 10 were delivered.

 ### Activity 36

Invoice from:	Supplier Account Code	General Ledger Code
Haddow Bros	HAD29	GL112
Jenson Ltd	JEN32	GL140
AJ Broom & Company Ltd	AJB14	GL110
JM Bond & Co	JMB33	GL130

12 Credit purchases – discounts and VAT

 Activity 37

(a) VAT = £400 × 17.5% = £70.00
(b) VAT = £650 × 17.5% = £113.75
(c) VAT = £425 × $\frac{17.5}{117.5}$ = £63.29
(d) VAT = £77 × $\frac{17.5}{117.5}$ = £11.46

 Activity 38

(a) VAT = £(850 − (3% × 850)) × 17.5% = £144.28
(b) VAT = £(600 − (5% × 600)) × 17.5% = £99.75
(c) VAT = £(325 − (2% × 325)) × 17.5% = £55.73
(d) VAT = £(57 − (4% × 57)) × 17.5% = £9.57

 Activity 39

Calculate the invoice value and amount paid by Z.

	£
Net price	600.00
VAT £(600 − (3% × 600)) × 17.5%	101.85
Invoice value	701.85
Less: Discount 3% × 600	(18.00)
Amount paid	683.85

Purchases

	£		£
PLCA	600.00		

PLCA

	£		£
Bank	683.85	Purchases + VAT	701.85
Discount	18.00		
	701.85		701.85

Bank

	£		£
		PLCA	683.85

VAT

	£		£
PLCA	101.85		

Discounts received

	£		£
		PLCA	18.00

13 The purchases day book – main and subsidiary ledgers

Activity 40

Purchases day book

Date	Invoice no	Code	Supplier	Total	VAT	Fabric	Header tape	Other
12/4/X1	06738	PL03	Fabric Supplies Ltd	1,097.22	160.62	798.00	138.60	
	0328	PL04	Lillian Fisher	107.74	16.04			91.70
	CN0477	PL05	Headstream & Co	(79.90)	(11.90)	(51.40)	(16.60)	
	07359	PL01	Mainstream Fabrics	330.04	48.52	281.52		
				1,455.10	213.28	1,028.12	122.00	91.70

Activity 41

Purchases day book

Date	Invoice no	Code	Supplier	Total	VAT	Wood	Bricks/ Cement	Consum -ables
3/5/X1	077401	PL16	Magnum Supplies	493.90	72.30		421.60	
	046193	PL08	JR Ryan & Co	118.47	17.64	85.08		15.75
	47823	PL13	HT Todd Plc	433.74	62.94	284.80	86.00	
				1,046.11	152.88	369.88	507.60	15.75

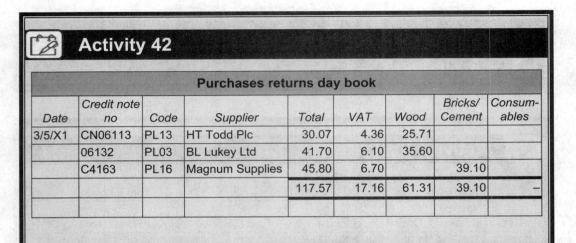

Activity 42

				Purchases returns day book				
Date	Credit note no	Code	Supplier	Total	VAT	Wood	Bricks/ Cement	Consum- ables
3/5/X1	CN06113	PL13	HT Todd Plc	30.07	4.36	25.71		
	06132	PL03	BL Lukey Ltd	41.70	6.10	35.60		
	C4163	PL16	Magnum Supplies	45.80	6.70		39.10	
				117.57	17.16	61.31	39.10	–

Activity 43

The entries in the purchases ledger will be:

Account name	Amount £	Dr ✓	Cr ✓
J D Withers	27.49	✓	
F Williams	164.50	✓	
K Bartlett	53.11	✓	

The entries in the main ledger will be:

Account name	Amount £	Dr ✓	Cr ✓
Purchases Ledger Control Account	245.10	✓	
VAT	36.50		✓
Purchase returns account – 01	60.40		✓
Purchase returns account – 02	23.40		✓
Purchase returns account – 03	108.00		✓
Purchase returns account - 04	16.80		✓

Activity 44

The entries in the purchases ledger will be:

Account name	Amount £	Dr ✓	Cr ✓
L Jameson	393.91		✓
K Davison	124.96		✓
H Samuels	109.79		✓
G Rails	180.93		✓
T Ives	192.98		✓

The entries in the main ledger will be:

Account name	Amount £	Dr ✓	Cr ✓
Purchases Ledger Control Account	1,002.57		✓
Purchases	853.27	✓	
VAT	149.30	✓	

14 Making Payments

 Activity 45

REMITTANCE ADVICE				

To:

Building Contract Supplies
Unit 15 Royal Estate
Manchester
M13 2EF

Nethan Builders
Brecon House
Stamford House
Manchester
M16 4PL

Tel:	0161 521 6411
Fax:	0161 530 6412
VAT Reg no:	471 3860 42
Date:	18 May 20X1

Date	Invoice no	Amount £	Discount taken £	Paid £
18 May 20X1	07742	199.47	2.55	196.92

Total paid	£196.92
Cheque no	200550

KAPLAN PUBLISHING

REMITTANCE ADVICE

To:	**Nethan Builders**
Jenson Ltd	Brecon House
30 Longfield Park	Stamford House
Kingsway	Manchester
M45 2TP	M16 4PL

Tel: 0161 521 6411
Fax: 0161 530 6412
VAT Reg no: 471 3860 42
Date: 18 May 20X1

Date	Invoice no	Amount £	Discount taken £	Paid £
18 May 20X1	47811	180.46		180.46

	Total paid	£180.46
	Cheque no	200551

REMITTANCE ADVICE

To:	**Nethan Builders**
Magnum Supplies	Brecon House
140/150 Park Estate	Stamford House
Manchester	Manchester
M20 6EG	M16 4PL

Tel: 0161 521 6411
Fax: 0161 530 6412
VAT Reg no: 471 3860 42
Date: 18 May 20X1

Date	Invoice no	Amount £	Discount taken £	Paid £
18 May 20X1	077422	740.85	12.65	728.20

	Total paid	£728.20
	Cheque no	200552

REMITTANCE ADVICE

To:

Haddow Bros
The White House
Standing Way
Manchester M13 6FH

Nethan Builders
Brecon House
Stamford House
Manchester
M16 4PL

Tel:	0161 521 6411
Fax:	0161 530 6412
VAT Reg no:	471 3860 42
Date:	18 May 20X1

Date	Invoice no	Amount £	Discount taken £	Paid £
18 May 20X1	G33940	500.46	–	500.46

Total paid	£500.46
Cheque no	200553

15 The analysed cash payments book

Activity 46

The entries in the purchases ledger will be:

Account name	Amount £	Dr ✓	Cr ✓
Homer Ltd	168.70	✓	
Homer Ltd	5.06	✓	
Forker & Co	179.45	✓	
Forker & Co	5.38	✓	
Print Ass.	190.45	✓	
ABG Ltd	220.67	✓	
ABG Ltd	6.62	✓	
G Greg	67.89	✓	

The entries in the main ledger will be:

Account name	Amount £	Dr ✓	Cr ✓
Discounts received	17.06		✓
Purchases Ledger Control Account	17.06	✓	
Purchases Ledger Control Account	827.16	✓	
Purchases	450.00	✓	
VAT	78.74	✓	

Activity 47

The entries in the purchases ledger will be:

Account name	Amount £	Dr ✓	Cr ✓
J M Bond	247.56	✓	
Magnum Supplies	662.36	✓	
Magnum Supplies	16.25	✓	
A J Broom	153.57	✓	
Jenson Ltd	336.57	✓	
Jenson Ltd	6.73	✓	
KKL Traders	442.78	✓	
KKL Traders	8.85	✓	

The entries in the main ledger will be:

Account name	Amount £	Dr ✓	Cr ✓
Discounts received	28.83		✓
Purchases Ledger Control Account	28.83	✓	
Purchases Ledger Control Account	1,842.84	✓	
Purchases	92.48	✓	
VAT	16.18	✓	

16 The Cashbook

Activity 48

The postings to the main ledger will be:

Account name	Amount £	Dr ✓	Cr ✓
Sales Ledger Control Account	5,230		✓
Sales Ledger Control Account	234		✓
Discounts Allowed	234	✓	
Stationery	200	✓	
Rent	1,000	✓	
Purchases Ledger Control Account	3,561	✓	
Insurance	450	✓	

The postings to the sales and purchases ledgers will be:

Account name	Amount £	Dr ✓	Cr ✓
H Ltd	5230		✓
H Ltd	234		✓
Q Ltd	3561	✓	

 ## Activity 49

The postings to the main ledger will be:

Account name	Amount £	Dr ✓	Cr ✓
Sales Ledger Control Account	2455		✓
VAT	5222		✓
Telephone	400	✓	
VAT	70	✓	
Motor Vehicles	5000	✓	
VAT	875	✓	
Insurance	4000	✓	
Rent & Rates	2000	✓	

The postings to the sales and purchases ledgers will be:

Account name	Amount £	Dr ✓	Cr ✓
ABC Ltd	2455		✓

Activity 50

The postings to the main ledger will be:

Account name	Amount £	Dr ✓	Cr ✓
VAT	214		✓
General Expenses	687	✓	
Purchase Ledger Control Account	189	✓	
Purchase Ledger Control Account	21	✓	
Discounts Received	21		✓
Electricity	200	✓	
Gas	540	✓	

The postings to the sales and purchases ledgers will be:

Account name	Amount £	Dr ✓	Cr ✓
TV Ltd	189	✓	
TV Ltd	21	✓	

17 Consolidation - Purchases

Activity 51

Purchases ledger

		Company A			
Date	**Details**	**£**	**Date**	**Detail**	**£**
30/6/X9	PRDB	528	30/6/X9	Bal b/d	11200
30/6/X9	Bal c/d	38167	30/6/X9	PDB	27495
		38695			**38695**
			1/7/X9	Bal b/d	38167

		Company B			
Date	**Details**	**£**	**Date**	**Detail**	**£**
			30/6/X9	Bal b/d	3720
30/6/X9	Bal c/d	5306	30/6/X9	PDB	1586
		5306			**5306**
			1/7/X9	Bal b/d	5306

Company C

Date	Details	£	Date	Detail	£
			30/6/X9	Bal b/d	28456
30/6/X9	Bal c/d	36387	30/6/X9	PDB	7931
		36387			**36387**
			1/7/X9	Bal b/d	36387

Company D

Date	Details	£	Date	Detail	£
30/6/X9	PRDB	105	30/6/X9	Bal b/d	50400
30/6/X9	Bal c/d	53467	30/6/X9	PDB	3172
		53572			**53572**
			1/7/X9	Bal b/d	53467

Main (general) ledger

Motor vehicles

Date	Details	£	Date	Detail	£
30/6/X9	Bal b/d	38700			
30/6/X9	Cashbook	19125	30/6/X9	Bal c/d	57825
		57825			**57825**
1/7/X9	Bal b/d	57825			

Purchases

Date	Details	£	Date	Detail	£
30/6/X9	Bal b/d	343600			
30/6/X9	PDB	34200	30/6/X9	Bal c/d	377800
		377800			**377800**
1/7/X9	Bal b/d	377800			

Purchases returns

Date	Details	£	Date	Detail	£
			30/6/X9	Bal b/d	1200
30/6/X9	Bal c/d	1740	30/6/X9	PRDB	540
		1740			**1740**
			1/7/X9	Bal b/d	1740

Purchases ledger control

Date	Details	£	Date	Detail	£
30/6/X9	PRDB	633	30/6/X9	Bal b/d	162094
30/6/X9	Bal c/d	201645	30/6/X9	PDB	40184
		202278			**202278**
			1/7/X9	Bal b/d	201645

Discounts received

Date	Details	£	Date	Detail	£
30/6/X9	Bal c/d	1800	30/6/X9	Bal b/d	1800
		1800			**1800**
			1/7/X9	Bal b/d	1800

Miscellaneous

Date	Details	£	Date	Detail	£
30/6/X9	Bal b/d	4000			
30/6/X9	Cashbook	920	30/6/X9	Bal c/d	4920
		4920			**4920**
1/7/X9	Bal b/d	4920			

Loan from bank

Date	Details	£	Date	Detail	£
30/6/X9	Cashbook	1125	30/6/X9	Bal b/d	31500
30/6/X9	Bal c/d	30375			
		31500			**31500**
			1/7/X9	Bal b/d	30375

VAT					
Date	Details	£	Date	Detail	£
30/6/X9	Bad b/d	12840	30/6/X9	PRDB	93
30/6/X9	PDB	5984	30/6/X9	Cashbook	12840
30/6/X9	Cashbook	160	30/6/X9	Bal c/d	6051
		18984			18984
1/7/X9	Bal b/d	6051			

Trial balance

	Dr £	Cr £
Plant & machinery	25530	
Motor vehicles	57825	
Bank		31171
Stock	15225	
Petty cash control	456	
Sales ledger control	237243	
Purchases ledger control		201645
Capital		6669
VAT	6051	
Loan from bank		30375
Sales		491325
Sales returns	2100	
Discounts received		1800
Purchases	377800	
Purchases returns		1740
Discounts allowed	360	
Wages	19400	
Rent	4575	
Heat & light	3900	
Rates	472	
Stationery	3060	
Telephone	933	
Insurance	4875	
Miscellaneous expenses	4920	
Totals	**764725**	**764725**

18 Petty cash

Activity 52

The entries in the main ledger will be:

Account name	Amount £	Dr ✓	Cr ✓
Postage	26.25	✓	
Staff Welfare	31.40	✓	
Stationery	19.40	✓	
Travel Expenses	33.01	✓	
VAT	7.98	✓	

Activity 53

The entries in the main ledger will be:

Account name	Amount £	Dr ✓	Cr ✓
Postage	20.01	✓	
Staff Welfare	4.68	✓	
Tea and Coffee	12.03	✓	
Travel Expenses	20.17	✓	
VAT	4.33	✓	
Bank	11.22		✓

KAPLAN PUBLISHING

Activity 54

Main ledger accounts

Postage account

		£			£
23 Apr	Balance b/d	231.67			
30 Apr	PCB	20.01			

Stationery account

		£			£
23 Apr	Balance b/d	334.78			
30 Apr	PCB	12.03			

Tea and coffee account

		£			£
23 Apr	Balance b/d	55.36			
30 Apr	PCB	4.68			

Travel expenses account

		£			£
23 Apr	Balance b/d	579.03			
30 Apr	PCB	20.17			

VAT account

		£			£
30 Apr	PCB	4.33	23 Apr	Balance b/d	967.44

INDEX

V

VAT – calculation of, 90, 98

VAT – credit sales, 93

VAT – registration, 89

VAT (Value Added Tax), 71

VAT, 63, 67, 70, 71, 85, 87, 88, 103, 104, 115, 200, 201, 212, 214VAT, 231, 265

Z

Zero-rated VAT, 71, 89